GW00630800

This book was written by two authors.

Where an author is expressing their own views, the section is headed by the author's name and is shown in italics.

Where a section is expressing the views of both authors, then it is shown without italics.

Written at the Villa Francia, Lanzarote, Canaries April 2013 and revised at Villa Junico, Algarve, Portugal April 2014

The authors would like to thank Villa Plus for helping us with the difficult Internet connections.

ISBN No: 978-1-5272-0505-5

CONTENTS

FOREWORD

Historically, meteorology and oceanography were taught in different departments in universities around the world. This was despite their shared fundamental basis of fluid dynamics. Only in recent years have the two disciplines merged with the ensuing graduate often labeled a climatologist. Radio and television, by contrast, were lightly touched subjects often embedded in a campus communications, marketing or public relations specialty.

In all of the classical subjects, and probably all of the arts and sciences, there have been champions. Oceanography has names like Maury, Ballard and Sverdrup. Meteorology has Hadley, Bjerknes, and Lorenz etc. When you come to the "crossroads" of meteorology and weather forecasting (particularly on television) the list of household champion names is virtually non-existent.

Until now ! From meteorology -- Bill Giles. From television production -- John Teather.

Almost like an arranged marriage, the U.K. Met Office went to bed with the British Broadcasting Corporation. The result was a BBC Weather Center that was admired and respected globally. But many a trained meteorologist had only a good head for radio when it came to TV weather broadcasting. Bill Giles was great in both mediums and became the U.K. equivalent of the late Walter Cronkite. The latter was once considered the most trusted television news anchor in the United States. The former became the most trusted and reliable U.K. television weather forecaster. For this, Bill Giles was awarded the Order of the British Empire by Queen Elizabeth II.

John Teather brought photographic and theatrical smarts to the BBC. He was a quick study in television technology and a very early adopter and developer of computer graphics. For John the broadcast was paramount. The weather forecast was a story and the presenter had to tell it well, tell it on time, and in synch with the graphics. Initially, for Bill Giles the accuracy of the forecast trumped the broadcast.

From their first acquaintance in 1975 to their respective retirements some 26 years later, and still today, Giles and Teather (another G & T if you please) have championed the marriage of weather forecast and broadcast. Their passion for excellence in both domains was not limited to their audition-selected few. With missionary zeal they set out to globally improve the public delivery of weather information.

They succeeded in doing this despite their respective bureaucracies. They realized the fundamental importance of accurate weather forecasting, while at the same time knowing and understanding that the general public has to be both educated and entertained.

Weather is universally described in academia as "randomly chaotic". Giles and Teather were never deterred by this and got it sorted quite quickly. This book is about how they did it, who they met along the way, and how these two unlikely bon-viveurs are now the pioneering champions of TV meteorology.

John L. Kermond, Ph.D Estero, Florida, USA

University Corporation for Atmospheric Research Visiting Scientist (Retired) at the National Oceanic and Atmospheric Administration Office of Global Programs

CHAPTER 1

INTRODUCTION

When Bill and John started writing this book, it was in the golden days when the state Broadcaster and the state Met Office worked together to provide a world beating service of excellence based on a partnership of skills.

However, that all changed in 2015 when the BBC announced that it was putting the weather supply contract out to competitive tender. Both felt that this was just a technicality, but were aghast when later it was announced by the BBC that the Met Office had lost the contract and that two preferred commercial weather providers were being considered. They straightaway worked with colleagues behind the scenes to get the decision reversed. In particular Julian Hunt who was previously the Chief Executive of the Met Office and had been ennobled by Tony Blair. This gave him the ability to ask parliamentary questions. But it soon became clear that the government would not intervene as they were giving the BBC a hard time with Charter Renewal negotiations and obviously did not want to be accused of interfering.

They also became concerned as to whether or not there was a level playing ground when the BBC appointed Nigel Charters as Director of Weather Procurement, later renamed as Project Director BBC Weather. His background was shown on Linkedin as coming from New Zealand. One of the preferred bidders was the NZ Company that had provided the weather graphics. Was there going to be a conflict of interest?

In the end the contract went to a Dutch company MeteoGroup who was founded in 1986 by Harry Otten who successfully lobbied the Dutch Government to curtail the activities of the Dutch Met Office to his commercial advantage.

John and Bill know Harry well, but fundamentally disagree with his proposition as they believe it the clear responsibility of all governments to have properly run and funded met offices to the benefit of their people.

But now the jilted bride has fought back, recently signing a new contract with commercial television (ITV) and launching a new graphics system that they say will surpass the BBC in quality and accuracy. They have played the BBC at their own game and given the state broadcaster's current death wish, they might well succeed.

So Bill and John's story is all about their relationship during the period when common sense prevailed at the BBC.

In May 1975 a young Met Office Scientific Officer and a BBC trainee Assistant Producer met for the first time. It was that day when Bill Giles auditioned for television and John Teather directed the studio. The day Bill learnt bowel control and John did the same.

But it was also the start of a 26 year working relationship building the BBC's weather broadcasts into world leaders and pioneered how science and broadcasting could work together to provide viewers and listeners with the best possible forecasts. Indeed a perfect working relationship where television and meteorology melded together to provide something truly greater than the sum of the parts.

Bill and John came from very different backgrounds that would require a mix of skills and talents that could eventually work together. For Bill it was a scientific discipline that allowed very complex physics and mathematics to be used to collect, collate and predict weather patterns. He honed his skills forecasting on an Air Force base where crews needed timely and accurate forecasts to allow them to fly. Then, on moving to London Weather Centre he needed to direct the forecast to public consumption.

John's path was very different where non-empirical taste and judgement were his disciplines. Having trained as a photographer he joined the BBC where programme making became his destiny, firstly through film editing and then into general production. But the ethos of public service figured strongly for both of them and a need to provide a first class service.

In the end it was their collective skills that enabled the mix to work. Bill was responsible for 25 broadcasters at the BBC Weather Centre, together with several support staff, and in the Nations and Regions a further 30 broadcasters. Recruiting, training, and motivating them into providing the very best weather forecasts possible. John was responsible for the multi-million pound self-contained 24-hour BBC Weather Centre with three studios, a £7m annual budget, together with a dozen BBC staff, and even more on contract providing engineering and graphics. But despite their very different responsibilities, they shared an office, as much a symbol that this was an equal partnership designed to produce world-beating weather forecasts on radio, TV and the internet. Bill always reckoned that sharing an office with John helped him learn emailing, as when the two of them were having one of their rare disagreements – the conversation always took place via email.

But this was also a period of change for both the BBC and the Met Office. Two very different cultures that had to find a way to work together. They both shared the vision of providing the best TV weather forecasts in the world, but getting there would be a challenge with the Met Office being forced from being a Civil Service department into a commercial agency, and the BBC facing competition from the growing number of digital stations coupled to falling revenues.

But, this does beg the question - why does weather broadcasting matter? Our climate is the major factor that describes who we are and what we are. It defines the country. People from the Mediterranean are very different from those in northern climates. Even life expectancy is dictated by the weather and the food we are able to grow and eat. The Mediterranean diet is well recognised for the contribution it makes to longevity. However, in the UK we chase the sun and the rain all the time. During long hot periods we seek the rain, and during the rain we seek the sun. This is not our fickle nature; it reflects the importance to all our weather sensitive industries, not least that of agriculture, to our very existence. The city dweller does not really get affected by the weather, but for those whose livelihood depends on it, it is of vital importance. The special 'Farmer's Forecast' broadcast each Sunday reflects the importance to the rural community of getting accurate forecasts to help them plan the planting and harvesting cycle.

Over the years Bill and John worked together with many well-known faces that were household names right from the 1950's through to this century. All of them were a bit eccentric – they had to be - as these meteorological scientists, were each evening, invited into the homes of up to 18 million viewers to deliver the weather news - both good and bad. Stardom was easy for some, but others found it very difficult. The public eye can be cruel and the constant scrutiny meant that it was too much for some when their private lives became the subject of newspaper gossip.

None more so than Michael Fish. He came to prominence in 1974 when he joined the BBC Weather Centre team at the same time as Barbara Edwards. Even before then Michael had an eye on self-publicity, which in itself is not a bad thing, and soon had a reputation for his outlandish dress sense. He became well known for his jackets, shirts and 'kipper' ties which over the years became more and more bizarre. He actually won the "Worst Dressed Man on Television" award a couple of times and the story goes that when he went to collect his prize of a suit made from his chosen material the sponsors of the award refused to accept his choice.

Michael was and is a survivor; his employers, The Met. Office, had tried on several occasions to sidetrack him away from the BBC Television Centre but to no avail, mainly because he didn't fit the stereotype image of a serious scientific meteorologist.

Bill remembers in 1982 they decided to send him on a short detachment to Southampton Weather Centre with the view of "forgetting" him and leaving him there forever. Bill was at a meeting in Bracknell when the director, Dick Ogden, and the Head of the London Weather Centre, Martin Morris, discussed their cunning plan. They thought it was brilliant until Bill pointed out that they didn't have anyone to replace him at the Television Centre and so the plan was shelved. Had Bill not spoken up for him all the stories known about Michael would never have happened including his immortal words on the storm of '87.

Michael lived close by at Twickenham and was always willing to come in at a moment's notice if someone went sick but would always study the duty roster with great care making sure that he had the same number of weekend duties as everyone else (they attracted extra money) but would constantly complain that he never had his fair share and in the next breath would complain that Bill never gave him any weekends off.

He was a great person for recycling weather maps rather than doing his own and it was fascinating to watch him broadcasting with the same map that Bill had made up the day before, but after saying that, you could always depend on him going into the studio and doing a very competent broadcast.

Michael took Bill under his wing when he joined the television team a year after him but I don't think he ever really forgave Bill when he became the boss in 1983. Bill was very disappointed that he refused to take any post of responsibility when we expanded to over 140 broadcasts a day as Bill was hoping that he would accept the post of managing one of the broadcasting areas and helping all the new broadcasters to settle and learn their trade. In later years he was to take some revenge on Bill by quietly backing Richard Edgar when he was accused of harassment. Still he has been very successful and famous even if it was for the remarks he made in October 1987.

Ian McCaskill broke onto our weather screens like a white tornado in 1978; he was like a breath of fresh air. His strong Glaswegian accent was different as was his approach to the viewing public. Unlike Michael he had spent some years at Prestwick Airport, in Malta and also Manchester so was an experienced forecaster before coming to the BBC Weather Centre. He was a bubbly enthusiastic communicator who developed his own style of telling the weather story. Whatever you thought of Ian he at least made us all think about how to grab the attention of the viewers. His one-liners at the beginning of his broadcasts have gone down in history. On one late evening broadcast he said that he now understood what the car advert "Vorsprung durch tecknik" meant.

He said it means "my car won't start". We understand that the manager of the nearest Audi dealer to him that night arranged someone to come out and fix his car - the power of television.

Ian had a great following but you either loved him or hated him. Many times people would say "I love it when Ian is on but I don't understand a word he says" Ian's style of broadcasting was so different from those back in the 1960s and 70s it was as though they were on a different planet and in many respects they probably were. Those days, however, also had their favourite weather presenters and there was none more popular than Bert Foord. Born in Appleby, Westmorland in 1930 Bert came across the screen as dour and humourless, but in actual fact away from the television he was the life and soul of the party. In one of his memorable forecasts Bert forecast that Apollo 13 would be struck by lightning on its launch to the moon and was proved correct.

He was also a very skilled union negotiator and in 1990 was made a distinguished Member of the Institute of Professionals, Managers and Specialists, the highest award the union could offer.

A keen sportsman he was a member of the Cheltenham Racing Club as well as a keen tipster on the horses. He also played golf on a regular basis with Jack Scott and the first weather broadcaster of them all George Cowling. So the dull two-dimensional Met man you saw on the screen was a completely different person when the camera was shut off - a wonderful exciting extrovert.

Jack Scott was completely different to Bert. Born in 1923 in County Durham, he was the first weatherman to be in charge of the team when he was promoted to Senior Scientific Officer in the late 1970s. Michael Fish, Barbara Edwards and Bill had some meaningful discussions with him when he tried to alter all the allowances they got for doing television but he had his way in the end.

Jack was there when the BBC moved to magnetic symbols and then in the early 80s he already had his eye on computer graphics; Bill took over from him in charge of the team when he retired from the BBC Weather Centre in 1983 to go and work, for the next 5 years, at Thames Television.

Barbara Edwards was the first woman to appear presenting the weather on UK television. She had a most wonderful speaking voice and when she left television after four years she took a six months attachment as a BBC Continuity Announcer before returning to the Met Office headquarters in Bracknell. Barbara had a rough time on television because she was a woman. The viewers didn't seem to mind Michael Fish's atrocious sense of clothes but they were very scathing about Barbara.

Even today you will hear people, especially other ladies, saying things about female presenters over what they were wearing rather than what they were saying. Apart from that, Barbara had an unfortunate habit of gulping while she spoke - eventually it got to her and she left. Nonetheless she was the vanguard for other women in the Met office to come and try their hand at television broadcasting, in fact there are more female weather broadcasters now than men - she was the start of the trend.

The next woman was Suzanne Charlton who joined in 1989. Although she was the daughter of Sir Bobby Charlton, she was determined to make her name in her own right. With a degree in Physics and Meteorology she became a forecaster with the Met Office. After a successful audition with the BBC she soon became a popular presenter with her clear voice and forthright manner. Behind the scenes she became an important part of the management team and was vital in helping with the development of the BBC Weather Centre.

John Kettley was a weatherman; in fact he still is and working as a freelance. John's main claim to fame was when the pop band 'Tribe of Toffs' went into the charts with their song "John Kettley is a Weatherman", which certainly increased his public profile. He has gone from strength to strength and now does a lot of forecasting especially for sporting events. He was a very good sportsman himself and probably still is, although he's getting on a bit now having been born in July 1952! and following in Bert Foord's footsteps was very keen on horseracing.

John Kettley hails from Todmorden which, when he was born, was in Yorkshire but Bill believes some boundary change in the past placed it in Lancashire and he used to take great delight in calling him a Lancastrian. Apparently it is nearly as bad as calling Devon born Bill, a Cornishman!!

Rob McElwee was on the same lines as Ian McCaskill but not quite so inventive. Over the years he had a large following and when, in a cost cutting exercise in 2011, he was taken off air there was quite an outcry. He found very clever ways of telling the weather story but was not consistent, so you could not depend on him continuing at the highest level. One morning he locked himself out of the studio thereby missing a radio broadcast. This was a cardinal sin, so Bill had him detached to RAF Odiham in Hampshire for a period whist he contemplated his mistake.

In 1997 the BBC Weather Centre expanded exponentially with the advent of News 24, who required 3 broadcasts every hour, every 24 hours. We needed someone to head this new concept of broadcasting into a live programme; 'cometh the hour cometh the man' and our man was Dan Corbett.

He had contacted John Teather just at the time when we were trying to form the new team. His performance style was exactly what we were looking for. He'd had a chequered career - born in the UK but educated in the USA where he became a weather anchor at a TV station in Tuscaloosa, Alabama and later in Waco.

Dan was different and there were early fears that his rushing style, so common and acceptable in the USA, would not be welcomed at the BBC. All through his career on UK television there was a nagging doubt in the background about this and this different approach did not exactly please the 'dye-in-the-wool' merchants at the BBC and the Met Office. He found working for the Met Office difficult and moved back to the USA on a couple of occasions. His final time at the BBC ended in 2011 when he accepted a job as a meteorologist with the New Zealand Met Office where he still resides and broadcasts on the state TV channel.

Helen Young who took over in charge of the Met Office Presenters when Bill retired, was born in 1969. Helen came to the BBC Weather Centre, after doing some television on HTV West and later BBC West, as the youngest presenter, aged just 24 years old.

She was different from the rest of the team with a Geography degree rather than mathematics or physics but that didn't hold her back. She readily accepted a management role when the weather centre expanded its broadcasting and easily adapted to filming with the daily six minute programme 'The Weather Show'. She left in 2005 to concentrate on bringing up her young family.

Good weather broadcasting requires an elegant mix of excellent presenters with detailed weather knowledge, understandable and supportive graphics and a drive and ambition to deliver the very best solution to telling the weather story of the day.

This book reflects that long journey through the stories that made both Bill and John laugh and cry along the way. It is not a history book, but more a reflection of the many factors that go to make good broadcast meteorology.

A shared passion was the driving force and the cooperation of the BBC and the Met Office allowed them to develop what became, at the time, the best centre of broadcast meteorology in the world.

It might also help future generations of weather forecasters and broadcasters understand where it all came from and certainly should reinvigorate the debate over how best to understand our complicated climate and communicate that to people, so that they can ensure that lives and property are safeguarded in times of extreme weather.

Bill and John were privileged to be able to put many of the building blocks in place and certainly had some fun in the process. But never was it more important than now for both Met Services and Broadcasters around the world to work even more closely together.

With our climate rapidly changing and the debate that surrounds the exact effects continuing, the need for excellent weather broadcasting becomes even more important. Not only do we need first-rate short-term forecasts, but a friendly face on our televisions to help us put it all in context.

Since their retirement from their respective employers they have continued to work together in particular on the international stage through the organisation they help found – the International Association of Broadcast Meteorology (IABM).

Our world's climate is rapidly changing and people are looking to weather presenters for help and advice. Let's hope, for all our sakes, they will step up to the mark!

CHAPTER 2

CLIMATE CHANGE

It's not rocket science to think that if the human species continues to grow in number and at the same time consumes the earth's resources at an ever increasing rate – that there will be a price to pay. In particular, in the way we burn fossil fuels to feed our enormous appetite for energy.

The global population has grown from 1 billion in 1800 to 7 billion in 2012. It is expected to keep growing to reach 11 billion by the end of the century. Each and every one of us burns something to keep alive, be it wood for cooking in an African village to fossil fuels making electricity to watch television. This all creates massive amounts of CO_2 which never leaves our atmosphere and acts as a shield that stops our earth naturally cooling.

But there is now a trillion dollar industry designed to convince us that there is no problem and mankind will be able to cope with it.

The industry is the oil industry.

BILL: *I wish I had never heard of the phrase "Global Warming" because by using that instead of "Climate Change" many non-scientific journalists and politicians believe that means the temperature of the Earth, and that of the United Kingdom in particular, should be rising at a very constant rate. Consequently when we have a cold winter or summer they latch on to the phrase "Global Warming" and ask what has gone wrong with the forecast. In the Hadley Centre of the Met Office, as well as many others around the World, research scientists were struggling away with Atmospheric and Oceanographic models trying to predict the effects of putting CO_2 and other greenhouse gases into the atmosphere in ever increasing amounts. In meteorology, as in mathematics in general, for many equations there are a number of answers and I am sure it is the same with the weather.*

We have studied many cycles as the Earth orbits around the Sun including the 100,000 year cycle as it wobbles on its axis right down to the 11 year sunspot cycle which also influences our climate.

The increase in global temperature that we've measured over the past few decades will not be down to one element but many; it is much more likely to be a combination of these, but modelling as best as they could, remembering things such as carbon emissions are more political than anything else, the research scientists are really looking deeply into the question. One thing is certain that no matter what your views on climate change are there is no disputing that at the present time the Earth is warming up.

The period 1983 to 2013 was the warmest 30 year period for at least 1400 years, so we just have to decide why we are warming up.

It could be natural variation, after all many scientists argue that we are still coming out of the last ice age and consequently warming up. It might be cosmic or solar activity. We already know that sudden warming of the stratosphere in the winter and early spring can have an effect on the North Atlantic Oscillation which controls whether, in the UK, we get mild wet westerlys at that time of the year or cold blocking easterlies as happened in the spring of 2013.

A few years ago some eminent scientists came up with a theory that cosmic dust was to blame for the warming of the planet. Their theory was that when a star explodes cosmic dust is scattered across the universe, some of it eventually arriving into the Earth's atmosphere. For cloud droplets to form there has to be a nucleus for the water droplets to condense onto. In the case of the UK it is normally sea salt particles but cosmic dust would do as well. Their argument went that because we are in a period of low cosmic dust there were fewer clouds than normal thus more sunshine and hence it would be warmer. Actually one of the reasons the mean temperatures in Western Europe are higher is because of the high night time minima that needs clouds to act as a blanket to stop night time radiation into space.

The warming could be due to El Nino, the warming of the Eastern Pacific, which in turn warms up the planet. One of the warmest years, some say the warmest, was in 1998 when there was a very strong El Nino event and one of the arguments that Climate Change sceptics put forward, is that no year has been warmer, so global warming has stopped. Actually in every year since 1998 the average global temperature has been higher than the 30 year average, and sometimes much higher so Global Warming hasn't stalled. Wait until the next strong El Nino and see.

And what about the greenhouse gases themselves, what the bone of contention is all about? In very simple terms the Sun's rays penetrate the greenhouse glass and heat up the soil inside. The greenhouse then radiates back out to space but because it is a different temperature to the Sun the radiation is at a different wavelength and not all passes back out through the glass. Some is reflected back and the greenhouse heats up. Actually it is a lot more complicated than that but it gives you a good idea as to what is happening. The Earth is very similar to the greenhouse; it doesn't have glass surrounding it but gases instead. Carbon dioxide, Methane, Water Vapour and others, which act in exactly the same way as the glass in the greenhouse. They allow the Sun's radiation to pass through; they heat the Earth, which in turn radiates back out to space. Because of the different wavelength of the radiation, not all of it passes through the greenhouse gases surrounding the Earth and some is reflected back to Earth again.

This is what keeps us all snug and warm and keeps the average global temperature to 15° Celsius. It has been calculated that if we didn't have the greenhouse gases that occur naturally in the atmosphere, the average global temperature of the Earth would be some 33° lower at minus 18° Celsius.

If that were the case we wouldn't be here today, or at least not many of us! The problem is that we have been putting these greenhouse gases into the atmosphere in ever increasing amounts since the Industrial Revolution reflecting more and more of the Earth's radiation back down to the Planet.

BILL: *The clever true research scientists at the Hadley Centre in the Met Office, and others around the Globe, came out with their pronouncement that if we kept putting greenhouse gases into the atmosphere in ever increasing quantities, the models were showing that by the middle of the century the Global temperature of the Earth would have risen by up to 2°C. As true scientists, that was the conclusion of their research, and as far as they were concerned the end of it. They were not interested in telling everyone the consequences but my job, and the job of my team, was to translate scientific information into a language that ordinary folk could understand.*

I thought long and hard about how to put the message of the forecast increase in temperature across, and what it would mean to people, and hit on what I thought was a very good idea. I looked at the climate across Europe and came up with the idea that if the researcher's mathematics were correct then the summer climate of London in 2050 would be the same as the summer climate of Nice, in southern France, today. This I thought would be an easy way for people to understand just what 2°C meant. I remember stating this on a Weather Show programme and was immediately called to the Met Office Headquarters to justify my claim. Several members of the scientific elite were there and said that I shouldn't say that the climate of London in 2050 would be the same as Nice of today. When I queried why I couldn't say that, the answer came back "Because it could be Lyons not Nice". I threw my hands up in disbelief; did none of them know how to get scientific messages across to the General Public?

One of the shattering statistics I remember reading about on climate change, if the mathematics was correct, was the possibility that in the United Kingdom the very hot summers we get now once every 50 years could, by 2050, be occurring once every 3 years and that the very mild wet winters, such as we have just had, that happen on an average of once every 30 years could, by the middle of the century, be happening every other year.

It is not climate change that we are all worried about, that happens all the time, but the rapid rate of climate change when many species of animals, fauna and flora might face extinction.

So, in my opinion, where the people in charge of getting the message out to the public have gone wrong is that they will often try and pin the temperature changes to one element, often just CO_2 emissions, and not considered all the other variables as well. The fact that the newspapers, in particular and journalists in general, call Climate Change Global Warming immediately makes none scientists believe that from now on the globe will be warming up in a uniform way. There will always be colder winters and summers but they will always occur less and less frequently if our mathematics are correct.

A Climate of Change

One way of checking the mathematical models is by starting the forecast way back in the past, say around the year 1900. We have a wonderful data base of the World's climate at that time. Now apply the mathematics and check the climate in, say 1925. Was the climate then roughly what we would expect it to be, by starting in 1900 and by continuing to check through the last century, we can get some idea that we are on the right lines. The mathematical models are being constantly added to and refined so give us a good indication that we are on the right lines for the predictions throughout this coming century especially if we do nothing to mitigate the use of fossil fuels.

BILL: *The main problem about getting climate change across to anyone, general public or Politicians, is the time scale we are talking about. Something that is likely to take up to fifty years to happen seems to be out of range of most people's minds, in the same way that it is difficult to comprehend the large numbers when considering vast distances between us and other galaxies. So my job is to use my skills, as a meteorologist and communicator, to find ways of getting the message across. Of course, by the very nature of things you will lose something in the translation and never completely satisfy the researcher.*

Many of the hypotheses I put forward about the consequences of the Climate changing, often during the' Weather Show' programmes, were looked at with great scepticism, but many are now mainstream and accepted. I don't know whether to be pleased that they are now recognised or very annoyed that I was pilloried for having them in the first place.

I remember stating I thought that because of the warming of the planet, the Sahara Desert could move north. In very simple terms my idea was that near the Equator the air is rising quickly forming huge cumulonimbus clouds and tropical downpours. At some 40,000 feet the air moves north in the northern hemisphere and south in the southern hemisphere as part of the Hadley Cell. Just taking the northern portion, even though frictional forces at that height are small, the air slows down and some of it starts to descend at about 30 degrees north.

Descending air warms up and tends to evaporate any moisture or clouds and is often an area of sunshine. If you look on an atlas many of the semi-permanent deserts are at this latitude. I thought, and said, what would happen if, due to extra heat being put into the atmosphere at the equator, the high level winds were just a little stronger. Perhaps they would go a little further north before descending at, say, 35 degrees north. And that is the Mediterranean. Could then, in time, the Sahara Desert migrate northwards into the densely populated areas of North Africa and southern Europe? If so the biggest problem facing the human race at the end of this century would be mass migration of billions of people.

Admittedly, many areas to the north, such as Canada, Scandinavia and Russia would be more accessible but would they allow the migrants in? At the same time, of course, the southern parts of the Sahara might just revert to lush tropical rain forest and this scenario could be enacted all across the World.

In the late 1990s I did a video link from Oxford for the British Council with Egyptian students in Cairo and Alexandria where we discussed Climate Change. I did mention that with global warming the Mediterranean Sea level would rise and because the flow of the River Nile has been slowed down by damming, its salt water would move into the delta regions making much of the fertile lands there infertile. So in a generation or two, what was the agricultural area of Egypt could become a salt marsh. It didn't go down too well, but already we are hearing of this happening.

I had a run in with Chris Huhne, then The Secretary of State for Energy and Climate Change, and wrote him a letter expressing my concerns in the way the message of climate change was being portrayed and that the Government really should use experienced weather broadcasters, such as myself, to get this very important message across. Not once did he reply to me directly, but passed it down the line and I eventually got a message from a Civil Servant pointing out that they had spoken with The Met Office who were happy about the way things were being done. I then pointed out that the reason they were losing the argument was precisely because scientists and not communicators were in charge of the message. I got no reply so I suppose the Civil Servants will continue to do it, badly.

Certainly the Climate change debate has changed from being a human problem to a political one. During the time of George Bush's presidency there was denial. Not surprising as his campaign funds came from the oil industry. Barack Obama has at least recognised there is an issue. The surprising thing for us is the number of weather broadcasters in the USA who deny there is any such thing. So for example, John Coleman, a co-founder of The Weather Channel, has called global warming "a fictional, manufactured crisis," and argued that "stamping out the global warming scam is vital to saving our wonderful way of life."

Perhaps he puts his finger on the real problem and that is that the people of the USA are really isolationists and don't want to do anything that would risk the 'American way of life'.

But there is perhaps a change afoot. Jeff Masters of Weather Underground recently said "The simple fact is, the climate is going to get warmer and warmer as we put more heat-trapping gases into the atmosphere. As that happens, the weather is going to get more extreme. People who talk plainly and credibly about climate change are going to be more successful and draw bigger audiences. Weathercasting is not an industry that can bet its future on denial."

The debate has been easier on the European side as the EU has actively encouraged both debate and action. In an attempt to drive the publicity for the campaign, the EU decided that the one person on television who has the trust of the viewers – was the weather presenter. They got together representatives from every EU member state to a series of meetings.

A Climate of Change

The inaugural one was held in an enormous conference room in Brussels, normally used by Ministers and Heads of States. Nicholas Hanley a senior member of the Environment Directorate, was giving a speech about the importance of communicating the need to reduce carbon emissions. John Teather was facing the wall of interpreter's booths that lined one entire side of the room.

He watched as a cleaning lady, entered each one in turn, switch on the light, empty the bins, and move on to the next. By the time she had finished, every light was now left on. At a suitable point he intervened. He explained to Nicholas Hanley and the meeting what he had witnessed and made the point that, once ordinary people like that lady understood the issues and automatically turned the light off when leaving – then we would be on the road to reducing emissions. However, Nicholas missed the point and we then had a lecture how the European Commission was reducing its use of electricity!

The group was then formed into the Climate Broadcasters Network – Europe (CBN-E) and met several times in some lovely places like Cannes. However, the money ran out and policies changed in the EU and what had been a promising forum for weather presenters to discuss issues came to an abrupt end. The whole subject has now fallen off the popular agenda as the financial problems in Europe worsen.

However the fifth assessment report of The Intergovernmental Panel on Climate Change, which was released in March 2014, has brought the whole subject very much back on the agenda.

Their conclusions that it is 95% certain that human activities are the dominant cause of the increase in global temperatures over the past century did not come as a surprise to many people in the United Kingdom who had suffered one of the mildest and wettest winters on record. The forecast many years ago, that as the atmosphere warmed so the increase of extreme weather would become more frequent, was very much in evidence in northwest Europe during the winter of 2013-2014. So will climate change be back high on the agenda? How will we, as humans cope with it until our scientists find a source of energy that is not dependant on burning fossil fuels? The warming of the planet and its consequent change in our climate will affect all of us in one way or another.

As we have already seen, the population of our Planet is expected to increase by 480% between 1900 and the year 2050 and with the possibility of many inhabited areas becoming uninhabitable the mass movements of many millions of people could become the biggest problem for humanity in the second half of this present century.

A conference in Cannes arranged by the climate section of the European Commission

The conversation continued over lunch with Bill Giles, Mike Fish and Gerald Fleming

A Climate of Change

BILL: *If I am right and much of north Africa and the countries surrounding Mediterranean Sea become difficult to live in, all those people will have to move and although there is a likelihood that countries to the north, such as much of Scotland, Scandinavia and Russia could become more accessible, would those areas wish a huge influx of uninvited immigrants? At the same time our holiday venues would change.*

In the second half of the 20th century and the beginning of the 21st as many peoples of northern Europe became more affluent, more and more turned to the Mediterranean and the Canary Islands for their summer breaks. However, by the middle of this century, if our mathematics is correct and no one finds a solution to the warming of the planet, it will be too hot to continue going there.

By that time we will also have persuaded people that their natural skin colour is the best one for them and that they shouldn't go out in the hot sunshine and get burnt. I am not the best advocate for that as I do go brown very quickly in the sun and I put that down to the fact that my grandmother was chased by a Spaniard and by the look of me probably caught!

With an increase of up to 2°C by the middle of this century or soon after, we could find that as well as people migrating northwards many tropical diseases could also follow. There is the possibility that malarial mosquitos, already the scourge of many sub-Saharan Africa may move northwards into mainland Europe and the British Isles.

Interestingly enough due to climate change the whole concept of retirement might well be affected. In northwest Europe, especially in the United Kingdom and Ireland a lot of old people die unnecessarily in the cold and damp winters, but as the climate warms up and we get far fewer of them, and as medicine becomes even better than it is at the moment, more and more old people will be living longer.

At the same time in Europe we have the suggestion, religion apart, that the higher the temperature the lower the birth rate. The combination of the two means that we have smaller and smaller numbers of young people and more and more aged and the working young ones pay for our old age pensions!

BILL: *So whilst the scientists are struggling to find new clean sources of energy we will have to consider how we might adapt to the change and mitigate its effects. We will have to look more closely as to how we manufacture the major greenhouse gases like CO_2 from coal fired power stations, exhaust from cars and planes, but that is easier said than done when the three largest polluters, namely China, India and the USA, seemingly do little to curb their output, although Barack Obama, the USA President, is facing up to the question. However, will future Presidents do the same?*

Planting trees may be some compensation but I looked at the problems on climate change of felling vast quantities of trees in the Brazilian rain forests (which currently lose about 1% of its area each year) and found that the amount of carbon capture by doing that, was almost exactly the amount that the USA puts into the atmosphere each year. The problem here, though, is political and we have to find some alternative employment for those destroying one of the best allies we have, in our search for slowing the rise of the temperature of our planet.

Obviously we will look at what we are doing at present with regard to wind turbines, solar panels, and ground heat sources as well as looking very carefully at Nuclear power that has got a very bad press since the problem in Japan after the tsunami.

One thing the engineers and scientists are working on is the ability to "capture" the carbon before it enters the atmosphere, compress it and pump it through pipelines into the wells that previously held natural gas.

The carbon dioxide then filters into the sandstone filling the very small spaces and is trapped by the large layers of rock above it as the natural gas was before.

Jetstreams could be the answer to our energy problems. There are four major ones, two in the northern hemisphere and two in the south, and are situated between 25,000 and 50,000 feet above the Earth's surface. They actually control the developments of high and low pressure that we recognise on the weather maps and that dictate the sort of weather we get.

Christina L Archer and Ken Caldiera as far back as the 2009 edition of the journal 'Energies' calculated that their total energy was in the order of 100 times of the World's present demands. By using very high flying turbines we need only to capture 1% of the Jetstream energy to satisfy all our needs and although it may sound very much like science fiction, scientists and engineers are working very hard to see if this could be a working proposition within the next 20 years.

Another alternative is to try and control the population growth of the planet, but I think that would be easier said than done. There has been some movement over the last few years in China, but even there the numbers are growing and trying to limit the growth in a democracy such as India would be a non-starter.

BILL: *I am a great believer that the scientists are giving us the very best reasons as to why the Planet is warming up but I am also a great believer that the human race is so clever that it will find solutions to our dilemma, but that in the meantime we should do all we can to mitigate the changes and adapt.*

CHAPTER 3

THE MET OFFICE

When Bill joined the Met Office on the first day of January 1956 it was almost like a family business. Virtually all the forecasting was done for the Royal Air Force, both at home and abroad because in those days the RAF had bases on every continent. They also had forecasters at most national and regional airports. The Met Office did some forecasting for the army, mainly low-level wind trajectories for shelling but nothing for the Royal Navy who had their own Met Department and still have to this day. Actually there was an attempt to merge the Met Office Training School with the Royal Navy one at R.N.A.S. Culdrose when they moved from Stanmore in North-West London to Shinfield Park near Reading, but nothing became of it because the Navy insisted that the dining room was segregated into Officers and other ranks which was not acceptable to the Met Office.

The Met Office, now over 160 years old, started life as an experimental government department under the Board of Trade to research the possibilities of forecasting the weather mainly for ships and their crews. Sensibly Captain (later Vice Admiral) Robert Fitzroy was appointed Head with a brief to try and establish the science of meteorology. He was very successful in developing a storm warning for shipping as well as instigating weather observation that could be transcribed to make a synoptic map which was the tool of every weather forecaster for the next 150 years. One of the early problems was getting the forecast out to the people that needed it in real time so that when wireless telegraphy on ships was developed in 1909 a new era of weather forecasting and distribution was born.

BILL: *Things moved gently on during the next fifty years with meteorology making great strides during both the world wars when the Met Office was moved to the Air Ministry and later The Ministry of Defence which, again, was a sensible move since most of the forecasting was for aircraft, both civil and military. So, that was the set up when I arrived in 1957 as a very junior assistant at Exeter Airport. In fact I very nearly didn't join because as I walked to the airport on my first day I took a wrong turning and nearly ended up in Clyst St Mary instead!*

The headquarters of the Meteorological Office, as it was then (in fact it has only changed to the Met Office in the last 20 years) was at Dunstable in Bedfordshire. It then moved to Bracknell in Berkshire in time for the first computer, a Ferranti Mercury, crunching numbers at 30,000 calculations per second, to be installed enabling the first numerical forecast to be produced.

As an observer or forecaster if you had any sense you stayed well away from headquarters and only went there when summoned. I well remember a very crafty ploy by the directorate in the late 1950s to move some assistants to Bracknell.

At every weather station every hour, sometimes 24 hours a day, the duty assistant would go outside to the Stevenson Screen and read the thermometers, check and describe all the clouds in the sky, both type and height, measure the wind velocity and calculate the visibility before coding it up in a five figure code and send it on a teleprinter to your Main Met Office. They, in turn, would collate all their outstation's observations and send on to headquarters. Every six hours, or sometimes every three, a certain number would be sent along a worldwide net to all countries in the world and every country would do the same. It was a marvellous system because for your one observation you received everyone else's, all in the same code. I always used to say that it was the only truly international body that actually worked. Once the observations were collected off the teleprinter, they were decoded and plotted by the assistant onto the relevant blank map using a double dip ink pen in red and black. This was then given to the forecaster to analyse and do their predictions.

This was time consuming since every single office had someone plotting these charts for much of the 24 hours a day. It was decided at headquarters, and kept a secret, that as they had the capability to plot a map there and then transmit it out on facsimile so that every office would receive it and not have to plot them locally. The 'powers that be' initiated a competition to see who was the neatest plotter at each of the outstations and made it such that it would be a feather in the cap of the winners. We had one very neat plotter at Exeter named Mike Collier and he found himself duly posted to Bracknell as a chart plotter, not a position anyone else at the office coveted.

Many years later, as I rose through the ranks, I found myself posted to Bracknell as a Senior Scientific Officer in the Public Relations Branch with my immediate boss Roger Hunt. The Assistant Director of the branch at that time was Dick Ogden, whom I knew as the Principal of the Met Office Training School whilst I was there teaching, and he was later replaced by a terrific Yorkshire man named Martin Morris.

Martin was larger than life and a great man to work for providing you were prepared to put 120% into everything you did. He was passionate about weather forecasting especially going back to first principles rather than taking the computer output literally.

Whenever you made a prediction about the forecast you would have to justify it to him and if your thoughts on how the weather would progress were wrong or badly argued, the wrath of God would descend upon you. I was lucky with Martin when he was the boss at the London Weather Centre because I had a terrific mentor, when at Strike Command, in a very senior forecaster called Len Ash. He was, like Martin, a stickler for detail and wouldn't let you get away with anything or try some short cuts.

Later Martin was promoted to Assistant Director in charge of the public relations and broadcasting and one of my jobs was to make sure that he had the best hospitality cupboard at Bracknell which we senior members of his branch would sample late on a Friday afternoon, but woe betide you if you asked for a whisky and not a beer!

In my opinion he was totally wasted running that department and would have been much better placed in charge of the Central Forecasting Office-the hub of the organisation and the reason the Met Office was in existence.

This was the time when the Met Office was moving away from being just a department of the Ministry of Defence to Trading Status (funded by customers rather than the Treasury) before later becoming an Agency and the focus started changing from forecasting the weather to selling their products including hardware and software. They were beginning to change away from their core business of forecasting the weather to selling it to the highest bidder and they needed to keep a strong grip on their forecasting skills. An opportunity to cement their position as the best weather forecasting team in the world was missed by not appointing Martin Morris as the driving engine. Sadly a few years later Martin passed away and the Met Office lost one of their great modern forecasters. John and I went to Martin's funeral and sitting at the back of the church we were obscured by pillars from seeing the pulpit. We were sitting quietly contemplating our loss when a voice boomed out from somewhere at the front of the church in a broad Yorkshire accent. The hairs on the back of my head stood up (and I am sure John's would have - had he had any!) because it sounded exactly like Martin. Not being able to see who it was, was very scary until we were told that it was his brother. The similarity in voice and volume was uncanny.

My involvement in the Public Relations Department at Bracknell was mainly looking after the Met Office at exhibitions, the visits to our 'world beating' forecast office and weather centre merchandise. As an aside, I had great fun running the exhibitions, which were mainly at the agricultural shows, but I did manage to get us into the Ideal Home Exhibition one year. I remember telling my boss, Roger Hunt, a most delightful man, that we should enter that exhibition to enable us to talk to a larger volume of the general public (it was at this time that we were trying hard to "sell" the weather and its products to everyone).

Reluctantly he agreed without realising that it ran for the best part of a month including weekends.

We had to man the stand with my staff from headquarters, who only worked Monday to Friday, and consequently they all enjoyed a bumper pay packet being able to claim overtime as well as weekend work.

I had a big problem with the budget for all the exhibitions that was far too small. So when discussing the shortfall with a colleague in London, who did all the design work for us, it was decided we should use some of the much larger budgets from the Army, Navy and Royal Air Force exhibition allocations and since we were part of the Ministry of Defence it seemed a very good idea to me.

I don't think anyone ever found out this arrangement until new people took over the shows for the Met Office and it was then that they started to cut back their involvement through lack of funding!

The Royal Show at Stoneleigh was my favourite. I always made sure we had some television broadcasters there to draw in the crowds (in fact although I was stationed at Bracknell I used to go back on BBC television once a month just to keep my hand in). The shows at Stoneleigh were great, full of very hard working farmers who knew just as much about the weather in their area as we did, as least for short term forecast. One year the Queen was on site and was designated to come to our stand, and since my boss Roger Hunt happened to be there that day, he was the most senior, and the only one she would speak to. He was duly briefed that he was not allowed to ask Her Majesty any questions but just to answer any she put to him. The moment duly arrived, and Roger was getting very agitated, his face was glowing red as the Queen approached. Before she has a chance to ask him anything he was heard to say (as he shook her hand) "Hello how are you?" The rest of the visit passed off without incident but he was all shaken up and the little red patches on his face (which incidentally are always there) became huge crimson blotches. Everyone came to congratulate him and I said "Well that was good - pity your flies were open" They weren't, of course!

Several years later when I was discussing my annual appraisal with Roger, tongue in cheek, I said I thought he should report that I was excellent at my job instead of very good. He didn't agree. I said to him well Her Majesty the Queen thought I was when she presented me with my O.B.E. "Well" he said "She was bloody wrong"

Talking about OBEs, I went out to Northern Cyprus to give a talk to a Church group. I settled in my room, had a shower and came down to the bar for a small beer before my hosts arrived and took me to the evening's venue. I sidled up to the bar and asked the Turkish Cypriot barman for a beer which he duly produced. "Put it on room 7 please, Giles is the name". This took longer than I thought and after a while came back and said it couldn't be done because there was no one called Giles in the room. I told him there was as I had just come out of it." No one of that name is in the room"" he said "in that room is a Mister Obe".

The Met office, at this time, was starting to sell their services to whoever would buy them and the farming community was one area that attracted us, so when we went to the shows I always included someone off the television (often myself) as well as experts in the field of selling Met office data. I devised a wonderful idea, as I thought, to get the people more interested in our stands at the shows, I would find something to sell them. After searching around I found a Ministry of Defence department near Ruislip in north-west London that could reproduce black and white satellite pictures for me at little cost. I selected about five different images from the close up pictures of the UK to one of Meteosat taken at some 36,000 kilometres above the equator and showing much of the western hemisphere. Once at the Royal Show, we would go into a set routine. I would be the "barrow boy" showing everyone the beautiful pictures we had (and remember they were the only place you could get them like that at the time).

After collecting a crowd someone else on the team would leap forward saying that he would have a couple. Then of course the rush started and at £1 a time we would make a killing. Not only that, but we had large numbers of people at our stand that we then passed on to the experts to sell the Met Office services. After the day's events, I would then, out of the takings, buy everyone a beer - just one - as thanks, but I did have a problem with all this money when I returned to headquarters to explain to the accounts department where it had come from.

I was ahead of my time in that department which also looked after merchandise for all of the Weather Centres up and down the country. I thought that what we were displaying was far too scientific for the average person so I tried to break away from the standard thermometers and barometers and looking through a mail order catalogue found just what I wanted. They were a new kind of thermometer that I thought would appeal to people wanting something to inspire their children and get them interested in the weather so I ordered two large boxes of them to be sent to me at my office on the second floor at Bracknell. Unfortunately they arrived whilst I was on a spot of leave. On returning I was called into Roger's office to explain the contents of the crates. They were thermometers all right but circular, bright yellow with Mickey Mouse emblazoned on the front with his hands acting as the hands of the thermometer. I think Roger secretly liked them but they had to go back because the person who would have had to take them to the centres and display them refused to do so. The name of my old fashioned dour Higher Scientific Officer was David Lee whom I would have more severe problems with at a later date.

Most scientific establishments, at that time, had a learned society to which their members could belong and so it was, and still is. In the Met Office it is called The Royal Meteorological Society or Royal Met Soc for short and later shortened even further to RMS. It was founded as The British Meteorological Society on the 3rd April 1850 gaining the Royal Charter in 1883.

For many years it appeared to be a society that mainly catered for research scientists and unless submitted papers had at least a double integration it was unlikely to be published - or that was how it seemed to many of us in the Met Office as forecasters and not research scientists. This has changed in recent years with a lot more emphasis on the "weather" as apart from "research meteorology." However in the early 1980s, when I was at Bracknell it seemed to me that most of the positions within the society were occupied by senior members of the Met Office and so there was a conflict of opinion on certain topics, and one I remember in particular.

For a number of years the Royal Met Soc had produced a calendar and were given permission on a couple of days in early November to come into the entrance hall of the Met Office to sell them to the staff. In 1982 I decided that the Met Office should also produce a calendar using the well known television team in many of the monthly pictures and I argued with Roger Hunt that it should be our calendar that was sold on our property not the Royal Met Soc. I think he agreed but the senior directors (who also basically ran the Royal Met Soc) disagreed and insisted they sold as usual.

The dates for them were agreed but I took our calendars into the hall and sold them a week before, whilst Roger was on leave, so that when the Royal Met. Soc. came to do theirs, no one wanted any. I was in the doghouse for a while but it set the precedence and from then on it was always our merchandise that was sold in our office and not someone else's.

The people that led the Meteorological Office, the Directors General, (later changed to The Chief Executive), were always eminent scientists well respected by the scientific community and were invariably Fellows of the Royal Society. It is the oldest scientific academy in continuous existence and comprises 1,400 outstanding individuals who represent areas of science, engineering and medicine.

At the beginning of my career the man in charge was Sir Graham Sutton, but all I can remember of him was that he was like a very genial grandfather and being very lowly graded and away from headquarters, most of us had nothing to do with him. He was succeeded by Basil John Mason, who actually reversed his Christian names on receiving his knighthood. He was a man larger than life; a great leader of men and a prolific writer of research papers. He led the Met Office through a golden age. He was followed by John Houghton, later Sir John, who, after leaving the office became co-Chairman of the International Panel on Climate Change and was a passionate supporter of the notion that the greenhouse gases we push up into the atmosphere will warm up the planet to unsustainable levels in the future, a hypothesis to which I fully subscribe. John Teather, later, invited Sir John to open the new training room at the BBC Weather Centre to brief all my forecasters and John's staff on the results of the lasts thoughts on Climate Change so that we were fully up to date on the subject should we be challenged.

Sir John had an elder brother, David, in the office that became such an authority on wind and wave forecasting for sailing that he attended several Olympic Games as the United Kingdom's weather expert, and through his expertise at micro-climate forecasting enabled the UK sailors to gain many medals. There is a lovely story about David Houghton when he was in charge at London Weather Centre. Until September 1991 the Television team came under London Weather Centre and successive bosses always made a great play of this fact when talking to people outside the Met Office.

David was a very outward going person and on this particular occasion, to impress his guests, he invited Jack Scott and Keith Best to accompany him and his visitor for lunch. They went to the local pub in High Holborn and on entering David went straight up to the bar.

He asked the cockney barmaid, who was the spitting image of Barbara Windsor in looks and voice, and enquired about the food." Excuse me" he said "I see you have curry on the menu" to which she replied they had. "Do you get rice with your curry?" he asked. She drew herself up to her full 5 feet 2 inches and in a very loud east London accent said to him "Do you get rice with your curry? Do you get rice with your curry? Of course you get rice with your curry you ignorant sod". To which David wobbling from one foot to the other replied, "Jolly good we'll have five."

After Sir John Houghton retired, we waited for his replacement to arrive, and to say we weren't disappointed is an understatement, as what appeared to be a clone of John Clease swept in through the main door with a haversack across his shoulders - Julian Hunt had arrived.

Julian, now Baron Hunt of Chesterton, is an eminent scientist gaining a first class honours degree in Mechanical Sciences from Trinity College, Cambridge and a PhD in 1967. He was a breath of fresh air and was tasked with restructuring the Met Office to become a Trading Fund in 1996. The thing I liked about him was that he was very approachable and John Teather and I had many a happy hour discussing television broadcasting with him. I remember an episode in the USA that showed what enormous standing he had within the worldwide meteorological community. It was at an American Met Society conference that Julian had been invited to talk by Dr. Joe Friday, then Director of the American National Weather Service, on the subject of meteorological data and data control. The Americans took the view that all weather data had been acquired using taxpayer's money and that the data, including weather observations and forecasts, should be free and freely available with no restrictions to anyone worldwide; they would only have to pay the transmission charges. On the other hand ECOMET, the Economic Interest Groups of National Meteorological Services of the European Economic Area, took a different view in that they wanted to charge all users, including the Americans, for weather data at a commercial rate.

The Director of the French Met Service was also invited to talk but I understand declined the offer. Imagine the scene in a packed auditorium with just two Brits in the audience, Bill and John, amongst a sea of Americans who were really angry on the stance taken by ECOMET, when Julian started to speak. All was going well until Julian, in his usual casual manner, looked straight at the audience and said "Well that's the way we do it in Europe, if you in the Colonies want to take a different attitude that's up to you." There was shock and disbelief at what he had said but he got away with it and I would suggest that he was the only person on the planet who could have done so, such was the awe and respect they had for him.

In those days when the Director General, or Chief executive, retired they were knighted soon afterwards. This didn't happen to Julian, and so there was quite a lot of ribbing he had to endure from his predecessors but he had the last laugh when he was ennobled by Tony Blair and made Lord Hunt, Baron Hunt of Chesterton.

John and I spent many a happy hour with Julian in the House of Lords discussing the demise of the Met Office as they moved away from their core business of forecasting the weather into an increasingly commercial company selling their wares. In fact we were all shocked when an advertisement appeared inviting people to apply for the position of Chief Executive of the Met Office with no requirement for the applicant to be a meteorologist or even a scientist because what they were after was a businessman. I am sure Admiral Fitzroy must have turned in his grave.

During our discussions in the Upper House, we invariably had lunch there and impressed as I always was with Julian's scientific brain, I was even more impressed with the way he could pick a quail clean in such a short time and I have it on authority, that I am the only commoner that has been allowed to pay for a meal in the Lord's dining room.

Peter Ewins took over from Julian in 1997 with his Director of Commercial Services, Bernard Herdan, whose directorate incorporated those of us at the BBC Television Centre.

I had many discussions about the radio and television output and being two grades above me he was the person to whom I had meetings to discuss the reports Roger Hunt did on me. It was important because my future pay and promotional chances were largely governed by those reports and I do remember saying to Bernard that I thought it was grossly unfair that as he was not even a permanent member of staff, but only on contract, should he be able to decide my progress within the Civil Service.

He took it all in good heart and we got on well and it was primarily him that made recommendations about me that got me an OBE in the 1995 New Year's Honours.

Bernard left sometime later to become Head of the Passport Agency and because there was a rumour that he might come back later as the Chief Executive of the Met Office, John decided, in the interest of the BBC licence payers, to make sure that he would be favourably inclined to the BBC itself. We duly took him out for a superb meal at The Old Plow, Speen in Buckinghamshire with no expense spared. The only problem for John who paid the bill on behalf of the BBC Weather Centre was that we all took our wives as well.

Peter Ewins was a very pleasant man and I got on very well with him, although he was the first Chief Executive who did not have a meteorological background. Incidentally he was the person who cleared me of the harassment charges that were placed against me in my final year but more of that later. I repaid the debt some months later when we were both invited to talk at the Grand Hotel, Torquay to a group of senior West Country county councillors. During lunch Peter was extolling the virtues of a brand new weather service on mobile phones.

He told the throng at the table that all you had to do was put in the place name and the time you wanted the forecast for and up would come the answer. He gave an example of Torquay, where we were all sitting, and announced that at three o'clock that afternoon, just over an hours time, there would be a shower at Torquay.

Well, three o'clock duly came and went and still the sun was shining brightly (although I must admit there were some lumpy cumulus clouds in the sky) and the delegates started to make fun of the new service until I remarked that the time had not arrived yet because Peter's phone was working on GMT and not BST and they had to wait until four o'clock to check the weather. Luckily the conference broke up by about half past three and we were away so no one ever knew if the forecast was correct.

CHAPTER 4

THE MEDIA AND METEOROLOGY

Good broadcast meteorology is a partnership between broadcasting companies and the Met Services. Unless there is a good working relationship then that elegant joining of skills doesn't happen. Over the years John Teather worked hard on the relationship between the BBC and the UK Met Office, it was difficult most of the time, and very difficult almost all of the time.

JOHN: *I have always thought it odd that the Met community have a blind eye when it comes to communicating the weather. You might produce the world's best forecast, but if you don't have the means to communicate it to the public, then it is all to nought. The real problem is a deeply imbedded cultural difference coupled with an almost paranoid suspicion. The two disciplines of the scientist and the broadcaster are very different. Certainly at the BBC, our mission was perfectly clear – to inform, educate and entertain. The public we served were very close to us, and through the many ways we encouraged comment, we had a pretty good idea of what their opinions were. That is not to say that we ran on a constant plebiscite, but, for example, one of the most widely read documents in television was the Duty Office log. It was on the desk of every producer, editor, controller and executive first thing in the morning. The Duty Office was part of the Presentation Department, and was tasked with taking viewer's phone calls and recording their comments. These were then typed up, and grouped by programme. So we were able to quickly take the heartbeat of the nation, and this certainly gave the BBC and instant contact with our viewers.*

The founding steps of the Met Office were based on public service, as it was in response to a growing list of losses at sea due to bad weather. The Met Office was established in 1854 as a small department within the Board of Trade under Robert Fitzroy, as a service to mariners.

The loss of the passenger vessel, the Royal Charter, and 459 lives off the coast of Anglesey in a violent storm in October 1859, led to the first gale warning service. In 1861 Fitzroy had established a network of 15 coastal stations from which visual gale warnings could be provided for ships at sea. So this basic purpose is what drives the whole world Met Community. What else can be more fundamental to the purpose of government than to help protect property and lives? It is even more important in emerging nations where one bad crop due to poor weather conditions can set back the GDP by five years and cause loss of life through starvation. So I have always argued that this fundamental principle must drive all consideration of how Met Offices are run and funded.

But this is where the principle departs from the reality. Almost without exception, Met Offices have a problem with the means of dissemination of their forecasts, as they are very suspicious of the media and the people the media employs. To serve the public properly in a timely manner requires a true working relationship between the Met Office and the Media. In the UK it is only right and proper that the publically funded Met Office and the publically funded state broadcaster should work tirelessly together to provide its paymasters with the best possible weather solutions across all broadcast media – by that I mean both national and local radio, national and local television and all new media such as the web and video player platforms. This obvious and self-evident principle, of a symbiotic relationship almost got there, but it was a rather tortuous route on the way.

The exception though is the USA, where they have a very different system from the rest of the world. They leave it to the private sector to broadcast the forecast, which is provided without charge. From our earliest visits to the States we were befriended by Ed Gross who worked for the National Weather Service. A no-nonsense guy with a Bronx accent, he helped us over the years to understand the way the American System worked.

Once he arranged for us to go and see their forecast office just outside Washington DC. What stunned us at the time, was when we were told that the duty chief forecaster had an element of his pay that was based on how often they got the forecast right. That sort of direct inducement, based on a pay by result, might well have been something the UK Met Office should have adopted. A wrong forecast was simply met with a shrug of the shoulders where perhaps a reduction in salary would have worked better to get it right next time. Until Ed retired in 1997 he was a tireless worker for the International Association of Broadcast Meteorology and was greatly missed. One treasured memory was when he took us to have a BBQ dinner at the home of Alan Eustis who he had worked with over the years. It was one of those 'Hollywood' moments as we sat on the veranda of his wood faced house drinking beers out of the bottle as the sun set. The steaks at dinner were so large they could have fed my family for a week. A night to remember.

My first introduction to the Met Office was way back when I first joined Presentation, and was summoned by my then boss, Hugh Sheppard, to join in the 'annual Met Office' negotiations. I was taken up to one of the grand hospitality suites on the sixth floor of TVC, where, the then Head of Presentation, Rex Moorfoot was entertaining the Met Office Secretary. If nothing else, the BBC hospitality department could lay on a good do. A tall patrician man of impeccable breeding neatly tailored in a fine three-piece suit, he was every inch a career civil servant.

I had been told in the lift coming up that it was reckoned that every gin and tonic we got down his throat was worth £10,000 off the bill. I am sure this was apocryphal, as at that time, with a small team of forecasters there was little expense for which the Met Office would need to recover. Following more drinks and a splendid lunch, a brief discussion agreed the deal, and the annual event came to an end. Any further contact during the year was merely to agree auditions etc., although that did not happen too often.

But matters were about to change, as the following year, he explained that the Treasury was putting pressure on their budget and had been told that they must recover more from their customers. The first time that word 'customer' had been mentioned. But, weren't we in a partnership serving the public? If the BBC paid the Met Office more, then surely the public was paying twice through their taxes and their license fee. A sort of compromise was agreed that would see honour done on all sides. But the scene was set for the amount paid to the Met Office to increase year on year.

The importance the Met Office placed on the relationship steadily grew, and I got to know the Directors General with Sir John Houghton 1983-1991, Julian Hunt 1992-1997, Peter Ewins 1997-2004, and Dr David Rogers 2004-2005.

My day-to-day contact was usually through whoever was the boss at London Weather Centre at the time, starting off with Dick Ogden, then Martin Morris, Francis Hayes and then Roger Hunt. Although from time to time, I did have to go and see their boss at Bracknell, Derrick Johnson. Derrick was a very dapper man, immaculate clothes, with no sign of dandruff, highly polished shoes, and a white clipped moustache, that even Hercule Poirot would have envied. The perfect civil servant. But he had an interview technique I have never seen bettered. After the initial handshake and welcome, he would sit down and say nothing. He would just stare at you waiting for you to start the conversation, even for meetings that he had called. This method would enable him to extract much more information out of you, as you struggled to keep the conversation going hoping he might join in at some point. I would have loved to have emulated it myself, but knew that I wouldn't be able to keep a straight face long enough!

When Roger Hunt moved to the commercial division he then took with him the responsibility for the weather team as Bill's line-manager. Over the years I had a great deal to do with Roger. He had a feel for the media, and although we did not always agree, at least he was a moderniser who could see the broadcaster's point of view.

It is true to say that without Roger's support and encouragement, the development of BBC Weather would have been much more difficult, if not impossible. He was involved in auditions, staffing issues and financial negotiations.

He came to 'away-days' and regularly visited the BBC Weather Centre. Roger was a good friend with the Director of Forecasting, Colin Flood, and that provided me with an easy relationship with that section. Roger only had one small weakness and that was – he could be a bit accident-prone.

I attached so much importance to forging good working relationships with the Met Office I regularly held dinner parties at home. One evening Roger, Colin, Bill and wives arrived. Roger was driving – and before he had even had a drink he demolished my gatepost on arrival. The evening was great fun and we didn't really notice the time, until Roger realised it was four o'clock in the morning. They were so late getting home that he was formally kicked out of his local baby-sitting circle.

These evenings were always lively affairs, and not least when a few years later we were entertaining some Met Office staff including Ewan McCullum and his wife and Roger and Chris Hunt. Ewan at that time was in the forecasting branch and seemed destined for greater things. Over a drink fuelled dinner Bill was telling the story of what happened at Ian McCaskill's leaving party. The BBC was always very good at saying thank you to its 'talent' who had served them well over the years. I had commissioned a bolt of specially woven tartan in the Clan McCaskill pattern.

Designer Liz Varrall had got it all sorted out and had spent a lot of time getting it right and writing the words that described it's manufacture. Ian's leaving do was in the high class 6th floor hospitality suite at TVC and was hosted by the Head of Presentation, Pam Masters who was not known for her sense of humour.

After an excellent meal and lots of fine wines, she thanked Ian for his broadcasts on behalf of the BBC and proceeded to present him with this special gift, to which Ian, who, by now was very well oiled, thanked her with the immortal words "at least it won't show the semen stains". At the exact moment as Bill delivered the punch line – Ewan was helping himself to more salad and fished out, for us all to see, a narrow plastic tube filled with white fluid. Later, when we had finally finished laughing we realised it was the sauce that came with the bag of Caesar salad.

Roger often attended the Paris Festivals with us, and standing in a bar one evening, after the festival show, we got talking about vasectomies – as you do. A few weeks earlier Bill and I had decided it was time we had the 'snip', but I wanted to have it done privately as I didn't fancy an amateur fiddling with down below. So we booked up together for the Marie Stopes clinic, in itself it didn't have an auspicious start as during the counselling session at the beginning, when asked what we were there for I got the wrong term and said circumcision – Bill almost left at that point! He went in first and after a few minutes all I could hear through the walls were screams of laughter, to which I assumed that Bill had taken down his trousers! It turned out that a team of Latvian doctors, observing the procedure, had a few too many drinks at lunch and were in party mood.

So, there in Paris at the bar, Bill was explaining this all to Roger, who had also gone through the operation recently, but on the National Health, whilst I was talking to an Icelandic weather forecaster about the number of sheep in Iceland. Roger was saying that he found giving a sample after the operation was the worst bit. Down at my end of the bar, the Icelandic was joking that some of the sheep in Iceland were 'very pretty'. I observed that it would be a perfect arrangement - you could love them and then eat them! At this very moment Bill was saying "didn't you go private – because the nurse dealt with all that for us" the Icelandic exploded in laughter and sprayed poor Roger with beer froth. To this day he doesn't know whether Bill was joking or not!!!

Sir John Houghton later became the Chairman of the Scientific Assessment Working Group of the IPCC (Intergovernmental Panel on Climate Change) and kindly came to TVC to give the team a lecture on the subject. Earlier I had been invited to attend a special conference on Climate Change held at Oxford University.

I had been keeping an eye on this growing debate on how mankind was irrevocably altering the atmosphere of the world, through the increasing emission of greenhouse gasses. It was only just beginning to hit the consciousness of the media and I was starting to think how this might impact on weather broadcasts.

The conference was a grand affair, with an audience of high level politicians, civil servants, scientific journalists and other movers and shakers. I didn't fall into any of those categories! It was chaired by the Swedish meteorologist, Bert Bolin who was the first Chairman of the IPCC. He started his talk with a slide show of the charts and analysis from the computer models that made up the results of the first assessment on climate change as published by the IPCC. I had seen all of this before and wondered what was going to be new. Bert soon got my attention. "We have all seen these before – and there is no doubt, I repeat no doubt, that climate change is taking place. The simple question is, what are we going to do about it?" This was the one question nobody was asking, and really woke me up to the fact that as a species we needed action. The conference continued with a discussion on the two key strategies – Mitigation and Adaptation. In other words, how to reduce it and how to live with it.

I felt it vital, that the BBC Weather Centre team, in particular the presenters, understood the science and would know how to answer any questions put to them by journalists, in particular from our own News Division. The sort of question, where, for example after a long period of hot weather, the question would be asked of them – 'is this the result of climate change'? Also I wanted the BBC Weather Website, which was one of the most visited sites on the whole of the BBC, to start providing information.

I needed Sir John's visit to the BBC Weather Centre to put the whole question on the map as far as the Weather Centre was concerned. Looking back I think we did a very good job. It is not an easy subject with which to deal, because the changes are long term and difficult to see.

Governments only take a short-term view, as they only see the world in five-year terms of office, when the policies they need to adopt are for 25 or 50 years hence. This was never clearer to me, as when I was invited by the Environment Agency to a reception at London's Thames Barrier. At this occasion, once a year there has to be a formal closing of the barrier to prove that it still worked. The guest speaker was the then Mayor of London Ken Livingstone, who told us that it had taken 25 years to win the arguments, get the money and then build the barrier. . So far that year, the barrier had been raised ten times more than usual, and the figures showed this was an increasing position. He said that the research had shown that with the predictions of sea level rise due to climate change, the current barrier would be breached in 25 years times.

The political will would have to be found to build a new and higher barrier further downstream, and raise all the flood walls from it, back to the existing barrier. He made that speech in 2000 and so far nothing has happened!

Julian Hunt took over from Sir John in 1992 and he was a very different boss for the Met Office. He won't mind me describing him as a John Cleese look-alike, with a Basil Fawlty manner. He was fearless and bold in his approach to everything. Once, at an AMS conference, Julian was due to speak after dinner, but there was no sign of him. Held in a huge ballroom with over a thousand sitting down to eat, the lights had dimmed and speeches begun, when suddenly a door opened at the back, and silhouetted in a shaft of bright light, like a visitor from space, was the tall outline of Julian. Carrying his little overnight bag, he worked his way in the dark to the stage, tripping over chairs and people, whispering "sorry, sorry!" under his breath, to arrive just as he was being introduced to speak. Not fazed for one moment, he gave a great and funny self-deprecating speech in his clipped perfect English accent. He was the instant star of the evening.

Julian's main claim to fame was to reorganise the organisation ready for Trading Fund status that started in 1996. The Met Office had to ensure that a new system of payments be devised. Up until that time the funding came direct from the Treasury. Now the income had to come from customers. So those clever civil servants came up with a solution that was worthy of a banana republic. Rather than the Treasury giving the money direct to the Met Office, they would divide it up and give it to the various agencies such as the Ministry of Defence, Home Office, NATS (National Air-Traffic Control) and the Coastguards and then they would give it to the Met Office.

When it came to the BBC we were already paying the Met Office almost £3 million a year. But there were other bits of income that made up the total the Met Office received in public services. This was approximately £800,000 that was transferred to the BBC, who then gave it back to the Met Office.

To ensure accountability, the Core Customer Group was formed, at which each of the funders had a seat. Their job was to scrutinise how the Met Office used its money and approve any development plans. Peter Ewins, who was then the Chief Executive, found this new exposure under the spotlight rather stressful. Until then the Met Office had sailed along doing what they wanted, only having to give a nod and wink at the Met Office Board, who acted on behalf of Government as the owners. But they were really, in all fairness, a concocted committee of worthies and weather 'luvvys'. The Core Customer Group was rather different, it was made up of people who actually used the services, and they wanted to know if they were getting value for money. Especially the representatives of NATS (National Air Traffic Service) who were going through a privatisation process themselves. They were concerned about the cost of Met Services and the charges they had to pass onto the airlines. There were several difficult moments as Peter Ewins tried to suggest that it was best to deal with it outside the Core Group, but to his dismay found that others shared NATS views.

During this time, there were discussions about the forthcoming move from the current headquarters in Bracknell to a new one in Exeter. We were not really being asked if we approved, it was more a case that it had been decided and we were being told. Outside the meeting I found many of the members shared my reservations.

We were told that there were structural problems with the existing buildings and a move would have to be made in any case. But it was the choice of venue that concerned me. London and surrounding areas housed two major universities, Reading and Imperial College both centres of excellence for meteorology and the associated sciences. There was also Oxford and Cambridge Universities not too distant. Coupled with the Royal Met Society with headquarters in Reading, I was concerned that for the Met Office to continue to be a centre for meteorological excellence, then, a network of scientific cooperation needed to be maintained. The Met Office already had a site at Shinfield Park in Reading. It was the Met Office training centre – and there was plenty of ground on which to build a new Headquarters. Also the site was next door to ECMWF (European Centre for Medium-Range Weather Forecasts) in itself a world centre of excellence. But of course this wasn't the game. Peter Ewins was the first boss of the Met Office with no background in meteorology and his appointment was much more to do with 'flogging' the information than making it. It is worth noting that a previous CE only has a business background. It's like appointing a butcher or a greengrocer to head the BBC!

I had, in the past, successfully used 'away-days' with my producers and some Met Office staff to brainstorm developments. In the summer of 2001, with the contract for the Met Office due for renewal later that year, and the BBC Weather Centre having new owners (BBC News), it would be a time to get together and talk through some options. I was still the BBC's representative on the Met Office Core Customer group and therefore had an overarching responsibility to smooth the way.

By now Roger Mosey, my new boss in News 'was too busy' to manage me direct and I had been passed to an accountant whose name I do not now remember and would rather not recollect anyway. Our initial session went well as we worked through the Weather Centre budget, how it was made up and where the income came from. I looked at the contract between the Met Office and BBC that was worth over £3 million and indicated that the BBC would probably be happy to settle around that figure. The Lunch was amicable, but over coffee I began to smell a rat. Had the Met Office already made contact with News? Had they conspired, behind my back, to short circuit me? Even Bill noticed something was up, as the Met Office representative, Stewart Wass was reluctant to engage in eye contact and even less in conversation. One will never know the truth. But I lasted until September that year, when at the age of 55 they made me an offer I couldn't refuse. But I subsequently learnt that BBC News substantially reduced its payment to the Met Office by over £1 million. So Mr Wass, if you are reading this - ha! ha! Serves you right!

JOHN: One of our biggest challenges was getting the entire BBC and Met Office staff based at the BBC Weather Centre together in one room for a meeting. We managed it about once or twice a year whenever Bill could arrange it on the rota. I would arrange for a conference room with a buffet meal and drinks. At 7.00pm we would start a photo session where a professional photographer would take publicity pictures of the weather presenters.

Then at 9.30pm after the forecast (later on it was 10.30pm when the news moved from 9.00pm to 10.00pm) we were joined by whoever had been doing that shift – and we had everybody, and could get down to business.

We were usually joined by Roger Hunt, or the Account Manager for the BBC. When Stewart Wass was appointed to the role, a blunt, loud Yorkshire man with the bedside manner of 'Attila the Hun', he was invited to a meeting. He quickly proved his diplomatic skills by telling the whole team that he seldom watched any television and he only had a black and white set.

Fancy saying that to a room full of people who earned their living broadcasting, and sitting in a room as a guest of the BBC.

For the locked drinks cabinet, Hospitality gave me a key so I could lock it overnight to save the contents walking. One time, I was sorting out transport home for the team, and when I arrived back to an empty room, the entire cabinet had been cleared. I was later told that Mike Fish was seen getting into a taxi clutching a bottle of fizzy water!

Strangely enough we got to know Julian Hunt even better after he had left the Met Office and Bill and I had retired. By this time he was now Lord Hunt of Chesterton, having been ennobled by Prime Minister Tony Blair for service to the Labour party when Julian had been leader of the Council in Cambridge some years before. Both of us were involved in the Weather Index and our own company The Weather People.

Both companies were competing for business, by value-adding to forecasts, packaging it in such a way to be targeted for a particular business. So, for example, doing a specific forecast for supermarkets, so that there was plenty of a salad available for a hot spell. Interestingly, without exception, the companies we approached were keen to talk as they found their dealings with the Met Office less than satisfactory and expensive.

The UK had a small, but developing private weather forecasting community, but they were finding it tough competing with the Met Office. On the other hand in the USA, the private sector was large and successful. Under the Freedom of Information act where all data generated by government was freely available, other than the cost of dissemination, companies had become very successful at adding value by packaging and targeting. But here in the UK the Met Office was the sole source of data and jealously guarded its supply and price. In conversation with Julian, who was now involved in Cambridge Environmental Research Consultants, we all expressed concern that we were not being allowed to work on a common playing field. He had found that the charge that was wanted for data supplied to his company was ridiculously high. Fine that there was a commercial section in the Met Office, but they should pay the same for data as the rest of the industry.

We knew from previous involvement that the commercial section raised less than it cost them to run the department. We decided to form an informal grouping of independent weather companies to better understand the issues. Julian agreed to host the first meeting at the House of Lords and in the end we got together about 20 companies ranging from one-man bands to larger companies who prepared forecasts for the press.

Over drinks and canapés in the grandeur of the House of Lords we learnt a sorry tale about dealings with the Met Office. There wasn't one company that didn't have a concern. So we decided to hold a further meeting with a view to then meeting the CE of the Met Office, Peter Ewins to discuss our concerns. Julian agreed to negotiate a date.

The meeting was held at Bracknell, and soon developed into a heated exchange, including Peter declaring that he was going to walk out of the meeting if anyone else complained about the Met Office. One colleague of ours, Simon Keeling, told the tale that he set up a new service providing forecasts for amateur pilots. He negotiated to buy the data with the Met Office, which they duly supplied. There was then some correspondence with another division saying that only the national Met Office should provide forecasts for aviators, and then they promptly released all the data on the web, effectively killing his business stone dead! But the more worrying stories were where someone had done a deal to subsequently find that the Met Office had gone in behind them and persuaded the company that they weren't dealing with anyone who knew what they were doing and then did a deal for less money!

To me this was a moral issue. In whatever guise the Met Office was trading, it was still a Government department. It was the politics of the mad house where a government, funded by the tax-payer, knowingly attempted to secure business at the expense of its own people by downright shady business practices. Where a government attempts to cease serving its people and deny the private sector the ability to thrive, then it is a very short road to perdition. Neither Bill nor I wanted to spend time in setting up a formal organisation to represent the private sector. We felt, at that time, we had done all we could and passed the baton to others.

Months later, we were invited to speak at a conference on Data Commercialisation in London. There was a growing concern that, what the Met Office was attempting to do, was also being followed by other government departments such as the Ordinance Survey and the Hydrographic Office. We did a fairly strong presentation outlining what we had already learnt from private weather companies, and finishing off with my concern over the morality of all this. Government against its own people. During the tea break we were sought out and congratulated for the stand we had taken. Also a lady from the Cabinet Office said that she was very interested in what we had to say.

A few days later she phoned me say that she had heard a whisper that the Met Office was considering suing the two of us for what we had said about them. Nothing came of it. I expect they were advised that if it came to court, the evidence we had would make the government look like idiots.

BILL: *While working as a Director of The Weather Index it was decided that we should look into the possibility of moving into the weather derivatives market. Weather derivatives are financial instruments that can be used by organizations or individuals as part of a risk management strategy to reduce risk associated with adverse or unexpected weather conditions.*

Basically this means looking at long-range forecasts for three to six months ahead or even further and then combining forecasting and climatology events connected to weather parameters, such as temperature. This 'long-range forecast' can be used and commodities consequently bought and sold. So, for example, buying large supplies of gas when the prediction showed there would be a cold winter.

Whilst in the United States at an American Meteorological Society conference we took the opportunity to visit an office in Kansas that specialised in the derivatives market and I must say we were very impressed with the totally professional way the work was conducted. Back in the UK we were sold on the idea of trying the same approach but who to get the data from was a big problem.

Sure we could get it from the Met Office, but at a great price even though that data was already paid for by the taxpayer, but unless we got it from the USA where all data was free and freely available, there really was no one else and besides we wanted to be seen to be supporting this country.

Simon Strong of Wpindex and I made an appointment to see my former boss, Roger, with a view to discussing all aspects of data but primarily those connected with derivatives. What we really wanted was a joint venture with the UK Met Office to go into this market in a big way but was told that it was not possible. Surprise, surprise when just a short while later, the Met Office announced that it had gone into joint venture with a company called WeatherXchange to explore the derivatives market.

Cindy Dawes, then Managing Director of the WeatherXchange, came to the Weather Index office for a meeting with me to supposedly discuss how we could work with them and the Met office on other weather projects. What she had really come to probe about, was what were our plans for the future and which markets we intended to seek out. But instead of that I tried to turn the tables on her to see what they were doing on derivatives. Unbelievably, since I had been on national television for 25 years and she lived in the UK, indeed went to Keele University, she did not recognise me or realise that I had spent my whole career of 40 years in the UK Met Office. She tried to impress me by saying that the past weather data held by the Met Office was fine for forecasters but too crude for her use and that the Met Office had allocated 20 forecasters to improve the data so it could be used. I knew at that time that the commercial hourly rate for forecasters of those grades to be something like £40 an hour and it didn't take a mathematical genius to work out that the Office was committing over £30,000 a week on this project. When I casually mentioned this she was more than surprised and quickly changed the subject.

Subsequent to this in 2005, The Met Office reported losing £4.5m in the failure of WeatherXchange, its joint-venture established in 2001.

They had invested £1.5m, and spent a further £3m in staff time and other costs. In May 2006, Peter Ewins, who was also chairman of the company, told the Commons Defence Select Committee, that he did not believe other participants in WeatherXchange made initial investments but had instead provided credibility and expertise.

"That sounds incredibly naive and amateurish," said Kevan Jones, a Labour MP. "If you had done that in local government, you'd have been shot."

JOHN: *I hope we haven't sounded too hard on Peter, as he was someone who we both liked and got on well with. The last time we saw him was in Geneva as he finished his term as the Permanent UK Representative at the WMO (World Meteorological Organisation) and after, in the time honoured fashion, was 'clapped out' of the building. He came back to his hotel where we were sitting having a nightcap. He joined us for one last drink. A little sad I think. Peter in the end, had been shafted by a government, who were trying to reduce their expenditure on meteorology, by making its world-leading Met Office become a business and not a centre of excellence.*

Peter's successor was David Rogers who we met in Geneva at a WMO meeting. We immediately got on with him. He was a breath of fresh air with lots of ideas. It might appear that I have gone to endless lengths to slag off the Met Office. My simple position was, when I was at the BBC, I desperately wanted them to be the best in the world. It was what the BBC tried to be. But with the move to commercialisation I became more concerned that they were losing their way. David shared this vision and asked what we thought of the new headquarters in Exeter. With us both retired the opportunity to see the building had not arisen. So a few months later we rectified this.

BILL: *Everything seemed to go well as we entered the large glass building in the aptly named Fitzroy Road just off the M5 motorway. We were met by David Rogers and given a tour around before settling in his office for a chat on all things meteorological and all things non-meteorological.*

On our way out I noticed in the foyer a raised round platform where people were sitting and chatting. On enquiring I was told it was where people could sit down and chat while having a coffee. I had been informed that it was called 'The Moon Café' and on enquiring why it had that name was reliably told that it was because "it has absolutely no atmosphere". I am also reliably informed that the fish in the large ponds in the grounds had to be taken out because so many birds came down to view and eat them and they were on the flight path to Exeter Airport just up the road.

Much later, when we were with David Rogers in Geneva at the World Meteorological Organisation, he told us that he had received a letter, whilst we being shown around, from one of the forecasters insisting that we were not welcome there and should be thrown off the premises immediately.

This was from the same David Lee who accused me of harassment at the BBC Weather Centre and so spectacularly lost his case and was subsequently posted to Exeter. Hell hath no fury like a forecaster scorned!

JOHN: *David Rogers only lasted a total of thirteen and a half months in post. The official line was that he was leaving for 'personal reasons'. "His recent marriage had" he said "brought a change in his domestic circumstances which had led him to consider his personal and professional future". To us it sounds like one of those confessions the secret service make you sign. Our view was much more that, he realised that what his masters wanted was a salesman and not someone to lead the meteorology. He now lives in Switzerland with his wife Haleh Kootval whom we have known for all those years through the WMO. One day I am sure he will set the record straight for himself!*

On our travels around the world it was only in the USA that there was an intelligent relationship between the Met Office and the media. Because there was no financial connection, it allowed both parties to do what they were best at.

However, in other countries there was an equal hatred of one another. The science based Met Offices considered the broadcasters to be shallow and staffed by arty people.

The broadcasters for their part found the Met Offices aloof and unapproachable. This was no more so than just across the water from us in the Republic of Ireland. Bill and I were asked to help set up a re-launch of their TV service as they were moving from magnetic rubber graphics to electronic ones. They had seen what the BBC was doing and wanted to try and emulate a bit of that. The first thing we found was that the relationship between Raidió Teilifís Éireann (RTE) and Met Éireann was non-existent. Although RTE had tried to open a dialogue, there really was very little cooperation. To move into electronic graphics meant that the weather presenter would have to be based at RTE's premises, rather than just travelling down from Glasnevin, the Met Headquarters, to do the broadcast. This meant that we would have to recruit and train the people to do this. To illustrate what RTE were up against, Bill and I had a meeting with the Director of the Met Service in his office. We had been told that he was a stickler for punctuality and because the meeting was late in the afternoon, we must finish at 5.30pm. There we were in the middle of the discussion, when he put on his bicycle clips and on the dot of 5.30, got up from his desk, put on his coat and left the office, leaving us sitting there. Unbelievable! Luckily, the Deputy Director Bill Wann, who was also at the meeting, was a very different person, urbane, well travelled and well read. He told us, that his Director wasn't really interested in the proposed changes, but he was and would lead the Met Office as best he could. I proposed to RTE that they host a lunch to cement relationships with the Met Office, and it had exactly the desired effect. I told the RTE people to refrain from talking "shop" and just socialise. Well, to an Irishman, that didn't need a second asking, and we had an hilarious, wine driven, lunch where we talked about holidays, families and told rude jokes. It was a talking point for months to come and formed a bond between Broadcaster and the Met.

Another example of difficult relationships was in Singapore where we had been invited to provide a training course, with a view that one day they would broadcast on TV. In many countries the broadcaster had given up trying to talk to their Met Service, and had done their own thing.

A Climate of Change

Using journalists, usually female and rather attractive, they used whatever weather forecast was issued in the public domain and spun it into a broadcast. This enraged the Irish Met Service, and so the disjoint between Met and Media just got worse. Several parts of the media, and in particular the press, complained that the forecasts were usually wrong anyway.

We soon got to the bottom of why. As part of any training session we run, it always begins with a Met briefing, so that those being trained have the story in their heads. The Deputy Director gave the morning briefing.

Earlier that morning I opened my hotel bedroom curtains to a brilliantly sunny morning. At the briefing we were told that "it would be fine in the morning and then thunderstorms in the afternoon". The next morning I awoke to a cloudy and dull day. The briefing was the same "it would be fine in the morning and then thunderstorms in the afternoon". Day three it was misty and foggy – the briefing was "it would be fine in the morning and then thunderstorms in the afternoon". We then realised what was going on. The Met Office was based at the airport and their primary job was as aviation forecasters. 'Fine' simply means the absence of rain. There is no meteorological term to discuss sunshine. We showed them that their problem was in terminology and they needed to use a 'bus-stop' language. Meaning what the weather would 'feel' like if you were waiting for the bus. So day one should have been "a lovely sunny bright day with thunderstorms in the afternoon". Day two "a cloudy dull day with thunderstorms in the afternoon". Day three should have been "a misty, murky day with thunderstorms in the afternoon". The look of realisation in their eyes was a joy to behold.

But perhaps the one thing that fascinates broadcasters more is when forecasters cling onto the weather story as described in the charts rather than the reality of what is happening outside the window. When we built the BBC Weather Centre I made sure that there were windows to the sky, so at least the weather presenter could check the conditions before going in to broadcast.

Nothing is worse than seeing somebody describe the weather as one thing, when viewing in your home, whilst outside it is quite different. When training in Kenya, the briefing forecaster was telling us that it was going to be fine, when outside the window to the briefing room it was raining. When challenged he persevered saying there was nothing in the charts about rain! Closer to home, John Kettley, after recording the late night weather was forecasting a dry evening. He closed up the office, coat on and made his way to the car, only to find when he got outside it was pouring with rain. Luckily for him, the crew in the studio hadn't gone, so he rushed back and managed to re-record his forecast.

Then, one early evening I was in the Weather Centre when we started getting urgent messages from the BBC Travel Unit saying that snow was falling in Bracknell (the Met Office headquarters.) I spoke to Mike Fish who was preparing for his 6.30pm broadcast and told him of the reports.

Not possible, he replied there is nothing like that in the forecast. As the minutes went by, more and more reports were coming in. So I asked Mike to call the Senior Forecaster at Bracknell and put the call on speakerphone. Mike told him about the reports the BBC were getting. No there was nothing in the forecast for snow. So I asked him if he had looked out of the window – reluctantly he agreed and you could hear his footsteps go off in the distance – then a faint "Christ!" was heard and the return footsteps were much quicker. "It's thick snow out there".

Pandemonium set in as Mike tried to adjust his graphics so that he could reflect the worsening conditions in his broadcast. When I drove home that evening I only got home by the skin of my teeth due to the heavy snow, and for a time Bracknell was cut off.

But the realisation that the world was changing was slowly catching up with some. For the 50th anniversary of WMO in 2000 a special conference was held in Geneva at WMO Headquarters, the International Weather Broadcast Festival with the participation of the IABM. It was a series of presentations and discussions on the main weather topics of the time. In particular one concentrated on the growing use of free weather reports on the web.

The Director-General of Météo-France, Jean-Pierre Besson was loudly complaining about all of this and called for laws to be passed to stop it, or at least charge for it. John intervened and explained that what he was proposing wasn't technically possible and that the world was moving on and if he didn't, then he would suffer the same fate as the dinosaurs! Like the former Russian President Nikita Khrushchev, Jean-Pierre rose to his feet and with his fist (rather than his shoe) he repeatedly hit the podium and berated John in French for a full five minutes with a wonderful colourful performance of hand waving and shouting. It is difficult to summarise the simultaneous translation, but it was something like "you don't know what the bloody hell you are talking about". Outside the building during the coffee break, John went up to Jean Pierre to make friends again. "Don't worry" he said "I enjoyed it – and can I beg a cigarette off you?" They became good friends and later after he retired from Météo-France he told John that he had to say what he did because that was what his political masters required, he himself strongly believed that all weather data should be free.

The story of Met and the Media has been played out over the years at the WMO. The formation of the IABM (International Association of Broadcast Meteorology) changed the whole debate. When it was granted consultative status in 1998 it provided an opportunity to lead the debate, because this gave us the right to speak during WMO debates.

The WMO was no different from the Met Services it represented in its structure and 'civil service' mentality. Many of the Met services were in countries originally in the British Empire where the civil service was run on British lines. Many of the Permanent Representatives who attended the annual meetings had never really had any dealing with the media. At first they were certainly suspicious of us, we dressed differently and the language we used during interventions was more direct.

But, as time went on, they slowly warmed to us, in particular at the many social occasions where they found that we were human after all! They shared the common problem of the need to get their forecasts out to the public, but found their relationship with the media rather difficult. The experience of the BBC, where we had found a way to work in partnership, was admired throughout the world, in particular, as many of them were able to see the result on BBC World News. There have been great strides to improve how the public around the world receive their weather. There are now specialist groups within WMO to deal with public services, on which many IABM members sit.

JOHN: *Both Bill and I have done many training sessions to try to raise the standard of broadcast meteorology. However, from the BBC being founding members of the IABM, recently they have pulled out completely and no longer take any part. Why, one may ask? I fear it goes back to 2001 and News Division taking ownership of the weather. It has now become rather introspective and the realisation that there is a clear responsibility on the BBC to take part in the success and development of world meteorology, as a world broadcaster, has long been forgotten. However, in all honesty it simply reflects what has happened to the BBC in recent years where it has lost its way, and forgotten its basic reason for existing – and that is to serve its viewers and listeners throughout the world.*

CHAPTER 5

AUDITIONS

There is a belief amongst scientists that they can do everything from explaining the origins of the universe to being able to 'walk upon water'. Most of them are optimistic, their glass is never half empty but always half full and it is the same with spreading the message about the weather forecast.

They believed that they know best about who should, and could, present the radio and television forecasts to the general public and that there was no need to involve the BBC or any other area of the media from newspapers to television. They also believed that they have the expertise to decide who, in the Met Office, would make a good broadcaster. In fact one very senior member of the Met Office was heard to say that a certain person would make a good broadcaster because he had a first class honours degree in mathematics from Cambridge! He was so convinced that he was right that he insisted this person went on television without realising that he had a speech impediment. This not only made the broadcaster unsuitable but completely destroyed his confidence to such an extent that it took him a long time to recover from the ordeal.

So convinced were the Met Office that they should decide who was suitable to broadcast, that in 1981 the Met Office held auditions for prospective radio and television broadcasters as people graduated off the initial and advanced forecasting courses. It is probably worth saying here that the expertise to become a national, or even regional, broadcaster on television is quite different from that of becoming a successful weather forecaster.

At this time no one who sat on the entrance board for those wishing to join the Met Office was looking at the candidate's potential as a broadcaster or, indeed, their potential communication skills; no one on these entrance boards had any of these skills themselves, in fact all they were looking for was the candidate's scientific background (especially if they had graduated from Oxford or Cambridge Universities) and what potential had they got for understanding the physics of the atmosphere or for meteorological research.

It was at about this time that the BBC was becoming more involved with the weather presenters. Up until then, although they always had the last say as to who would appear on their screens, they only looked at those who had been at London Weather Centre as radio presenters. Television presenters, of course, need quite different skills to radio but they only auditioned those who had done national radio.

Television was becoming increasingly personality focussed and the existing weather presenters were 'national treasures'. It was very important for the BBC to ensure that it selected the right people. It was very much the policy at the BBC that it would only use trained meteorologists, in the same way that the newsreaders had to be journalists. However, the meteorologist had to be able to communicate the weather in a way in which viewers and listeners could readily understand. As the state broadcaster it was absolutely right that these weather presenters were drawn from the state meteorological office. However, the majority of those offered for audition, might be first class meteorologists but lacked any communication skills. At this time Bill was still involved in training and could see what the BBC wanted.

BILL: *I had, for some time, been arguing that communication skills, and in particular those needed for broadcasting, should be part of the initial and advanced forecasting courses in the Met Office and with my unique position of working at headquarters, but also presenting television broadcasts, I started to look at the possibility of devising a syllabus to cope with this new trend.*

All weather forecasters, even to the present day, are taught their trade based on weather for aviation. This is perfectly reasonable since weather forecasting really took off during the Second World War even though some modern form of trying to forecast the weather started way back in the nineteenth century, especially for shipping.

In aviation meteorology you need to be precise and concise concentrating mainly on those aspects of the weather that are important to the people flying the aircraft whereas for the general public it is not necessary to be such. A pilot wants to know what the height of the base of lowest cloud and maybe the direction of the wind and its strength whereas someone watching on television is more concerned about rain, sunshine and temperature. In fact we have one hundred ways of describing the weather from nothing happening right up through fog, rain, snow and severe thunderstorms with hail but there is no mention at all about sunshine. This is not important to people flying planes but very important to the general public.

So it was with this background we started a new approach to get the newly qualified forecasters to understand how to get the weather message across to those who had little or no knowledge of the physics of the atmosphere. Times were changing for the weather forecaster too as modern aircraft became less and less sensitive to bad weather and could fly and land in foggy conditions. We were also beginning to open up weather centres in some large cities across the country with forecasters becoming more and more involved in local and regional radio and television.

Teaching those on the forecasting courses how to communicate verbally in a language everyone could understand was relatively easy but producing a system for showing weather maps was more difficult.

This was at a time just before computer graphics came onto the scene and at the BBC Weather Centre (the only television station at that time that did a national weather forecast) we were still using the wonderful magnetic symbols and by placing one on top of the other we could show how the weather would change during the day using a single map. However, at the Met Office we did not have any large metal maps to put the symbols on, and they were BBC copyright, but I still wanted something to show the movement or changes in the weather throughout the day or night. The ability to show how the weather moves and develops came into its own with computer graphics but, at this time, it was still a little way off.

So we developed a metal cube that could be rotated around a vertical axis and by placing different maps on each of the four vertical sides and moving the faces around we could get some semblance of movement. This allowed the members of the courses to begin to get the idea of telling the weather story in a more interesting way and also allowed me to have some idea as to the individual forecaster's ability to communicate. This was the start of getting people to go to the BBC direct for television auditions without first having to spend a few years at London Weather Centre on radio.

Apprenticeships have gone through a turgid time over the last few years. Before the modern era, completing a professional qualification took several years of hard graft but now it can be done in what appears a recklessly short time. Such is the same in weather forecasting. When I was learning my trade we started with an initial forecasting course lasting seventeen weeks. This was followed by about three years at a large Met Office under the watchful eye of a senior forecaster. This, in turn, was followed by the advanced forecasting course lasting some six weeks and after a further training period of six months you were signed off as an independent weather forecaster. Now all of this is combined into a much shorter period.

In the 80's there was not often a need to audition as vacancies only occurred on retirement or if someone was promoted by the Met Office and had to leave. When Bert Foord and Graham Parker both left in 1974, they were replaced by Barbara Edwards and Michael Fish. Barbara was an important milestone for the BBC as she was the first woman weather presenter on British TV. However, her career was dogged by nerves when on-air; this manifested itself in a gulping for air. The BBC sent her for specialist training, but it was not really greatly improved and she left on her own request in 1978.

But in that time she, acted as a role model for many aspiring young women. But a new phenomenon also happened – the press became obsessed with what clothes she wore for her broadcasts and poor Barbara suffered with this attention as most of it was rather unkind. The reverse was true for Mike Fish who revelled in the attention given to his strange choice of ties, jumpers and jackets – always the showman and never slow in coming forward.

Once we started to expand with new services coming on stream, auditions became more frequent. The Met Office was still only looking for meteorological qualifications, but for John that had to be coupled with personality.

JOHN: *A weather forecast only lasts a couple of minutes, and so it is vital that in the first 10 seconds the viewers like who they see. If they don't they will cease listening and miss the forecast. The presenter has to be a welcome guest in peoples' homes. A smiling open face opens doors – a frown doesn't. It is even more difficult for female presenters, as women viewers can be very critical and start looking at what they are wearing. The successful female presenters were the ones who looked good, sounded good and wore sensible clothes. They could get over the first 10 seconds with ease.*

I tried many different ways of carrying out auditions from simple ones when the candidate did a forecast in studio Pres A to ones that involved an interview. I think my favourites were the ones we held at the BBC's Elstree Studios.

The format was to start with a buffet lunch, then one by one, they did a 4-minute TV interview with Bill, and then a fairly short recording with weather charts. There were usually about twenty candidates and at Elstree parking was easy and the hospitality room very pleasant. During the lunch, I had a chance to observe people. If, for example you are in a bar, it's the ones that you notice, that may have potential, and not the ones by themselves in a corner. Remember, I was looking for extroverts with big egos. Roger Hunt would normally join the day, to ensure the auditions were fair. The buffet lunch normally included chicken vol-au-vents and we always reckoned that you would know where Roger had been standing as there would be two footprints on the carpet visible through a sea of pastry flakes. In the studio each person went through a sit-down one-to-one interview with Bill. From these I could judge fluency and body language – and simply did I like them? Bill would then take them through a simple set of weather charts and then get them to do a forecast. This tested whether they could relate to a camera and finish on time.

So, that was a day of auditions, and subsequently we would have a session at TVC (TV Centre), usually at least a week later, so that when each candidate's tape was reviewed it was fresh.

Both Bill and I would be there, a Met Office account manager, who at this time was probably Gordon Higgins, Barrie Gilmour or Mervyn Hardman and perhaps someone from Met Office HR. I would have the remote control and often after a few seconds on one candidate I would fast forward to the next. "Hold on" would come the response from the Met Office, "we haven't seen the whole audition." I would simply tell them that if I had been bored in the first 10 seconds it wasn't going to get any better in the next five minutes!

My job in the BBC was to simply represent the viewers and put myself in their place. Bill would refer to it as the 'John lean forward factor'. If I intuitively leaned towards the screen, then the candidate had captured my attention. It begs the question as to whether anyone else in my position would have made different judgements.

47

I doubt it, as it is very much part of any producer's training to recognise and nurture talent. It's what we do, and by the time you reach that position you would have gone through years of working on programmes and learning the grammar of broadcasting. The Met Office never really did understand the process, all but perhaps Roger Hunt who was much more media savvy then his colleagues. In later years Bill and I simply made the decision together. I don't regret any decision I made as many of those I chose are still broadcasting and I think they are all fantastic. My only exception to this would be David Lee who I didn't like on audition, but Bill persuaded me that he would be OK and that we were desperate on numbers. Shame I didn't stick to my guns when you think of all the upset he subsequently caused us both.

The BBC has always bent in the wind of political correctness. It goes with the territory for a state broadcaster. My boss Sandy Maeer summoned me one day to say that the BBC felt that it was under-represented with ethnic minority people on air. The Board of Governors and the Board of Directors had decreed that this must change. Radio 4 already had its first 'black voice' and now television must follow. Someone in authority had noticed that there were no black faces doing the weather. I wasn't going to be caught on the back foot with this. I told her that if I had seen an ethnic minority meteorologist at audition then I would have already taken them on. I wasn't interested in skin colour, only their ability to broadcast. I carried on and explained that the overwhelming source for meteorologists was in the Met Office and they simply did not have any black meteorologists. The black community do not tend to study for science degrees. Her response was the usual Sandy "I'm not going to argue with you – just do it."

I fell on the mercy of Roger Hunt and explained my new problem. When he got back to me, he said that they had one black assistant, Everton Fox who they could accelerate onto the necessary forecasting courses. I asked for him to come to TVC for an on-camera test, and found him a most charming man with great potential. In all, it took about 12 months for him to be ready. At the same time Jay Wynne had just joined the Met Office with an MSc in Applied Meteorology, and after seeing him on camera he joined us a few months later. Job done!

CHAPTER 6

FINDING THE BROADCASTERS

The first weatherman appeared on BBC television on 11 January 1954. George Cowling was based in London and travelled to the television studios by tube train clutching the weather maps under his arm. Once there he transferred the information on to some boards using china graph pencils. At this time there were three weathermen, George, Tom Clifton and Philip McAllen and the only people who decided who would do the weather broadcasts were the Heads of Department at the Met Office Headquarters. These were eminent scientists, experts in their field, but had no idea or understanding about television or the skills needed to get the weather message across. In fact the broadcasts were really Met Office weather briefings using scientific language that would have been used whilst briefing RAF and airline pilots. The only weather symbols they had to describe the weather were the ones used by meteorologists around the world but these were a simple code totally unknown to the general public. For instance an upside down triangle denoted rain showers and three horizontal lines meant fog. This system of 'recruits and symbols' lasted for the next twenty years with little or no involvement of anyone at the BBC.

BILL: *Even when I went for my television audition in 1975 the BBC had no input as to who would go for that audition although, by that time, they had the final say as to whom, of the candidates, would appear, even so the only people that were put forward for selection were forecasters at London Weather Centre who had appeared on national radio. No one within the Met Office could apply unless they were stationed in London. This all changed in the early 1980s when the BBC Weather Centre took over the responsibility from London Weather Centre for national radio.*

After that anyone working as a weather forecaster in the Met Office could apply, when a vacancy occurred, to become a television broadcaster without having been on national radio first. Although this opened up many more potential recruits it also presented its own unique problems. Remember that, by this time, all forecasters were assessed as to their broadcasting potential on all forecasting courses using the dreaded cube so I had some idea of what they were like.

Incidentally one young forecaster, Claire Martin, a niece of Barbara Edwards the first lady weather broadcaster, did the test during her advanced forecasting course. My remarks were "that she had an engaging smile but very little else!" Claire has gone on to be one of the most successful and recognisable weather broadcasters in Canada.

She reminded me of my remarks when presenting me with an award for Outstanding Achievement as a Broadcast Meteorologist in 2008 from the European Meteorological Society.

I wouldn't let her get away with that so in my reply I said I was wrong in saying that about her because she really didn't have an engaging smile! It was all in good fun and we laughed about it over a drink later in the evening.

The fact that we could now, theoretically, look at every weather forecaster in the Met Office as a potential broadcaster seemed a great advance, but what we found was that if an Officer-in-Charge of any Met Office dotted around the country didn't like a particular forecaster they could recommend them to come for a television audition hoping against hope they would be successful and move away from their office. Under this system we had some most unsuitable candidates and I must admit that the Met Office Directors couldn't understand why the BBC rejected so many.

At this time we moved into computer graphics, and indeed, led the world but with daytime television starting as well as BBC World and BBC Prime we suddenly realised we were going to go from three broadcasts a day to well over fifty a day and soon to be over 140, including all the radio broadcasts.

BILL: *Up until this time there was very little financial incentive to come and work on BBC Television.*

Since most of us were Higher Scientific Officers in the Ministry of Defence we were doing a job graded at a more senior level and we all received a responsibility allowance and little else and if and when you were promoted to a Senior Scientific Officer you were posted away. This happened to that doyen of broadcasters Bert Foord who was posted to Strike Command at High Wycombe and another stalwart, Graham Parker went to Gibraltar on promotion.

But there came a time when it seemed rather silly to lose the talent and all the training as a broadcaster on promotion so it was decided that we could have one senior man in charge and that person was Jack Scott. However, since he was then at the higher rank, he was not entitled to the responsibility allowance. So, on his promotion he had a cut in salary and thus a review of payments and allowances came into being.

Even though we now had a person in charge we still were part of London Weather Centre and did two weeks at the Television Centre and then two weeks at London Weather Centre; it wasn't until I took over as the boss in the 1980s that we broke away from them and became an independent office in our own right.

A meeting was arranged with our Union the Institution of Professional Civil Servants and Met Office Directors to decide on a different system of rewarding the television broadcasters and it was agreed that we would be paid per broadcast. This went on for several years; Jack Scott retired and I took over as the Senior Broadcaster.

Actually that was somewhat of a fiddle because exactly three years before Jack Scott retired I was promoted to his grade and so had to leave and go to our headquarters in Bracknell in the Public Relations Department. However, I used to come back on television just once a month to keep my hand in so that when Jack retired I could come back as the boss.

A Climate of Change

Now, the Met Office thought the BBC had agreed to this arrangement and the BBC thought the Met Office had. But in actual fact, the only people that had agreed to this was Jack and myself so that I would be ready to take over in three years time on his retirement; and that's precisely what happened.

One of the reasons was that he didn't want Michael Fish to have the remotest possibility of taking over as officer-in-charge. Luckily for me the BBC also wanted me to take over. The green eye of jealousy was always there from the staff at Headquarters many of whom were higher graded than the television people but earned less money because of the allowances. So I was summoned to Bracknell once again to talk about them. They agreed that the arrangement of so much per broadcast was a better system than a blanket allowance and since we were only doing three broadcasts a day the £17 per broadcast seemed small enough for them to cope with. I readily agreed with this figure and on the way out casually mentioned that these allowances would be pensionable to which everyone, wanting to get home for the weekend, readily agreed.

What they didn't know, which I did, was that there was soon to be an enormous expansion at the BBC Television Centre with Daytime television coming on-stream, BBC World Service, BBC Prime, Super Channel as well as British Forces Broadcasting Service needing forecasts for our troops around the world. So almost overnight we went from those three broadcasts a day to almost one hundred – all at the agreed £17 per broadcast and pensionable! After all of that, though, I never remember even one of my staff saying thank you!

Actually it didn't cost the Met Office a single penny since all the extra allowances were paid for by the BBC through its many customers and even the pensions are paid by the Treasury but it really upset the powers that be at headquarters when they realised National Television Broadcasters with much lower ranks than they were, had much higher salaries and pensions and, would you believe, from that time on I could recruit people of any high grade to do television if they were suitable.

Needless to say none were, although some of us at the Television Centre went up in grades as the office there expanded. This has changed since I retired and the accountants took over because all they now want are the young ones who are a great deal cheaper.

In fact, in my last few years in charge I was repeatedly requested to get rid of Michael Fish and Ian McCaskill and bring in much younger people at half the salary. Needless to say I refused as the BBC would never have agreed, but it was a tough battle to fight and as soon as I retired in 2000 the accountants had their way – and still do to this day.

At the initial auditions for entry into the Met Office no one was assessed as to their potential for broadcasting or indeed their potential for communicating information understandable by the non-scientific general public and so when we, at the BBC Weather Centre, moved rapidly from three broadcasts a day to over one hundred, we found it impossible to recruit enough forecasters from the Met Office to fill the posts.

BILL: *During my career only 1% to 2% of the Met Office forecasters were deemed suitable for broadcasting at the national level. Actually assessing forecasters on their advanced course was a difficult job because by this time we had been opening up weather centres in many major cities across the country where broadcasting was part of their routine daily programme. I found that we could train about 80% to do local radio; then there were a few who might eventually come to TV Centre but I was after making sure I spotted two other groups. One very small number of people were considered not suitable for local broadcasting because of their strongly held political views and it was deemed a bit of a risk allowing them to have access to being live on air. The second group, I used to feel very sorry for because these were the ones who were perfectly capable of being forecasters but had a speech impediment and it would be very unfair on them if they weren't identified early, so that they would not be posted to a weather centre where they had to broadcast as part of their duties.*

Actually there was another small group I had to be aware of and that was those individuals who were very nervous and broadcasting affected them.

The way I found out about this little group was when I was at London Weather Centre and we had one person who proved to be a very good forecaster and later a manager but broadcasting upset him so much that when he was on the broadcast shift would keep nipping to the toilet it affected his bowels. It was disconcerting at the end of a night shift when we would be preparing for the main live morning radio weather forecasts that he would keep disappearing to the toilet two floors up to write and practise his scripts. I remember standing there one morning, not realising he was in there, when all of a sudden his voice boomed out from inside the cubicle "Good morning here is the weather forecast" The number of times I came out from there shaking my foot was unbelievable! So I had to make sure that those in that little group did not have to broadcast.

When the monthly roster was produced at London Weather Centre, all the radio forecasters would eagerly see which shifts they had been given because there was two days in each month that were crucial; the middle of the month and the last day. These were the days that the monthly long range forecast were issued by the Met Office Headquarters and BBC Radio 4 always did a pre-recorded interview and paid the forecaster £11 so it was a real bonus to be on shift at those times.

I remember one day early in May 1975 looking at the newly produced roster, that one of the days had a small 't' on it. When I asked the boss what it meant he said that I was to go for a television audition. I said that I didn't want to go, as I was perfectly happy just doing the radio. He said "well you have to go, it's on the roster" I said "Of course it's there you've just put it on". "Well you'd better go then" and that is how I went for a television audition.

Four of us went for this television audition, I got the job and driving home that evening I thought well done my old son, 3 to 1 against and you did it. Then I looked at the others. One of them was six foot seven and they couldn't get him into shot and he proceeded to do the forecast like the Hunchback of Notre Dame.

One of the others came for every audition, not because he wanted the job but because he liked the BBC hospitality. So actually there were only two of us in contention and I later found out why I got it.

The auditions consisted of three maps. The first was a large Atlantic map on which were the isobars and fronts, the second was a map of the UK for tonight and the third one for tomorrow. Timing in television is paramount and to make sure no one overran there was a clock beside the camera where the floor manager stood and when you got into the last minute of the broadcast she would put her finger on it showing when you had to finish, so you could watch the second hand moving around and end your piece spot on time.

The biggest fear in the early days of your television career, and this applied to the auditions, was to end up on the last map with not enough to say and then dry up. So the trick was to spend a little less time on the first two maps so you had plenty to talk about on the third while you were waiting for the time to finish. However for the other forecaster in contention, Michael Bibb, who eventually had a very successful career, as television forecaster at BBC Bristol, there was a problem. The clock dictating the length of his broadcast had stopped but he didn't know it. He had spent quite a time on the big Atlantic map and kept glancing up to look at the clock expecting to see the floor manager's finger pointing out his 'out time' but nothing was there so he continued talking until he had exhausted his knowledge on it and was forced to move across to the tonight map. The same thing happened there; he kept glancing up to see how much time was left. Finally he had told us everything, and more, about tonight's weather and so had no option but to go onto the last map.

Meanwhile the engineers had worked to reset the clock and put it to the correct time so that when Mike looked up at it as he moved to the last map he saw the finger on the clock with just two seconds remaining. He knew the biggest sin in broadcasting was to over run your time so he looked into the camera and said "and tomorrow's weather will be similar". That is how I got the job as a trainee television weather broadcaster!

Finding new weather broadcasters at this time was a comparatively easy task. Vacancies did not occur that often and there always seemed to be suitable people to hand. The auditions usually meant that we saw someone we could bear in mind for the future.

When it came to the start of Daytime TV, Bernard Davey and Suzanne Charlton were available, and then with the start of BBC World we took on Peter Cockroft, Rob McElwee, and Helen Young. Richard Edgar was the first 'outsider' in the sense that he had been broadcasting at Thames Television as Jack Scott's deputy, but he was a good broadcaster and just about had sufficient meteorology from his military service.

But the continuing expansion at the BBC Weather Centre really made the traditional route for finding new weather presenters unsustainable.

The BBC's general policy was that anyone broadcasting weather should be qualified sufficiently in meteorology to enable them to be authoritative and knowledgeable. The dividing line in the future was whether it required a fully qualified independent forecaster, or someone with sufficient training that they could present the weather with support from a forecaster. John's view was that in an ideal world everyone should be a forecaster, but that wasn't in reality going to be possible. He even tried recruiting from overseas with the excellent Irwin Kroll from Holland and Tom Huff from New York who were brilliant. On each occasion they were auditioned and their tapes referred upstairs to the Director of BBC Television. Each time there was the same reply "we don't think British viewers are ready yet for foreigners".

Each new service we added provided a new headache as to where we were going to find the presenters. News 24 presented a particular problem, as not only did they want their own graphics look, but also wanted their own presenters. So we had to find five 'new faces'. The demise of the US backed Weather Channel provided us with Carol Kirkwood, Louise Lear and Victoria Graham. None of them had any meteorological training, but were accomplished performers. The Met Office was not at all happy about this idea, as they didn't fit into any existing category. They were worried that, if for some reason the BBC no longer wanted them, there would not be any job for them back in their organisation.

However, up until this point, all weather presenters on the BBC were Met Office staff and they really didn't like the idea of the BBC employing them on presenters' contracts. So a way round was found and they all were employed by the Met Office on special contracts. As to their lack of meteorology, it meant they would never be able to broadcast on peak BBC1 and that we had to be careful that there was always a qualified forecaster on duty at the same time. But, they were very bright, and with Bill a good teacher, quickly learnt sufficient meteorology to help them become very accomplished performers. Another 'new face' we were lucky to find was Daniel Corbett. He had written to John asking if there were any opportunities at the BBC. He was currently broadcasting in Waco, Texas, but as he was British by birth felt that he would fit in well. An audition was held and within ten seconds John knew that Dan was going to be a success on News 24.

Although a meteorologist and the Met Office employed him, he always felt that he was viewed with suspicion and was never accepted into the organisation. He now works in New Zealand for their Met Service.

This 'up against the fence' recruitment policy was really getting too much for Bill and John, and with the ever growing demands for new services, they felt that it needed a radically different approach that would give some sort of 'built-in' safety margin. To be fair to the Met Office, they were finding the ever-increasing demands difficult to deal with too.

Until now, their recruitment process for forecasters was only really interested in scientific qualifications and not presentational skills. Now the BBC needed both qualities in equal measure. John was also aware that there was an increasing need for some additional support behind the scenes in the Weather Centre. Our online services of the website and Ceefax needed daily data inputting; the research into world events to feed the BBC World services needed more and more attention, and there was a growing need to make up specialists graphics for broadcast.

So the idea was hatched to create a shift of 'Broadcast Assistants' who would provide this support, but more importantly, that they would be recruited on the basis of both their scientific and presentational skills. We would seek to find people with good science degrees, who had passed an audition that they were suitable for broadcasting. During their time as Broadcast Assistants, they would be trained not only in broadcasting, but also in meteorology so that at a suitable time could qualify as independent forecasters.

So it was really a role reversal on the normal Met Office recruitment as now we recruited people who would be excellent presenters and who had the scientific background to become meteorologists.

It took a bit of time to re-work the budget to be able to afford this shift, but eventually a joint BBC/Met Office advert was placed in the national press. We had over a 1,000 applicants and eventually took 6 people to make the first shift. This strategy proved to be our saviour, as when we had a vacancy we had a choice of people ready and able to broadcast. But also, by the time they did go onto broadcasting, they already had background experience in how all the systems worked including the graphics. It is worth noting that they have now become the mainstay of the current BBC team – and jolly good they are too!

The sudden need to find over 20 broadcasters for the regions, in the end, went very smoothly as we followed the same basic recruitment policy, although we could be a bit more relaxed over the scientific skills as they would always have the support from a forecaster based in London to coordinate the forecast and ensure consistency across the whole country.

CHAPTER 7

GRAPHICS

One of the biggest challenges for televising the weather is the graphics. With radio broadcasts the art is to paint a picture in the minds of the listener with words. However, on TV they have to be much more literal and visually show the weather. In the 1950s Computer graphics were really a dream, and so an entirely physical system was used.

When TV restarted after the war, a simple hand drawn chart was shown with an announcer reading the weather. With the decision to use a meteorologist in vision, in 1954 with George Cowling, the BBC supplied large Perspex covered maps onto which symbols could be hand drawn. In 1967 symbols were introduced to show the weather and they were ones used internationally by the whole meteorological community. They had been developed to brief meteorologists and not the public. So, for example, an apex down triangle was to show a shower, and three horizontal lines for fog. With the UK post-war economy growing and an increase in the sales of refrigerators, the BBC was readily able to get supplies of 'magnetic rubber'. This was what was used to hold the fridge door closed. But it could also be used to make synoptic (pressure) charts. So the BBC had made a large 5ft by 4ft sheet steel chart with the Atlantic map stove enamelled onto it. By placing the magnetic rubber on it the isobars could be easily shown. Magnetic sheet rubber was also available, so sets of the meteorological symbols were made, and two smaller steel charts of the UK fabricated. One for 'tonight' and one for 'tomorrow'. This provided clearer and sharper graphics than the hand drawn ones, but still did not really help viewers understand the forecast.

Hugh Sheppard, who was in charge of the weather at that time, received a letter from a student in Norwich, Mark Allen, who as part of his design degree had developed a set of 35, easy to understand, weather symbols that covered every aspect of weather conditions. The BBC readily adopted them, and on 16th August 1975 Bill Giles presented the first broadcast using them. John had directed a special programme with Jack Scott that explained the changes. It is not an exaggeration to say that these new symbols captured the imagination of the nation. Gone was the 'meteorological briefing' and in came true television weather forecasts designed for the general public. These symbols remained as a mainstay of broadcasts right up to 2005 when a 'new look' set of graphics made them no longer viable. Although it is worth noting that they are still used in printed material.

BILL: *John and I were so keen that the weather story using these new magnetic graphics was almost self-explanatory. In my opinion it is no use giving the best weather broadcast in the history of the universe if no one can understand it. But we wrestled with one problem which was how to show, in simple terms, probably the greatest weather hazard we experience in the UK – that of dense fog. We did what we had done on many previous occasions when contemplating these complicated problems, John announced we would have to book a conference room where we could get peace and quiet away from the day to day tribulations of the office. We looked at every conceivable solution, from a special symbol to using sheets of tracing paper cut to shape and stuck on the map. We finally came to what I think was a monumental decision, that, when we were forecasting dense fog on the weather maps we would put on the letters F O G. This seemed fine and straightforward but we forgot about Ian McCaskill! He was broadcasting one day and on the final map had put the letters G.O.F. Now, I am convinced that he did that on purpose because if you watch the recording back he seemed to have said "oops" long before he got to the map.*

On another occasion during a local broadcast the first letter of FOG was crooked. I used to get very cross when this happened, my argument being that "we get the forecast wrong enough times without the symbols being crooked" Any rate the broadcaster carried on with the forecast and had almost finished when he turned to the weather map and the offending graphic and said "I'm sorry about the F in Fog" but he got his message across - just that once!

Satellite pictures became available in the late 70s, firstly biked across from London Weather Centre until a 'Mufax' machine was provided at TVC. This huge machine scanned the image onto pre-impregnated paper rolls. Health and Safety was not an issue then, and it was simply stuck in one corner of the weather office. Some years later, John managed to get a bigger office, and decided to partition it off so that the machine had its own area and the noise it made, suppressed. After a couple of months, he got a painter in to smarten up the offices. He asked the painter to do all the walls in magnolia. But on his return later found the partitioned area was a light green. He pointed this out with some vigour only for the painter to provide a demonstration. As he applied his brush of magnolia paint to the walls, after a couple of minutes, the wall went green. Obviously the Mufax machine had impregnated the plaster with its chemicals. The next day John had a door added to the little room and an extractor fan inserted into the window. Heaven knows what harm had been done to the weather team in their previous office!

The means of showing the satellite pictures were equally crude. The weather presenter marked the coast of the UK in red felt tip pen, and then it was held onto a metal music stand by some odd strips of magnetic rubber. The spare studio camera was trained onto it and then locked off.

The early broadcasts used the weather presenter's finger. But, that really didn't work, because some of them didn't have 'photogenic digits', and also the pictures were only about 12 inches by 9 inches and the hands looked grotesquely large.

The solution was at hand, when producer, Orwyn Evans, (who incidentally took over from Hugh Sheppard when he in turn left to start up the International Unit), borrowed, from his Grandma, a long knitting needle and painted it yellow. This simple innovation revolutionised the broadcast of weather satellites. John had worked with Orwyn in Cardiff, so knew him well, but is convinced to this day that the knitting needle innovation is why he got Hugh's job and not him!

They became an instant hit. For the first time the British public could actually see the clouds that covered the UK and how the patterns they made fitted in with the rest of the graphics in particular the pressure chart. On one broadcast Ian McCaskill forgot all about showing the satellite picture. By the time he came off air, the Duty Office was alive with calls of complaints from viewers wanting to know why the satellite had not been shown. Ever inventive, the next night Ian apologised for his mistake, and opened his jacket to show it pinned to the lining "I've made sure that I won't forget tonight!" But it did show how powerful TV could be at that time. It wasn't unusual for the weather forecast at 9.25pm to get up to 18 million viewers. Ian made his reputation by some clever one-liners. But his career in one-liners came to an abrupt end, when he made some political remarks. John had already been instructed to warn him off, when in one broadcast, at a time when Mrs Thatcher was in Europe negotiating some important change with the EU, it was a very rough night at sea. "It's so rough in the North Sea tonight that even Mrs Thatcher couldn't walk on water". The next morning John had a call from the Head of Department to say that she had been called by a member of the Board of Governors, and if Ian ever made a remark like that again, it would be the last broadcast he would ever make!

In the early 1980s there was a growing interest in using computers to make graphics for television. The Quantel Paintbox, which was a dedicated computer graphics workstation for the composition of broadcast television video and graphics, was launched in 1981, and it revolutionised the production of television graphics.

In January 1983 the BBC launched Breakfast Time, with weather presenter Francis Wilson who had been poached from Thames Television. Although he had been trained in the Met Office, he was young, ambitious and no longer constrained by the Met Office's rigid civil service mentality. He was refreshingly different. Under the flamboyant American producer Tam Fry, he developed his own style and was soon talking about "fluffy bits" – a term the Met Office would never have allowed. But more importantly, he used computer graphics.

The programme used a suite of Paintboxes to produce all their graphics for the programme. But they were labour intensive, needing a skilled graphic artist at each machine. It took a fair degree of resources to make up the weather charts. But when done, they looked fantastic in comparison to the magnetic rubber.

It was certainly a wakeup call for the Presentation Department. John was convinced that magnetic rubber must go and be replaced as soon as possible with computer graphics. The problem would be cost and practicality. Francis Wilson only broadcast for a comparatively short period from 6.00am until 9.00am, so once the graphics had been made they didn't have to be updated. The cost of the Paintbox and a designer was easily lost in the overall budget of a live current affairs programme. To do the same thing for the main weather broadcasts would involve having an expensive designer on a 12-hour shift, 7 days a week. So to cover holiday and sickness it would mean a team of 5 designers. It was just too much.

But tucked away at Television Centre was a small, but clever team called Computer Graphics Workshop (CGW). It was managed by a mad, but brilliant Scotsman Bill Gardner, who proposed that they could develop the software which would allow the duty weatherman to make up a stack of weather graphics using an Apple Lisa Computer as the interface to a Paintbox.

Apple had developed an operating system that provided a very user friendly screen display which could be configured to make the job of the weatherman easy. John realised that this would be the way forward, because the 'one-man' operation of weather would continue without additional staffing. In effect the weather presenter would also be the graphics artist, although the system contained all the graphics elements already drawn and agreed. This would ensure that all the weather graphics would have the same look – even if Ian McCaskill was on duty!

But the implications of this new technology were even wider than perhaps John and Bill first thought. By now Bill had taken over from Jack Scott as the Senior Forecaster and team leader. Together they spent a great deal of time brainstorming its potential. To start with there was no limit to the number and type of graphics that could be used. The magnetic system always had the same format – Atlantic Chart, Satellite, Tonight and Tomorrow. On a Friday evening the Tomorrow UK chart was replaced with a European one. They realised that there was a whole new visual grammar here. Not only was it about quantity, but also about order. The weather 'story' could be illustrated in the right way.

JOHN: *Both Bill and I had long believed that a weather forecast was a story. It had a beginning, middle and an end. I believed that the job of the graphics was there to illustrate that narrative. So if the story of the day, on say a Monday, was that by Friday it was getting very much colder with snow, then the 'weather story' was snow and not what was happening on Monday.*

It wasn't my job to prescribe what graphics should be used when and in what order, it should be led by the 'story'. This basic policy that I established with Bill at the start of computer graphics in 1985 underline how we did, what we did, in all our broadcasts for the next 20 years. That was until May 2005 when the 'new graphics system' was introduced.

But, back to those early beginnings, John got busy and persuaded the BBC system to fund a Quantel Paintbox dedicated to weather and the cost of the development of the software. The new system would be like a slide-show with a stack of graphics that could be shown in order. The graphics would be of two main types, those that the weather presenter had prepared themselves, such as symbol charts or league tables and graphics automatically drawn up from data supplied by the Met Office. Luck was on our side again as the Met Office had some very clever software people, in particular Bob Ellis who led a team to develop the means to send to Television Centre, on an agreed timetable, data such as pressure charts, humidity charts, temperature charts, satellite images etc. Once received at the BBC, the Paintbox would automatically draw them up ready to be selected by the duty weather presenter.

For many years John had worked with graphic designer Liz Varrell. He had first met her during the days of magnetic rubber. She worked for the centralised Graphic Design Department, and each time he had some weather work to do, he asked for her. The design aspects of weather graphics are more complicated than they appear at first sight. There are a lot of technical issues to do with map design.

So, for example the TV format at this time was 4:3, so wider than it is high. When you look at the map of the UK, Scotland is almost half the length of England, and the whole area is long and thin. So on magnetic charts we had squeezed down the UK overall and shortened Scotland. The Shetlands were also an issue as they were so far north.

We opted to put them in a box and bring them down the map. In fact the Shetlanders were so upset about being 'put in the box' beside Aberdeen that they devised a T-shirt on which was a detailed map of the Shetland Isles with a box on the side of the shirt in which was printed BRITAIN.

This was easy to do on a steel chart, but when it came to computer graphics it was a different story altogether. The background maps would have to carry data such as pressure charts and if the BBC map was a special one, then the data would have to be re-mapped. Luckily Bob Ellis at the Met Office worked well with Liz and a compromise was reached. There was also a complication over the area for which data could be supplied. John wanted to ensure that both satellite and Met Office data appeared over the same area. However, it all, in the end, came down to map projections. Some were polar stereographic and others Mercator projections. On the initial design the area appeared to John to be too tight, in particular, it needed some space in which the presenter would stand.

So the idea was developed of using a boxed area for the data leaving the rest of the map to act as a surround.

However, there was another hurdle to overcome. To show the weather presenter standing against computer graphics required us to use Colour Separation Overlay (CSO) or as it was known in the rest of the world – Chroma Key. Basically, if you stood against a blue screen (we used blue to match in with the sea, but green was more commonly used) then wherever the camera saw blue, you could replace that with the weather graphics. As you could never wear blue clothes using this method, Bill had to arrange for a special clothing allowance, as many of the team had blue clothes. We organised a weather presenter fashion show one day in the studio so that we could establish what would and wouldn't work. Following this, a special clothing allowance was agreed, so that new clothes could be purchased that were 'CSO safe'.

The other main issue was how to prompt the presenter. To the viewer they would be seen standing against a lovely weather chart, but in the studio all they would see would be a plain blue screen.

So pointing to a particular area on the screen would be impossible. Bill Gardner came up with the idea of a translucent screen mounted in a frame, lit from the back with blue lights, and also behind was a video projector that would project a faint image of the graphics. From the front, the camera would see a blue screen, and if the settings were right, it would not detect the projected image of the graphics. Initial experiments showed promise. John then had to sell it to the staff in Pres 'A' who would have to operate it. Needless to say they were less than enthusiastic! However, John persevered and also added another idea, and that was to use an autocue head on the camera. Autocue was a long established system for putting a script in front of the camera so that a presenter could read it without it looking as if they were reading. It's what makes newsreaders look as if they know what they are talking about.

In this case, there was no script – just the final mix of presenter and graphics just as the viewer would be seeing, plus another innovation in the top right hand corner – a countdown clock.

No more 'finger on the clock'. In the gallery the director started an electronic countdown clock that began with the full duration of the broadcast and then counted down to zero. So when the weather presenter turned to look at the camera, they could see what the viewer was seeing and also how much longer they had to speak. It was the end of over-running weather presenters!

To control the replay of the graphics in the studio a trolley mounted Apple Lisa Computer was supplied with a lockable door on the front to prevent anyone having a 'play'. Attached to this was a long lead with a push button on the end by which the forecaster triggered each graphic.

It had been thought that this could be done by someone in the gallery, but it worked much better with the presenter doing it, as they had made and rehearsed with the graphics, it gave them total control of the broadcast – something that John was keen to encourage.

There were some experiments with using a button connected by radio, but it was too dangerous. It would only need a local taxi on the same frequency and chaos would have reigned. There were several pilot runs to ensure that the system was stable and predictable. Bill scheduled all of his team to have training days with the ever-patient Tom Hartwell of CGW. We were finally ready, and the first broadcast was on 18th February 1985 presented by Bill Giles.

BILL: *It took a little time for many of us older broadcasters to come to terms with the new computer system and indeed the computers themselves. We knew that both had to be robust and over the years whenever a new system was proposed Computer Graphics Workshop had to make sure that it was "McCaskill proof."*

If when working with the computer you did something incorrect it would come up with a little caption that said "illegal activity." Ian was sitting at the machine one day merrily working away, John and I were watching to see how he was coping when to our horror a floppy disc shot out onto his lap. He jumped up and in his usual breathless delivery looking at John he said "I did nothing illegal"

We were now leading the way in computer graphics for weather but being the leader in anything you have to put up with the teething problems. In the very early days, one of those problems was that for no apparent reason the whole system would lock solid and it was impossible to move the graphics on.

I well remember one broadcast where the graphics locked out right at the beginning of the broadcast and the only thing I had on the map behind me was the word Scarborough 21°C 70°F because what we always tried to do was to build up the map as we went along thereby drawing the viewers' eyes to that part of the country that you were talking about. Nothing I could do would move the graphics on, so I had two minutes to fill and that, I can assure you, is a good laxative. There is no such thing as a constipated weatherman – or lady for that matter.

I used to get very cross when the system failed us on air because it was me, the weather presenter, who ended up with egg on my face.

In those early days one of the system analysts would be in the studio during the broadcasts, not that they could do anything once you were on air but really needed to immediately analyse the reason for a fault if it occurred. After one horrendous broadcast I struggled through to the end and turned on Robin Vinson, the attending system programmer. I approached him with my hands outstretched and being then a President of St John Ambulance knew exactly where the windpipe was located. He, startled at this, said that it wasn't a computer fault but an engineering one.

I immediately turned around and headed for the engineer's windpipe. He denied it and they bounced me back and forward until Robin was heard to say that it was because of a bug in the system.

I thought deeply about this and wondered if there was a bug in the system who de-bugged it? I spoke with Tom Hartwell telling him that next time it happened to me I was going to blame them 'on air' for the bug in the system. I told him that I would look straight into the camera lens and say to the viewers "I am sorry we have a bug in the system we will have to de-bug it then I would turn to the analyst and say "Would de-bugger in the corner please come and fix my machine" I never did, of course, because that way I might lose my pension.

Trying to sort out the problems wasn't from any want of trying and Tom Hartwell recalls racing down corridors in TVC with engineer Nick Gill one night looking for a faulty Ethernet connection SOMEWHERE that they suspected was causing an intermittent problem. It was late at night after transmission had finished, and the corridors and cableways dark and spooky.

At one point Nick said "it could be the Vampire Tap has developed a fault" – Tom's heart almost stopped at that point. "What the hell is that?" "Oh, it's a spike they drive in to connect thick Ethernet cables ..." Ahhhh!!!! They then spent the rest of the night pulling out cables like spaghetti looking for this.

Early on with this new system, Ian McCaskill had a brilliant idea. The forecast at teatime on a Saturday was only 1 minute long and it was difficult to get everything in and finish on time. The system allowed the forecaster to mark each frame as to whether to cut to the next image or mix, and whether to stop or automatically run to the next frame after 2 seconds.

The idea of this was to allow a sequence of charts like satellites to run in a sequence automatically. Ian was certainly very bright and worked out that if he set up his 'stack' in the right way, he could get it to run automatically and last just one minute from the first push of the button.

He rehearsed and rehearsed and it all worked perfectly. One thing John insisted on was that the presenter got in the studio in sufficient time to rehearse and check everything was working. Everything was excellent, the two minute flashing red lights started. Ian made sure he was in the right position on camera, mentally practised his opening words, when by mistake, with about thirty seconds to go, he pressed his hand push button. The sequence started. He lent over the computer on the trolley to try to reset it – but had forgotten that it only resets after it has completed any sequences- and his whole broadcast was one long sequence.

As he went on air, all that the viewers could see was Ian's backside as he frantically tried to stop the machine. He realised he was on air and as he turned to peer at the camera, he just said 'hello' as the graphics changed remorsefully behind him!

Considering that there was a requirement of having a system that would operate without constant intervention, it did prove remarkably stable.

There were a few times when the system froze on-air, and so we developed a routine where 'key' charts from the graphics system were copied onto another device in the studio gallery called 'Slide File'.

The idea being that, if the weather system failed on air, then the director would cut to this other device and replay the key charts. On one broadcast, Bill was about 30 seconds into his forecast when the graphics went to black. In the gallery they went to the stand-by, but nothing came out of it, until the operator realised that she had electronically 'locked' the machine by mistake.

On releasing the lock, the images starting playing so fast they looked like a fruit machine behind Bill. There was a lot of public reaction, but Anne Robinson said on 'Points of View' praise was due to Bill for calmly getting through the broadcast.

But, there is another important point here. The idea of having the duty forecaster making up their own charts, meant that they were ensuring the weather story was really well into their heads. So they could easily do a full broadcast without any graphics at all. On some rare occasions they had to do exactly that!

In 1993, the BBC Weather Centre won the Royal Television Society's award for Technical Innovation in operational systems and John Teather together with Ewen MacLaine accepted the prize at an awards ceremony at the Dorchester Hotel. Ewen was now leading the Computer Graphics Workshop, another Scot, but not this time completely mad! He cleverly negotiated all the twists and turns as we continued to develop the weather graphics system.

JOHN: *But a real sudden advance for us was when we were told that a new 'Daytime' look was being proposed on BBC1 that would entail a news summary on the hour, every hour, followed by a weather forecast. There was no way that I could do that from Pres 'A' as during the morning it was used for trailer making. My solution would be to build a small self-operate studio that could service this new requirement.*

Finding accommodation in TV Centre was always a challenge, but I managed to get my hands on an office on the 5th floor which had a small outer office and a bigger inner office, that didn't have a door to the corridor. This would help with noise penetration. The existing weather office was being eyed up by Press and Publicity, who were expanding their empire, so they exerted their pressure on the system to get us out. It would not be possible in this new space to use a blue screen type presentation, so I asked for a desk by the window, and a switch that would allow the forecaster to cut between either a shot of themselves or the weather graphics direct.

At the start, it was a desk-mounted switch which was in view, but shortly after that Computer Graphics developed the ability for their software to drive a vision mixer direct, including mixing between the studio and the graphics and finally we replaced this with a foot switch.

The office had a large window overlooking the roof, so I asked design department to come up with a scheme of artificial plants to dress the view, including a display on the desk of seasonal flowers. Using the window had the added advantage that viewers could actually see what it was like in West London, and gave a chance for the weatherman to describe what was going on such as "it's a lovely day out there at the moment, but by lunchtime it will raining hard". They could then cut to the graphics to explain why. Selling the idea to the weather presenter team might have proved difficult.

But when Bill explained that their broadcast responsibility allowance of £17 was for every broadcast they did – you could see the wheels turning as they calculated how much extra they would earn. I was also concerned that there may be a union issue with them turning on lights and doing a vision cut etc. But on checking the broadcast unions said that as they were Met staff it was up to them and the Met unions couldn't find anything to object to. So, the era of one-person weather broadcasting began in October 1986. Parallel to this, a Presentation producer Martin Everard, left to head up a new TV Channel – SuperChannel. He realised that with the development of the self-operate studio, I might be interested in providing a commercially sponsored weather report.

This was a very new departure for the BBC and it took some time for the 'wise men' of BBC management to agree that it would not break any rules or conventions. However, we had to be careful not to look as if the BBC was endorsing any products. The sponsor was to be the tyre manufacturer Goodyear. So, in the early days we took it very carefully. Martin developed some opening titles that sold the tyres, which he then edited onto the front of the weather before transmission. Some of the graphics were changed to include the sponsor's logo. I briefed the team, and agreed that their opening announcement could only be a statement of fact such as "Welcome to the Goodyear Weather", but there was to be no reference after that. I threatened Ian that if I ever heard anything like "it's been another good year for weather" then we would have serious words with him! The major broadcasts continued to come from Pres 'A', but that little self-operate studio increased its workload, as we took on BBC Prime (a commercial entertainment channel) and SSVC (the new names for BFPS who broadcast to troops overseas). Later on we added 'Weather to Ski' an early Sunday evening broadcast that followed 'Ski Sunday'.

This was done in association with the Ski Club of Great Britain. I had to ensure that the ski conditions we broadcast were accurate. We could have readily got data for free off the Internet, but this was inputted by the local Tourist Boards, who rather exaggerated the conditions, in particular when they were poor. With the Ski Club, they had their own representatives in each resort that phoned in the actual conditions to headquarters.

After several meetings with Rosemary Burns of the Ski Club, we struck a deal to supply the BBC with all the data. Rosemary's knowledge and enthusiasm was infectious and rather important as neither Bill nor I had any idea about skiing and had never skied.

Together with Liz our designer and Computer Graphics we developed a new suite of graphics that looked fantastic. I was also keen to test out how better to animate graphics and add sound. To show the list of snow amounts we used a table, but it only just faded the list on line-by line. So Liz re-designed them so that each resort tilted like horizontal Toblerone bars, the sort of thing you would see at the airport.

As each country appeared there would be the sound of a whoosh of a ski. Also she designed opening and closing titles both with music, and coupled with this, Tom Hartwell supplied a 30 second countdown clock, complete with tone that cut off at the appropriate time. Now we could produce a complete, sophisticated little programme entirely operated by one person – the weather presenter. The snow depth data was faxed to the BBC Weather Centre by the Ski Club after lunch on a Sunday. The weather presenter entered the figures via the Mac interface computer, and then operated the studio, including getting the programme recorded for transmission. For me I had proved an important point.

By investing in clever software, then the overheads of production were really only the cost of the weather presenter, who was already on duty to do other weather reports during their shift. With a growing list of clients I was able to spread the cost of Computer Graphics across them, as, if I developed a trick for one customer, then I could use it for others.

True economy of scale.

But with the computer graphics system on air, work did not stop there. Behind the scenes John was working with Computer Graphics Workshop and Tom Hartwell on the next release. In May 1988 more technological advances were made to allow the introduction of 'Radar Rainfall' where the heaviness of the rainfall could be shown as an animated sequence. At the same time we introduced topography to the flat map, featuring mountains.

Parallel to all of this was the growing development of the BBC Weather Web site under the leadership of Jeremy Hall. The BBC were pioneers in the development of the World Wide Web and were keen to drive content into this new media. The BBC had an online presence supporting its TV and radio programmes and web-only initiatives since 1994, but did not launch officially until December 1997, following government approval to fund it by TV licence fee revenue as a service in its own right. Jeremy was in there from the start and built the site up over the years to become one of the most visited. In the early days he had to learn programming skills to keep the site on-air.

It was fully integrated into the Weather Centre and Liz ensured a commonality of design. Also we eventually took responsibility for the weather on Ceefax (Teletext) to ensure a consistent forecast was delivered across all platforms.

John receiving the Royal Television Award for the new Weather Graphics from Bill Cotton

It was received together with Ewen McLaine who was Head of Computer Graphic Workshop who pioneered the technology behind the system.

Although graphically there was little you could do with Ceefax due to the low resolution, Liz did make some small changes to ensure it looked like 'one BBC.'

In 1996, we introduced new animations and graphics including Weather Advice and a subtly modernised set of new symbols. The maps also showed more topographical definition and natural shading on the land. A year later in 1997 with the introduction of the new BBC logo, the weather also adopted the BBC corporate typeface Gill Sans.

Behind all of this, the means of making weather graphics was rapidly changing as new technologies became available. The Apple Lisa Computer was superseded by Apple MacIIs and Mac Fxs and allowed the interface used by the weather presenter to be in colour.

The move from Quantel Paintboxes was made in 1995 when the new Alpha Digital computers arrived, which allowed the pictures to be made and then transferred to a Profile which by now was a standard device used in TV for playing clips. It had two outputs and was used to play both clips and stills giving the ability to integrate movie sequences into weather reports. Software was also developed to allow a vision mixer to be controlled. The first use of Matrox video cards, (an electronic circuit card that plugged into a computer) that were of broadcast quality and fitted in a Windows NT PC was pioneered by Computer Graphics Workshop for use in the 1996 Olympics. Weather took advantage of this development and used these in 2000 and also in the regions and nations to provide a standalone weather graphics system.

In November 1997 BBC News 24 (now the BBC News Channel) launched. News wanted the weather graphics used on the new channel to look different to those seen on other BBC output. Despite John trying to persuade them otherwise, and the Presentation Department insisting there should be one look to reflect the BBC Brand – we were up against the News Division who basically felt that they were apart from the rest of the BBC and could do whatever they wanted. So we designed a whole new suite of charts with a predominantly blue and orange colour scheme.

To do this we had to basically have two computer systems to produce charts in two different colour schemes. Every chart we made up normally was then automatically redrawn to be used by the News 24 weather presenters. Sense finally prevailed and News 24 was brought back in line in 2000 with the Weather 2000 relaunch.

The move by the TV industry from 4:3 aspect ratio to widescreen 16:9 meant a substantial change for weather broadcasts. The introduction of widescreen forecasts in 1999 caused us major problems. Liz had said that she needed a new source of map backgrounds, as it would not simply be a case of "adding a bit more at the sides".

Bill broadcasting from the Weather Office Studio with a very snowy outlook behind him

Ian McCaskill getting ready to broadcast in this poor quality photo taken from high level to show the camera and prompt monitors, together with all the control equipment

She eventually found a company in the USA who were selling high-resolution maps taken from the Landsat satellite. Not only did these show superb topography on land but wonderful contours and colours of the sea. The very high definition was vital, as at this time we were responsible for regional weather and had to be able to produce the 12 close-up maps of the UK.

But there was a big problem – the map images were very expensive and John didn't have the budget. After some horse-trading he managed a deal where they would defray the cost across three financial years.

JOHN: *I don't know the total number of maps that poor old Liz had to make in the end, ably assisted by Tricia Hylton but every time I walked into her office she growled at me! So no change there then!*

By this time the BBC Weather Centre had expanded so much that I now employed Liz fulltime, and Tricia part time in their own fully equipped office, just producing weather graphics for the weather forecasts and the recently commissioned Weather Show.

One morning I was summoned to Sandy Maeer's office (my line-manager) to be told that she and Pam Masters (Head of Presentation) had been at a routine with Controller BBC1, Peter Salmon. He had just come back from holiday in the USA, and was struck by the fact that every weather forecast he had watched had a 'fly through' and why didn't we? I explained that I had been looking at this for some time, and had seen it in the States on many occasions over the years.

At every conference we attended in the States there was a fierce debate amongst the broadcasters that they were being forced to use fly-throughs by their News Directors whether or not it told the weather story. I explained that my main concern was that it was style over content, as it didn't really add anything the comprehension of the forecast. There was also the added downside, that the viewer was denied seeing their part of the country until the sequence got to their region or area. But, I said that I had been working with Computer Graphics Workshop on the concept and it may be that we have to purchase a separate graphics machine such as one from Kavouras (a leading American weather computer graphics company), just to do that bit.

Although sympathetic to my concerns, Sandy was insistent we demonstrate that we were actually doing something so that it could be reported back the Controller. She suggested that Bill and I go to the States and do some research and visit some TV Stations with the Kavouras machine and gauge reaction from both weather presenters and news directors.

I spoke to Kavouras and asked them if they could put together a tour of typical stations that were using their graphics system. They came back with a list that took us to San Francisco, across to Sacramento, down to Los Angeles and across to Las Vegas. From there we would fly to their headquarters in Minneapolis and meet up with Roger Hunt from the Met Office to ensure that their system could ingest their data to make our fly-throughs. Oh dear, I thought, it's a tough life having to go on all these trips!

We had indeed been very lucky with overseas trips in our time at the BBC. Normally production staff would never the leave the country, but the international dimension of weather, coupled with the input of commercial funds, had allowed us literally to see the world. However, with very few exceptions, it was always budget travel, in the cheapest seats and in mainly downtown hotels, unless it was a conference hotel, when we could enjoy a little more comfort.

Arriving in San Francisco airport we picked up a car, and after some time eventually found our hotel. For the first-time visitor the very hilly nature of the city, coupled with roads that just literally stop dead at a hill, makes navigation a nightmare. Several times we could see the hotel, but couldn't find a road to get to it. But then our record of navigation is pretty appalling. It's safe to say that we have got lost in every city or country we have ever visited – without exception! It also applies to the UK!

Only by chance later that day, we were lucky enough to find the TV station that we were booked into and meet the lead meteorologist who was preparing for his next broadcast. He showed us around the station, and then concentrated on his area and how he produced the report. He was very well equipped with briefing displays that ensured he understood the weather situation. On the subject of fly-throughs he suddenly got agitated "I hate the f***ing things – I only use them because our News Director insists. He says that 'because the machine cost so much, then we have to get our dollars worth!" He went on to explain that the other down side was how long it took the graphics machine to render the fly-through and during that time he couldn't do any other work. We watched his broadcast and departed.

The next morning we drove to Sacramento for our next appointment. We eventually found the TV station on about the fifth time of driving round the town. The notable thing was how much alike were all the stations we visited. The newsroom and studios were almost identical and all the staff were delightfully friendly and welcoming.

Our conversation with the duty weather forecaster was an echo of San Francisco, and he did all he could do not use fly-throughs until he was forced to.

We then had a long drive from Sacramento down the route N1 to Los Angeles. I had worked out that it was considerably cheaper for us to drive rather than take internal flights. It would have been more than double in costs even having included car hire and extra hotels. It did though afford us the opportunity to drive down that famous Pacific Ocean road. I had put a Beach Boys tape in my luggage just to get us in the mood for the long drive! We did allow ourselves one moment of indulgence when we stopped for coffee in Carmel hoping to see 'big girls on roller-skates'. It was worth the stop.

We had been to LA before, and got very lost. This time was no exception, as I hadn't taken the Sat Nav option on the car because it was too expensive. It proved to be a false economy. That evening we took a taxi from the hotel to the TV station. This was a much larger affair then the previous two as there were studios making programmes. It was on a large plot with high fences and barbed wire.

The newsroom though was as familiar as before and again, we had the same story from the weather presenter. He was even more vehement than the previous two and said "the bloody things should be banned!"

After an interesting chat and watching the news and weather going out, we asked them to book us a taxi. We said we would see ourselves out down to the main gate as it was getting busy in the newsroom with a breaking story of a shooting. At the motorised gate we said to the security guard, that if he let us out now, we would wait in the street for our taxi. "No sir" he said forcibly "I would rather you wait here with me where I can ensure your safety. This is not a good area." We didn't need a second asking!

The drive across the desert to Las Vegas was stunning. We forget the sheer size of the country. When we could see the pyramid of the Lexus Hotel - we were still 20 miles away. Las Vegas is a crazy town, sitting in the middle of a vast desert, it is simply a city built for pleasure. As the sun set and we sat round the hotel pool, the air temperature was 120°F or in English 49°C. Our station visit was not scheduled until the next day, so we went to dinner in the Lexus, which is worth a visit just by itself. This huge Pyramid is hollow inside with the bedrooms hung round the insides. The strangest thing is the lift. Once the doors are closed, the car moves sideways first before then going up, as it steps it's way up the apex. Very odd, but it made the first-timers like us scream! We ate in one of the two, three-star Egon Ronay restaurants at the Lexus - the total bill was only $60 – it was superb! The next day we drove to the station and actually found it first time! The smallest of all of them, but again, with a familiarity to the rest. It was very much the same story. The duty forecaster used fly-throughs but didn't much like them as with his climate it was all about temperatures and seldom rainfall. But his news director liked them!

So, after visiting all those stations, the conclusion was clear. In Minneapolis at Kavouras Headquarters we had very useful discussions over how their machine worked and how it might be possible to get Met Office data into it.

BILL: As usual we could never meet and talk with people from Kavouras without them extending lavish but discreet hospitality on us. This time, my boss, Roger Hunt, was with us and after a sumptuous meal all ended up in a nightclub which turned out to be a lap dancing club as well. John and I had been entertained by Kavouras before, but Roger was obviously new to it. The drinks came and the dancing started, all very professional and choreographed, and with the girls being so beautiful it was a joy to watch. The little red patches on Roger's face were growing larger as he enjoyed the music when he was invited to go onto the stage. Reluctantly he was dragged up there but because his musical rhythm didn't fit the musical beat he soon retreated. Nonetheless I still have some good photos of the event that, needless to say, kept my job secure!

JOHN: *I did, sometime later, eventually buy a Kavouras machine, but it was a cut down version, that allowed us to ingest US radar images and map them over one of our high-resolution maps. I never did see fly-throughs in my time at the BBC. I continued to work with CGW on the concept and just before I left, saw some brilliant trials that Tom Hartwell showed me.*

One of the big issues that we had with Kavouras was getting the resolution of the maps at the same high level as the static ones. Tom's solution was to separate the map from the data, as not only did it make the render very quick, but also kept the high resolution.

By this time the Weather Centre had been given to the News Division as the Presentation Department had been privatised! Also both Bill and I had retired in 2001. I had always argued that any changes to weather graphics should be by evolution and not revolution. Over those 20 years we had many upgrades and enhancements, but they built on what was already there and did not replace them. In 2005 those 'clever people' in News launched a new graphics system that immediately met with criticism and derision. They had literally thrown out the bath with both baby and water. Typical of News they went for style over content. Our green and pleasant land was suddenly brown as we zoomed all over the country. All very clever, but it added nothing to the understanding of the weather. Indeed, as you were flying over Scotland you couldn't see what the weather was doing in your own area until it came into view. But the biggest sin – was that the forecast became prescriptive. The graphics were always in the same order. Forecasters were instructed not to use pressure charts as 'they confused the viewers' and that flashy fly-throughs must be shown in every forecast whether it was relevant or not.

News Division, with its 'money is no object' gung-ho attitude to licence payers, threw out Computer Graphics Workshop after their 20 years of most brilliant development, and went to the New Zealand firm Metra. We will never know the true cost, but over one million pounds has often been quoted. It still galls me that all previous investment was abandoned in favour of a commercial company.

But these were changing times, and the fashion of competitive tendering was in vogue. In the end even the Met Office had to go through a tendering process. What had happened to those basic principles of public service broadcasting where the state broadcast would by nature use the state Met Office?

But what really makes me cross, is the cavalier 'not invented here' syndrome that belies the BBC's News Division. All of the years of experience and development were just dismissed as 'the old way of doing things! When on April 1st 2001, the Weather Centre moved from Presentation to News I knew my days were numbered. I had not made friends there. When News would phone up to ask the weather to cut back because they were over-running I always said no! To take one minute of the weather was to half the duration and do a disservice to the viewers. Viewing figures over the years had consistently shown an increase at the end of the News just before the weather.

I knew what our viewers wanted even if News didn't!

CHAPTER 8

A BIT ON THE SIDE

There have been lots of things that have gone on in parallel to our work at the BBC Weather Centre, but don't really fall into any other chapter. So, for the want of anything better we are calling this 'A Bit on the Side'.

BILL: *In the early 1980s, not long after I had come back full time to the BBC Television Centre, John and I were invited to Brest in northwest France to a conference designed to look at "Safety at Sea". We were not sure of the relevance, but looking at the schedule there might be something useful, and after all they were paying. We duly arrived as 'green horns' on the conference circuit so it was really our job to observe and advise on severe weather conditions. The organisers were especially worried about the number of injuries occurring on the long haul fishing boats that went from the shores of Western Europe, mainly from Spain and Portugal. We sat around the large oval conference table listening to mainly university professors and other graduates working on their respective PhDs and who were justifying the grants they had been given.*

Very little of the conference was concerned with the practicalities of fishing in winds of gale force 8. In fact I am still convinced that the conference missed the main reasons for most of the injuries and they were tiredness, boredom and particularly alcohol. Nonetheless we were introduced, for the first but not the last, to French hospitality. Sitting in the conference with the sun streaming in through the windows was stifling and as we glanced across the table it was obvious the man opposite was wearing a wig. Fine but he had not fitted it correctly and it slanted over his left ear. That afternoon, he had changed it, but we were certain it was then on back to front. Looking and guessing what he had done wrong made the session go more quickly but John is prone to having a little doze in the afternoons.

He had drifted slowly into the land of nod with his earphones on, listening to the simultaneous translation, when I changed it from English to Italian and turned up the volume. He shot up straight listening to it and stayed awake for the rest of the afternoon.

On the morning of the second day we were all taken along to the harbour at Brest to watch and talk to the local fishermen as they landed their catches. It seemed to us very unfair that the UK fishing fleet had been decimated over the past few years and yet there in France were so many small fishing boats that they had to moor up alongside one another.

That apart, watching these muscular men moving their catches from boat to the quayside made me wonder who, from the conference, would dare tell them they needed to straighten their backs when lifting the heavy baskets; not one of the PhD students I'm sure!

We came upon on a boat that intrigued us with its large catch of langoustine and as we watched them, a member from the conference, a Hull Trawler captain, sidled up to us and said in a broad Yorkshire accent "They're dirty buggers here they don't even take out the shit sticks before they cook them" When we enquired what he meant he told us that before cooking langoustine you have to take out the long thin gut which is the elementary canal. You have to do it before cooking because after, it all breaks up and you can't remove it and it is that piece that can give you food poisoning. We thanked him for his advice and thought no more about it. That evening we were treated to a sumptuous banquet by the Mayor of Brest only to see that the highlight of the feast was a huge mound of freshly cooked langoustine - all still with their 'shit sticks' in place. The old Yorkshire sea dog was quite right you couldn't get them out when they were cooked. We went rather hungry that night!

Our trip back to Gatwick was equally eventful. We climbed aboard what appeared to be an aircraft left over from the Second World War. Because of John's height we were shown to the front of this little plane and as we took off the hostess asked John if he would stick his feet out to keep the door to the flight deck open so as to circulate the air. There we were sat with the door open looking at the French pilots smoking their Gauloise cigarettes when quite suddenly John turned to me and told me that he thought he was having a 'funny turn' He said he seemed to be gasping for breath. I replied so was I, as we were flying at 10,000 feet in an unpressurised plane, so only had about 70% of the oxygen that we were normally used to. We both sat back wheezing away until we descended into Gatwick Airport and sea level again.

But Brittany was to figure again when John Teather got summoned up to see, the then Head of Presentation, Malcolm Walker.

JOHN: *Malcolm had taken over as Head of the Presentation Department on the retirement of Roger Greenwood on grounds of ill-health. An imposing figure, always immaculately dressed in a three-piece suit sporting a handkerchief in his top pocket. Like his predecessors and successors, he was very supportive of weather and championed it all he could. As Malcolm was some way up the BBC food chain he also commanded an impressive office, and me being rather junior in the department would visit him in some awe.*

I seem to remember that his secretary Audrey always seemed to be slicing up runner beans at her desk, but perhaps it was only the once. Malcolm told me that he had asked me up, as he had received a letter from the Brittany Fishery Association asking if they could buy the British Shipping Forecast. Apparently their captains always listened to the UK shipping forecast, but reception was sometimes poor, but they were convinced that it was more accurate than the one they got from Météo-France. They had recently got caught in some serious storms and there was a real need to get better forecasts.

The 'Safety at Sea' conference in Brittany

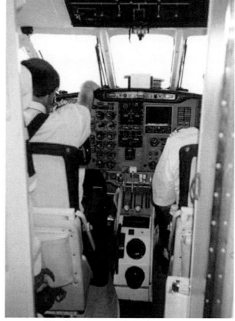

A plate of non-treated langoustine and an interesting flight back with Air France

A Climate of Change

Malcolm wanted to know what I thought. I could see that delivering it would be no problem as we could fax it to them, but they would have to arrange their own translation. I was sure the UK Met Office would be happy for a small fee.

One of many things I learnt from Malcolm was 'style'. He always did things 'properly'. He told me that the French had invited us to go to Brittany to discuss and it would be rude to say no! On arrival we were met at the steps of the plane by a delegation that treated us as if we were members of the Royal Family. We were taken by fast car to our hotel. It was at that point that we realised that none of our hosts spoke any English. Malcolm's French was better than mine, although at best, it was only schoolboy French. That evening, we were treated by our French hosts, to a lavish banquet at a restaurant, that they had opened especially. Toasts were made and speeches attempted all in this 'Allo Allo' language punctuated by a lot of arm waving and nods and winks. We gathered that they had just opened a municipal golf course, and challenged Malcolm to a match. He hadn't played for a while and was rather rusty, but if I would caddy for him, he felt that the honour of the BBC was at stake and we had no choice.

Early the next morning the match began. Tenacious is the best way to describe Malcolm's style, he wasn't going to let the French chap win, and by golly, he didn't. Triumphant over lunch, we started talking about the Shipping Forecast for the first time since our arrival. Luckily, we were joined by an English-speaking lady and so the business was easier to transact. The deal was done, the money agreed, but by now we were getting late for our plane home. They told us not to worry, as the plane would wait for us. Half an hour later we arrived to find the plane, with its other passengers sitting waiting. We climbed the steps, waved to our hosts and the 'Royal Party' departed.

So, on the appointed day, the new service started, but within a few days the Met Office rang to say that it had to stop. When Météo-France discovered what was going on they went berserk, saying that the English were encroaching on their territory and complained formally to the WMO (World Meteorological Organisation).

The hundred years war never really ended!

Malcolm Walker arrives in France by plane to be made very welcome by our hosts. Our French was rusty but the lady translator helped and we had a splendid dinner.

The next morning we realised that Malcolm had agreed to play in a golf competition. Eventually we got to our plane that had been waiting for our arrival.

A Climate of Change

In the early 1980s our thoughts had turned very much to computer graphics and Bill and John went on the short trip across to Brussels where a demonstration was to take place, by the American company Kavorous, showing their latest ideas on computer graphics for the weather. At this event there were two weather broadcasters from Germany with whom we became very friendly and have continued to do so right up to the present day. They were Inge Niedek and Dieter Walch who both, at that time, worked for ZDF television as Broadcast Meteorologists. The demonstration, however, developed into a bit of a farce as the graphics machine was using American model data and showing a forecast that was physically and scientifically impossible. Kavouras brushed this aside by extolling the virtues and beauty of the graphics, but for the meteorologists in the audience they had just blown it. Inge and Dieter's knowledge of meteorology and understanding of weather broadcasting were very similar to ours and over the years we have had many useful conversations on the way that the information should be put across to the general public. In true German precision, Dieter always maintained that there should never be more than four facts in any broadcast. We begged to differ over this. But our friendship developed over the years, as we all became founder members of The International Association of Broadcast Meteorology (IABM) in which both John and Inge have taken a leading role. Over the years we have spent time together at conferences both in Europe and the United States, more often than not agreeing on the main points driving broadcast meteorology forward. On the lighter side John and Bill have been guests of Inge and Dieter in Germany and only a short while ago had a very enjoyable time being shown around Berlin by Inge and her husband. Both of the broadcasters have also visited our homes in the UK. Bill remembers one occasion sitting in John's back garden putting the world to right and also when they came to his house in Oxfordshire when Bill's wife Maureen thrilled them with a roast dinner including Yorkshire puddings as a starter. They are both, especially Inge, still very involved with IABM so we see them on a regular basis.

BILL: *At the same meeting in Brussels we were introduced to Jules Metz, known affectionately as Monsieur Meteo, who had been on Belgian television for a number of years, and rumoured to be the longest serving TV weatherman in the world. Our friendship nearly didn't get off the ground because unbeknown to me his wife had a little dog, which as I shook her hand, I very nearly trod on. Jules was trying very hard to ingratiate himself telling us that he knew me well since they were able to get BBC Television. He invited both of us to his television centre and upon arriving there told us that the whole building was split in two, with mirrored facilities divided by a central atrium.*

On one side RTBF the French speaking service and on the other BRT the Flemish speaking service. Protocol dictated that if I was to appear on Jules's television broadcast, then I had to go into the other side as well. The difference between the two arms of the broadcasting channel had to be seen to be believed. I was asked to go and do a piece on the Flemish side first, so was taken to the studio through a corridor with little or nothing on the walls. There we met the Flemish weather forecaster who was not quite so famous as Jules. The studio was functional but sparse, however they made us very welcome and we recorded a piece for that night's new broadcast. It wasn't difficult, they were happy for me to speak in English – actually I did tell them that I knew a couple of phrases in Dutch, one was 'I love you' and the other 'will you marry me?' but they wouldn't let me use them probably because I had a strong Devonian accent! It happened to be the wedding anniversary of the King and Queen of Belgium and all we did on-air was chat and drink a toast to the happy couple.

We were then taken back to the entrance foyer and passed to someone from the French speaking side. As we walked down the corridor towards the studio it was a massive change. There were pictures on the wall, potted plants and music playing gently in the background and it seemed as though everyone we met was in party mood. Sitting with Jules in the 'green room' we talked about what he would like me to do during his weather broadcast and I thought this would be easy as I had just done one on the other side of the building. Not a bit of it. Jules, apparently, always ended his broadcast with a proverb and wondered if I would do it tonight –in French! Reluctantly I agreed when he said it would all be on autocue and I would just have to read it.

After his weather forecast it came to my turn, and remember this was live, and I was to speak in a language that I hadn't used since my boarding school days, I looked into the camera to see the words they had written for me. I couldn't believe what I saw; yes it was in French but they had put abbreviations on it and not written the whole word. I stumbled through, came off air glad that that was over only to be told that what I had said in French was nothing like what was written. My proverb had translated into 'A breadstick on an Elephant's back'. Still, with a laugh and a delightful glass of French wine all was soon forgotten.

Sitting in our office one day John said to me "How's your skiing?" Now, being a lad brought up on the banks of the River Dart in Devon I said "probably about as good as your Russian" "Good" he said because we are going to start doing a programme on Ski resorts after 'Ski Sunday' and we will have to do some promotional work for it. "I've booked a skiing lesson for you at the ski slope at Hillingdon"

So, there we were, a few days later at the slopes in west London. I was kitted up with all the gear and with an instructor, shown how to move down hill but more importantly, how to stop.

John all dressed up for the occasion with his woolly hat, was getting impatient because he had great difficulty funding this and after just one hour wanted to see if I could ski down the big slope.

Being a Scorpio I managed it but would get very few marks for style. His next venture was to take me, now an 'accomplished skier', to the slopes of a ski centre at Sandown Park, where I was to ski down the hill, stop on a prearranged mark and deliver my piece to camera. After a lot of shouting from the producer, still in his woolly hat, that he wanted me to move more quickly down the slope, I eventually did manage it. We were now ready for real snow and with Rosemary Burns of the Ski Club of Great Britain as our host, we jetted off to the French resort of Megéve.

On the first morning, after breakfast, we got ready to go out on the slopes in real snow for the first time. Being, by that time, an 'accomplished skier' with two hours of dry slope skiing under my belt, I dressed full of fear and excitement. I paused for the expected photographs as I embarked from my chalet only to see that I had been beaten to the lower slopes by John's researcher. Shirley Edwards was fully kitted out in what would have been far too much clothing even for the top of Everest, in fact glancing across at her I felt positively undressed. As I was searching to see where she had hidden her oxygen mask she inadvertently stepped backwards and with a scream of terror, that I remember to this day, fell flat on her back. Like the Michelin Man, with all the clothes she was wearing she couldn't move and reminded me of a turtle on its back. We all rushed forward to help her up, which was a struggle, but it all came good in the end as we sat her down in an après ski cafe.

Here John wanted to film me going up on the ski lift, which in itself was dangerous to a man of my meagre experience, meet me at the top of the mountain to which he and his researcher had arrived in a huge luxury cable car, and do some gentle filming up there. I enjoyed that until he told me that, with a Ski instructor he had hired, I was to ski down the mountainside to the bottom, where they would be filming me on the descent.

They then proceeded down the mountainside again. The mountain was huge and to ski off it meant going over what looked to me like a precipice. I followed the instructor over the edge and down the mountainside we went.

I struggled to stay upright but managed all the way down and as I told John later, the only reason I did so, was that the instructor was French and I was damned if I was going to allow a Frenchman to beat me.

Whilst there I had another first, ice-skating. Rosemary helped me around the rink and as someone remarked later I looked like a stuffed penguin but I never fell over once!

The UK skiing market was opening up more to the North American resorts and, funded by the resort of Crested Bute, we went there together with Suzanne Charlton, because she could actually ski. We set off, business class, on British Airways, to Denver, Colorado. Arriving at Crested Bute we were so overwhelmed; it looked to us like a scene on Christmas cards. The main part of the resort was at a height of some 10,000 feet above sea level, much the same height as John and Bill flew back to Gatwick from the Brest Conference, with the summit of the mountain towering another 1,875 feet above it.

BILL: *There was plenty of snow and my first reaction was that when global warming kicked in these high-level winter resorts in North America would have a distinct advantage on some of the lower slopes across Europe. We took a day or two acclimatising to the altitude which Suzanne took advantage of by taking me up the mountain and making me ski down to the nursery slopes. Actually, I wouldn't tell her but I was petrified and exhilarated all at the same time. Talking of nursery slopes, Suzanne managed to persuade the 2 metre tall John to put on a pair of skis and have a go. Very reluctantly he did, and to start him off Suzanne gave him a gentle push. He was on the nursery slope so it only had a very gentle incline but as we watched, he headed straight for the kindergarten nets that protected the very young ones from other skiers. Not knowing how to stop he slid gently and very elegantly into the kindergarten, falling over and ending up in the safety fences like a salmon caught in a fisherman's net.*

JOHN: *I got my own back just the next day. Suzanne and Bill were doing a piece to camera advertising the coming ski forecasts that we were going to do when we got back home. The idea was that as Bill being the second most competent skier of the three of us, would stand on his skis in the snow while Suzanne descended towards him at a rapid pace, brake hard to be close to him and then they would talk to the camera.*

Unbeknown to Bill I wanted to liven things up a bit to get my own back for the episode in the kindergarten the day before. So, I asked Suzanne to ski down a bit quicker on the next take and crash into Bill. She did this with a vengeance knocking Bill off his feet and falling on the ground herself but she was a pro to the end - lying there in the snow she still did her piece to the camera. That was another 'out-take' that went out on the programme 'It'll be Alright on the Night'!

To end our short stay there, we were all invited to a party in one of the skiing lodges halfway up the mountainside after which we would all ski down holding flaming torches. We weren't quite up to that so we would be taken up to the lodge on the back of snowmobiles. We had been on a snowmobile just a day or so before when a group of us, with instructors, rode across a frozen lake and up into the mountains.

Bill drove and John sat on the pillion. It was soon obvious that John had never ridden on a motorbike because as Bill leaned into his left to go around a corner John leaned to the right and instead of turning to go up the incline we carried on straight ahead into a massive snowdrift. On the way back we had a race with Suzanne who, much to Bill's annoyance, beat us, but there was one consolation for Bill - she is also a Scorpio.

BILL: *So there we were ready for the party, John on the back of one snowmobile and me on the back of another. The drivers took off like something out of Formula One motor racing and we soon arrived, rather harassed and quite out of breath.*

We had a glorious evening with plenty of food and drink singing songs we had never heard before, and also teaching them some old rugby songs I remembered, when, all too soon, it was time to go back down the mountain which in places was very steep. Remembering the shattering ride up I was surprised to see John's driver taking it very gently down back to the hotel and asked him why. "Well" said John "as I got on the snowmobile to go back down the mountain I said to the driver that if he drove down at the same speed as he drove up, then all of the evenings food and drink would be down his neck!"

We flew back from Crested Bute to Denver to wait for the flight back to London. They were announcing over the tannoy that the flight was overbooked and they were looking for volunteers to forgo the flight in exchange for $1,200 and a guaranteed 1st Class seat the next day. Golly and ours were on complimentary seats anyway! But unfortunately Bill was on duty the next day and there was no way he could miss it. Then our names were called out to go to the flight desk where we were asked if we would consider being upgraded to First. As Bill said "can a duck swim?" Of course we would be delighted to help them out of this predicament. So we three, and a journalist who was covering skiing at Crested Bute for the Daily Mail, climbed the stairs to an area in a plane none of us had ever ventured before. We found out during the flight that the journalist was over with his wife and child but they were travelling in economy in the back of the plane. But, as John always said, journalists were animals! As Bill said "I wouldn't have dared do that".

As all three of us settled down for the long flight we noticed someone vaguely familiar next to Suzanne. He obviously wasn't as famous as she was but nonetheless it intrigued us. Suzanne did try to make some conversation with him but he was a bit surly if not rather rude in his manner so, she didn't bother anymore. Half way across the Atlantic we realised it was Mark Thatcher son of Margaret Thatcher the Prime Minister.

We all slept well during the night flight and what a pleasant way to be woken in the morning with a beautiful air hostess speaking softly and gently in your ear and asking "how would you like your eggs this morning Sir?"

BILL: *The trip was very successful and we went on air soon after with our skiing forecast immediately after the programme Ski Sunday. I remember on the very first programme, I had to mention the snow conditions in Crested Bute, which I did, with a little smile on my lips.*

Bill cuts a dash on the ski slopes getting ready for filming. The team with Suzanne Charlton

But the real fun was on the snow mobiles as we travelled over a frozen lake

A Climate of Change

As all three of us settled down for the long flight we noticed someone vaguely familiar next to Suzanne. He obviously wasn't as famous as she was but nonetheless it intrigued us. Suzanne did try to make some conversation with him but he was a bit surly if not rather rude in his manner so, she didn't bother anymore. Half way across the Atlantic we realised it was Mark Thatcher son of Margaret Thatcher the Prime Minister.

We all slept well during the night flight and what a pleasant way to be woken in the morning with a beautiful air hostess speaking softly and gently in your ear and asking "how would you like your eggs this morning Sir?"

BILL: *The trip was very successful and we went on air soon after with our skiing forecast immediately after the programme Ski Sunday. I remember on the very first programme, I had to mention the snow conditions in Crested Bute, which I did, with a little smile on my lips.*

CHAPTER 9

ON THE ROAD

Broadcasting the weather live on the BBC was always a very lonely business. In the early days only one person at a time would be on duty in a small room where they would prepare the weather maps before going to the studio to dress the magnetic boards. They would then, after a telephone conference with the Senior Forecaster at the Met Office Headquarters, go back to the studio and present their forecast to the nation. They did this for two weeks and then returned to their parent office, London Weather Centre, for a further two weeks on national radio.

At no time did any of them meet with the general public that they broadcast to. Bill got increasingly worried about this isolation and started to give talks to outside bodies and tried to encourage his team to do likewise.

BILL: *I started to give talks very early on in my broadcasting career and although initially it was very intimidating, I carried on becoming more and more confident.*

I thought it was essential that all the team got out to visit the people who listen to and watch their broadcasts, to increase their confidence, act as a public relations exercise and to get feedback on what we were doing.

Unfortunately it was not that easy to persuade the team to do this and enjoy this aspect of their work for two main reasons. Firstly it is quite different talking to a hall full of people than to an inanimate television camera or radio microphone and many felt intimidated by people looking at them. Secondly, at that time, permission had to be given by the Assistant Director at HQ for them to go ahead.

There was a great deal of "green eye" jealousy too from those of a higher graded desk job at Bracknell towards my staff at Television Centre.

I remember Jack Scott was asked to give quite a prestigious talk, but on asking permission from his boss at the London Weather Centre was astounded by the answer from this forthright Yorkshire man Martin Morris who said, "Why have they asked you? They could have had me - the boss of London Weather Centre"!

He obviously then, and later, did not understand the power of television. However, as I got promotion to a much higher grade and John became an Editor we changed all that so that permission was granted directly by us.

Mind you, there were some terrible mistakes and faux-pars especially by Michael Fish. In those early days many of the talks were to the County Women's Institutes - and wonderful audiences they are too. As you went around, you heard snippets of news about other speakers and the word had got around to me, that although they enjoyed Michael coming to talk to them, he was a bit boring. I always, to this day, believe that to engage an audience you need humour to get your message across, but Michael didn't seem to be putting too much of that in his talks but concentrated more on slides of the headquarters building in Bracknell.

I had a word with him about injecting some lighter moments into his talks only to be told a few weeks later of a newspaper headline stating "Blue Fish" What had happened? Apparently, instead of injecting some subtle humour during his talk Michael had stood up at the beginning and said something like "before I give you my lecture on meteorology have you heard the one about the copulating pigeons?" In all fairness to Michael the story of the pigeons was a true one. At that time we had a studio in an office on the 5th floor at the Television Centre where we did some broadcasts sitting at a desk with a window behind us. On one occasion when Michael was in full flow, behind him appeared two pigeons in the course of creating the next generation.

Another time I had an irate call from a lady near Liverpool who rang to complain. What allegedly happened that time was that Michael had given a talk to a society of Carers and had said the wrong things as far as they were concerned. Sitting near him on the top table was an attractive young lady and I understand Michael referred to her "warm front" just a little too often. At the same talk he rather foolishly mentioned that if you dropped anything on the third floor at the BBC Television Centre, where the male wardrobe dressers had their offices, you either left it or kicked it to the side before picking it up. This did not go down well with his audience and when I questioned him about it he did say he noticed some people leaving the room.

One morning I had a phone call at home from an agent telling me that the famous actor David Kossoff had been booked to give a talk that evening in Tunbridge Wells to a Confederation of the Women's Institutes, but had lost his voice and had to cry off. Would I please act as a stand in and do it instead? I couldn't on that particular evening because I had arranged to attend a ceremony where my PA was graduating and that there was no possibility of me missing that. The agent was distraught until I came up with the solution; I would ask John to do it. I phoned him at Television Centre where he was in the edit suite making another Weather Show programme. His initial reply when I asked him was "You must be joking" or words to that effect. He said he was in the middle of an edit, in casual clothes without even a tie! I said that whoever did it would be paid £750. His reply was "Who is it? Where is it? What time do they want me there?" And that was how John found himself that afternoon driving to Tunbridge Wells!

JOHN: *I eventually found the car park to the Theatre and after a long drive rushed inside to find a toilet. The first one said Ladies, then the second one said Ladies, then the third one said Ladies. By this time I was desperate and realised that, as this was an all female event, they had changed all the toilets to ladies only. Too late – I listened at the door and when I could hear no voices I dived into the closest cubicle. Having completed my mission, I suddenly heard voices as two ladies came in to powder their noses. "Shame about David Kosoff and then Bill Giles was not available, so we have got some unknown BBC Producer instead – don't know what he will be like?" Before they had time to speculate, I coughed, unbolted the door to see two rather shocked ladies.*

I quickly explained who I was and that I could not find a gentleman's toilet, but I hoped that I had not scared them and that they would enjoy my talk. I left rapidly.

When I found the organiser of the evening she was so grateful that I had come, as she did not want to disappoint the 1,500 ladies in the audience. Giles what have you done to me I whispered under my breath. She explained the proceedings, where she would introduce me after prayers and notices, then if I could speak for 45 minutes and then 15 minutes of questions that would be fine. It is difficult to describe how my stomach felt. I had done a lot of amateur drama in my time and was used to making speeches in my role as Chairman of Harrow Arts Council, but this mattered. The reputation of the BBC Weather Centre was at stake! At the appointed time we climbed the stairs to the spot lit stage - it felt as if I was going up to the gallows. After the notices, I was introduced and thanked for saving the day. I walked to the microphone and faced a sea of expectant faces. I paused for a time and then lent close to the microphone and said "little did I know when I got up this morning......" They laughed and after that it was really quite easy.

After this initial success Bill and John decided to go into the business of a double act where they would go on stage and talk about the weather and the BBC Weather Centre.

BILL: *This seemed a good idea at the time and I managed to get an agent to take us on. Not long after this I had a phone call from him saying that he had booked us a gig. I thanked him and turned to John - we shared an office at Television Centre, actually a huge office, and said to him "we have a booking - the Albert Hall". "The Albert Hall " he sounded delighted and scared at the same time thinking of how are we going to fill that illustrious building in Kensington, when I added "The Albert Hall, Bolton".*

We duly arrived at the venue and were shown the dressing room where we sat down thinking what have we let ourselves in for. At this stage in the proceedings we weren't sure exactly what we were going to do for the hour and a half we had been booked for. John had always said that it was best not to be too rigid on the programme but make it up as we went along.

The curtain rose with John already on the stage and he proceeded to tell the audience what we planned to do. After about forty five seconds he then announced "The Star of the Show – Bill Giles" I then came on only for John to take the mickey and insult me throughout the evening which went down very well with the audience.

JOHN: *One joke that always went down very well, centred on a mobile phone. We had found a way to get it to ring in Bill's pocket without the audience seeing us trigger it. So whilst I was talking to the audience, it would go off and Bill would answer it in a loud whisper "I can't talk now we are on stage in the middle of a show". I would carry on telling my story. "Yes of course I love you but I can't speak now".*

Still I continued, but seeing that by now the audience had ceased to listen to me and were really listening to Bill's phone call. "I can't wait to see you too" he went on. The trick was to spin this out until I came to the end of the story whilst Bill kept telling the caller on his phone how much he loved and wanted her, until at this point he would hand the phone to me and say "it's your wife".

BILL: *We did many of these shows over the years and thoroughly enjoyed them and one of the more memorable occasions was at the Royal Geographical Society. Standing there on the stage looking out through the auditorium that would have been familiar to many of the world famous explorers of the 18th and 19th centuries was totally overwhelming. The thought of standing on the same platform as people as well respected as Henry Morton Stanley announcing he had found Livingstone and many of the Antarctic veterans were awe inspiring and we both became very nervous as the auditorium began filling with many learned people. Our talk went well with John insulting me in his normal light hearted way which was a ploy that worked well because the audience were always fascinated as to who is this giant of a man insulting Bill Giles the well-known television weatherman? All, that is, except my wife, who hadn't seen many of our talks together and I could see her getting more and more upset until it dawned on her that this was part of the act. We were all invited to dinner and one of the ladies present obviously took a shine to John, as now he is a Fellow of the Royal Geographical Society!*

One of the very early talks I gave was in Monte Carlo. John and I flew to Nice, picked up our bags and were met by a tall Frenchman who escorted us to his helicopter for the trip across the bay into Monte Carlo.

The hotel was magnificent but what John hadn't told me was that the conference organisers stipulated only one room per speaker. What normally happens at these events is that the speaker comes on their own but John, not believing I could cope or more likely he just wanted a nice trip to the Mediterranean, came as well, believing in his ability to talk the receptionist into letting us have two rooms.

On this occasion he failed and we had to settle for a shared room - but it was a big one. He always reckoned he discovered the true meaning of flatulence after that!

The next morning we rang the BBC Weather Centre in London to find out what the weather was likely to be in Monte Carlo for the coming few days and spoke to the duty broadcaster which happened to be Ian McCaskill. Now as weather forecasters, we have two set vocabularies; one we speak to each other using semi scientific language and the other when we translate that into conversational English for the General Public including members of the BBC production team. John spoke with Ian and asked him a simple question about the weather and had a jargonistic reply from him about "warm and cold fronts over Ireland occluding as they transferred east, increasing the precipitation over Central Southern England". John was so confused when I asked him what the answer was that we were none the wiser for asking.

Talking of using scientific language, I remember the Head of the Presentation Department at the BBC, Malcolm Walker, coming back from a trip to Scotland where he heard a radio weather broadcast which he didn't understand. He said the forecaster had said during the broadcast "there will be some solid precipitation in the upper atmosphere" and asked me what that meant. I replied, "Some snow on the hills"

After breakfast John and I went down to the conference room. The plan was that I would give the talk and John would make sure the graphics I was using came on at the correct time. The conference started and almost immediately things started to go wrong. The slide projector went out of focus and a little later fell apart and at that time I felt very sorry for the eminent medical professor giving his very interesting and important review of his latest research. These problems kept cropping up and eventually the organisers called a halt to the proceedings and declared a coffee break so that the engineers could sort the problem out. I was scheduled to speak just before lunch so I knew my allotted time would be cut back a little which was a problem because the organisers had requested a script before hand for the translators to use and we were told under no circumstances were we to depart from it.

My turn eventually arrived and I started with completely unscripted words "I have some good news and some bad news. The bad news is that you are going to be late for lunch, the good news is that I don't have any slides to show you!" Luckily for us John had previously decided against using boring slides but had made several video pieces to accompany my talk that he ran from the control centre and it worked perfectly.

After a very successful day we were tired so decided not to paint the town red but to stay in and enjoy the in-house entertainment. We went down into the bowels of the hotel where they had a plush theatre and as we walked in through the entrance an usher said to us in English "Bachelors Sir?"

We were rather startled at this and just grunted a "yes" reply and we were placed right in the front row. I settled down to watch the show knowing that John, with his acting and directing abilities, would be looking at the technical side of the show. It was very good and we saw various acts although I didn't get a great deal out of the comedian since my French is very limited. The final act was something different. A beautiful girl appeared from the wings smiling and cavorting around in quite a suggestive manner. We both sat up straight at this point so as not to miss anything when she started to take her clothes off! I was enjoying the background music as she gradually took off more and more clothes.

Both of us were getting hot under the collar at this stage but when she revealed her top we knew we were looking at a particularly beautiful girl. I leaned across to John and enquired what he thought of her and his reply was that he had never seen anything so beautiful. At this point I started to think that something wasn't quite right but couldn't put my finger on it until she took her off last garment, her hot pants, to reveal to all and sundry that this beautiful girl was in fact a boy. John went deathly white as the blood drained out of his face. But then I thought he's led a very sheltered life!

A Climate of Change

As we moved out of the theatre and into the foyer of the hotel we met a group from the BBC who just happened to be there on another assignment so we all sat around a table for a drink and chin wag. The BBC Head of Graphic design was holding forth on some new project in which he was involved and drinking and smoking, when all of a sudden he sat up straight, became very flustered and thrust the cigarette he was smoking into my hand. It burnt a little as I caught hold of the wrong end! Wondering why this had happened and happened so quickly, out of the corner of my eye I saw a lady moving towards us. It was his wife and he had supposedly stopped smoking some time before and had agreed with her that he would never restart 'on pain of death'. The only pain that evening was the cigarette burn to my hand that I carry to this day.

Once after giving a particularly successful talk I was approached by Arthur Martin who said he was from an agency called Giantpatch. He booked celebrities for talks and personal appearances and said he would like to represent me. I told him that I had a more than full time job and certainly didn't want to go on the after dinner circuit other than just occasionally. Nonetheless he persisted and I eventually capitulated and said that I would give it a try. Over the next few months he got me several jobs and announced that he was setting up a weeks tour for me around the country.

All went well until we ended up in Manchester one evening where he had booked me into "The Blue Room". Unbeknown to me it was a strip joint and I found it extremely difficult for 45 minutes to engage with the audience, as they had come into the club for an entirely different show. Later that evening, we had a very meaningful conversation, when I told him, in no uncertain terms, what I thought about his booking arrangement that day.

After that he started looking more towards the local arts centres and small theatres but, as I pointed out, if I were to do that it meant talking for at least one and a half hours rather than a twenty minute humorous after dinner slot.

Thus came into existence my two hour stage act "The Bill Giles' Weather Show." I came to enjoy doing these because there were so many different topics. Starting with all about the weather maps and showing the audience how to do their own weather forecasts, followed by climate change and ending with television broadcasts and the things that can go wrong on live television. The only problem about this long show was what to do in the interval because in most other shows people could come and buy DVDs or CDs but I had nothing like that. However, I managed to acquire some printed satellite pictures and teamed up with a firm called MetCheck owned by Jeremy West operating out of north Buckinghamshire who had the licence to use the BBC Weather symbols.

These we printed on to some sweatshirts, which we sold at the theatre shows. I couldn't do the selling, although I was always there to sign the satellite pictures, so I employed a friend, Willy Wilson (and later on my step-daughter Karen) not only to look after that commercial aspect but also to act as my driver.

With this arrangement we could afford to travel much further from my home base in south Buckinghamshire, as after the show I could curl up in the back of the car and be driven home. But after a while things went downhill as Arthur branched out in new directions. He decided to get the sweatshirts printed in Pakistan more cheaply than in the UK and invested a lot of the money I had earned from the shows, only to find out that when they arrived all the weather symbols were out of focus. Things went from bad to worse until Jeremy and I, fed up with being fobbed off with another excuse, decided to take the matter into our own hands. Realising that this would be the parting of the ways with Giantpatch we went to London in his Land Rover to Arthur's office and took all the satellite pictures I could find and also all the UK produced sweatshirts. They lasted me for several years.

Even to this day I still enjoy performing the weather shows but these are more often than not on P&O cruise ships as a guest speaker.

CHAPTER 10

BROADCASTING TO THE WORLD

During the 1980s there was growing public interest in European Weather, in particular for holidaymakers. This was easily provided using the magnetic symbol system, and European forecasts became a regular part of the schedule with Holiday Weather every Friday evening. However, it proved more difficult to do this in an electronic graphics system.

The development of European Maps and data proved to be a considerable challenge to both the BBC and the UK Met Office. Not only were there technical issues, in, for example providing satellite pictures, but questions began to emerge over who owned the data. The BBC was already broadcasting into some European Countries, and local Met Services started questioning the right of the BBC to use data that effectively they had provided.

A commercial contract secured by the BBC Weather Centre to provide daily European forecasts for 'SuperChannel' for broadcast in Europe, added to the debate. Also BBC Enterprises had started 'BBC Prime' an entertainment channel, for which we made European weather reports.

In 1991, the BBC launched BBC World Service Television, a commercial news and entertainment channel for broadcast outside the UK. At this time, the international news service was dominated by CNN operating out of Atlanta USA, who included a global weather forecast in their schedule. Chris Irwin, the Chief Executive, and Hugh Williams, Director of Programmes of BBC World Service TV were both convinced that from the start of the new BBC service, world weather reports were an important part of the schedule.

Fortuitously, the work that we had put into providing European coverage meant that a great deal of the software had already been developed by the BBC and the UK Met Office. This included a full palette of graphics including pressure charts, land temperature, sea temperature, satellite and precipitation (rainfall) charts. But this doesn't minimise the enormous achievement of providing a whole suite of graphics to cover the entire globe, in particular for the Met Office sourcing all the data sets by which the BBC Weather Graphics System could then automatically produce the graphics ready to go on air.

But that would only be half the problem. BBC World Service was a 24/7 service and producing that number of broadcasts each day and every day would need special production facilities.

Also the production of specialist forecasts for BBC domestic services, BBC Prime, and the Services Sound and Vision Corporation, were putting strain on the small, self operate studio on the 5th floor.

John had been working on the concept of a dedicated Weather Broadcast Centre, but had been unable to attract the funding. Now with the needs of BBC World, the time was never better. All of these things needed a stroke of good luck. The studio through which the weather had been transmitted since 1954 was coming out of service and would no longer be able to be used for weather broadcasts. So the die was set – the weather would just have to have its own studios!

The first thing was to find the space at Television Centre. A scheme of this size would need the support and talents of the Engineering and Projects Departments. Luckily John had a good working relationship with them. A chance phone call to John from a colleague in Engineering suggested that there was a plan to close the Technical Store on the 2nd floor. This area kept all the spare parts for cameras etc. But with the advent of digital devices, repairs were no longer a soldering iron job and so parts were no longer needed.

To judge its suitability, it was arranged to visit the area after it had closed for the evening, so as not to alert the staff working there, who were not aware of its possible demise. So the next time Bill was on duty John took him down to the area and explained his plan. They were like excited kids in a sweet shop. Plans were then advanced at some speed as the start date for BBC World Service was getting closer.

There were also some important internal politics to be negotiated by John's Head of Department, Pam Masters, who had been very supportive through this period. She helped steer it through the appropriate committees and the first phase of the BBC Weather Centre opened on 1st September 1991 with a forecast office, automated weather TV studio and a radio studio. This facility would provide the means to generate a considerable number of forecasts, efficiently and cost-effectively using a high degree of automation. In broadcasting terms it was a first.

By the end of the 1990s and the completion of phase two, the Centre had a new larger forecast office and an additional TV studio. It also provided a higher level of automation with each weather presenter having their own settings. On entering the studio and pressing their button, it would switch on the studio lights to their own setting, adjust the microphone volume and adjust the camera height to suit. It was soon producing 140 tailored weather reports every 24 hours. A considerable achievement and the biggest facility of its kind in the world.

Editorially, world weather was a challenging concept. Mindful of the very general 'wave of the hand' presentations on CNN, John and Bill were determined to provide a distinctive and detailed forecast that would be expected of the BBC brand. Also, the BBC was very mindful of its authoritative voice, and the accuracy of the forecast would be very important.

There were many issues to consider, for example the need to ensure that city names were appropriate to receiving the countries. Was it to be Mumbai or Bombay? Peking or Beijing? We also needed to ensure how place names were pronounced. We had to be sensitive in describing the weather in a way that was appropriate to people in their own countries. Phrases such as 'another hot and sunny day in Dubai' would appear rather crass. Understanding local conditions and concerns were vital. For example, knowledge of drought or flood conditions would enable the broadcasters to contextualise their forecasts.

Garnering all this information in itself became a major task as we had to ensure it was accurate and readily available. As far as the broadcasters were concerned this added a new dimension for them because suddenly they had to become geographers and climatologists as well as meteorologists. It also kept designer Liz Varrall busy, with not only producing the new map backgrounds, but John wanted to see the national boundaries on the maps. You will never believe how many boundaries there are that are in dispute around the world. In the end we used the United Nations listing as being the safest bet.

Obviously we were going to need to ensure, that for each broadcast made for BBC World, the duty forecaster knew precisely what was expected. With the advent of the opening of the BBC Weather Centre John had been able to make the case for an Assistant Producer, and Andrew Lane joined the team. His experience lay mainly with radio, but he was excellent at systems and processes. Together we developed a system of 'Style Guides'. So for each shift there would be a book containing a sheet for each broadcast to be done. Normally a BBC World shift would consist of nine broadcasts, and each one would be slightly different so that it targeted each part of the world that was at peak viewing, at the time of broadcast.

Not only were there details of this, but also local information such as religious festivals and holidays. The trick was to make the broadcaster sound as if they were fully conversant on the country for which they were forecasting.

In the end we extended this concept to all the shifts, as some on them had different customers, and also included radio broadcasts. It was a major task to keep all these guides up to date and relevant, but they certainly worked very well.

You could say that this broke our 'one-man operation' concept, but this research was done during normal office hours. We weren't there at 4.00am in the morning when BBC World recordings were being done. There was just one person on duty and that was the weather presenter.

Quickly the weather reports on the BBC World produced a great deal of international reaction and interest. For many viewers, particularly in developing countries, this was their first introduction to quality broadcast meteorology.

For local Met Services and TV stations it was a considerable challenge. Many Met Services became concerned that they could become marginalised by global TV weather forecasts. We were soon getting concerns expressed by the Hong Kong Met Service.

JOHN: *By chance, I got a phone call from Hugh Williams of World Service, asking if Bill and I would be prepared to go on a 'service visit' to Hong Kong.*

He explained that BBC World was transmitted in China via the Star Satellite, which was owned by Rupert Murdoch. The Chinese government was putting pressure on Murdoch to take the BBC it off his service, as they did not like the BBC's open editorial policy. In other words they did not like the BBC telling the truth about China!

Not being any friend of the BBC he was open to be leaned on by the Chinese. Hugh wanted us to go to Hong Kong and generate some nice, good feeling stories in the press and local TV and Radio. When I asked Bill if he would like to go, there wasn't even a breath before he said "yes." But more seriously it would allow us to go to the Hong Kong Met Service and allay their fears and also when I told SSVC (previously BFPS) they insisted we went to their local radio station in Hong Kong to be interviewed.

As BBC World was a commercially funded service and not from the licence fee; when the tickets arrived we had been booked in business class. After years of flying stowage, this was going to be a real treat. It was for a while. Wherever I flew with Bill he would invariably be recognised by the cabin crew and we would get special treatment. Most pilots were weather nuts and keen to talk to Bill. This flight was no different.

As soon as we boarded we were treated specially. The Chief Purser came to speak to us to say that the Captain would appreciate us going up to the flight deck after lunch for a chat. Duly, after an excellent lunch, we were escorted up to meet the Captain. Sitting at 35,000 feet with the summit of Everest just off to one side – it was magical. The Captain explained that it was rather boring on these long flights as there was little to do. They simply followed a rather tatty, much folded map that in schematic terms showed them where to turn.

Air Traffic Control came on the air, and agreed a course change. He turned a dial on the autopilot and the huge 200 tonne Jumbo Jet gently changed course as we continued chatting for over an hour and a half.

Back in our seats and gently snoozing we were awoken by the Chief Purser telling us that "all hell had let loose and the shit has hit the fan". Gosh we thought – what's the problem! He explained that they just had a report that a China Airways plane had fallen off the end of the Hong Kong runway and had closed the airport until further notice. He also pointed out that the plane would never fly again as the sewerage outlet was at the end of the runway. The plane was literally in the shit! The Captain was trying to negotiate another country in which he could land us and find hotels for the night. It was the 4th November 1993.

We diverted to Bangkok. After a three-hour drive through the congested city we finally arrived at a hotel. It had only just opened, but the third floor and above was not finished although the rooms were made up. After a very welcome dinner we found our rooms at the end of a plain concrete corridor, knowing we only had 2 hours to sleep before we were being collected to return to our aircraft and then hopefully Hong Kong.

The approach to the runway at Hong Kong's Kai Tak airport, accepted as the most difficult in the world, was a very frightening experience. As you descended close to the mountains the plane literally skimmed the rooftops and as it did an almost 90 degree turn you could actually look upwards into peoples' apartments. The plane descended lower and lower at an alarming rate, because, as the captain had told us earlier, you need to get onto the runway early and pull up sharply unless you wanted to follow the Air China plane into the sewerage.

Our hotel, the Conrad Hilton towers to 61 stories in the business district and fully refreshed after a good night's sleep we sat having breakfast looking out through a floor to ceiling window over the bay. The trials of yesterday seemed a long way away.

One of the main reasons for going to Hong Kong was to pay a visit to the Royal Hong Kong Observatory which changed back to its original name of The Hong Kong Observatory in 1997 when Hong Kong was handed back to the Chinese government. It observed a large increase in the local temperature there between 1980 and 2005 because of the loss of surrounding vegetation due to rapid building construction in the area. It is a prime example of the urban heat island effect that some sceptics worldwide try to use to counter the climate change argument. The building lived up to its Royal name, as many other observatories around the world, and we found ourselves moving from the hustle and bustle of the city to the tranquillity of a bygone age.

After being shown around these impressive gardens and buildings we sat down to discuss their worries. Their problem was again our World Service broadcasts. Already, at this time, the meteorologists there had a very sophisticated model to forecast typhoons.

Typhoons, Hurricanes and Cyclones are all the same weather phenomena but called by different names depending in which part of the world they are in. In the Atlantic and Northeast Pacific, they are called Hurricanes, in the Indian Ocean, Cyclones, and in the western Pacific Typhoons but they all have one thing in common, when they hit a populated area they can cause devastation.

The winds are exceptionally strong in excess of 74 miles per hour with gusts considerably higher. In fact Typhoon Wanda, which hit Hong Kong in early September 1962, had wind gusts of 160 mph and in the 52 years between 1956 and 2008 they had six very strong Typhoons.

In addition to the destructive winds, when these severe storms move inland they dump copious amounts of rain as the winds slowly ease down. They arrive in southern China regularly with Typhoon Ugasi a fairly recent arrival on the 24th September 2013. It is with this background that the forecasters at Hong Kong Observatory were worried about our broadcasts on BBC World. They thought, quite understandably, that we could undermine the excellent work they had done in forecasting typhoons, their strength and movement, by giving different information about the severe storms on our weather broadcasts for that region.

We came up with a wonderful compromise that Hong Kong themselves would send us their forecasts of coming severe weather direct and that we would use only that on our broadcasts, enabling us to make sure that there was no conflict of opinion. One of the big problems we had was, that although the UK Met Office received all official forecasts of severe storms worldwide as part of the World Weather Watch, it would have been very difficult to strip that data out from all the rest sent to the BBC.

Later we negotiated this system with all the world weather centres that had responsibility for forecasting these severe storms and used that local information when compiling our world forecasts.

While in Hong Kong we were delighted to be invited to the radio studios of SSVC (Services Sound and Vision Corporation) whose job it was to broadcast to our troops overseas.

In fact back at home we regularly did a broadcast for all our troops overseas and it was an immensely difficult to do because we had to talk about the forecasts for troops in Germany, the Middle East, Hong Kong, Belize and the Falkland Islands all in one broadcast and trying to link all of them was sometimes a nightmare.

We duly arrived at the studio to be feted as part of the family and had a very pleasant time chatting to all the broadcasters and backroom staff there, but the time had come for us to do an interview that would go out on air the next day. What to do and what to say? We talked about weather and weather forecasting and the difference between radio and television broadcasting but, as always, ended doing our usual double act that we normally performed on stage which consisted of getting the wrong end of the stick about a subject and going into a diatribe of complete nonsense. It seemed to have worked, but we would have liked to be a fly on the wall in the studio offices after we had left.

One of the other main reasons for our visit was to help World Service generate some good news stories. A meeting was arranged between a Chinese lady reporter and us. She proceeded to set up her recording equipment without smiling or giving any indication that she was looking forward to talking to us. We went through the usual questions of what we did and how were we enjoying our visit and had we been to Hong Kong before.

We got onto the subject of the Chinese languages finding out that Mandarin was the main language in China and spoken by most young and middle-aged people, but in Hong Kong the main language was Cantonese. She told us that Cantonese was much closer to the ancient Chinese in pronunciation but that both languages had much the same grammar so that they could both understand each other's written work but not when they spoke their respective languages.

Bill said it all sounded exactly the same to him and then went into a version that 'Monty Python' would have been proud of and ended up with the song from the Goon Show that Prince Charles made famous. At this her normal inscrutability left her and she broke into a wide smile and into hysterical laughter. That broke the ice and we continued to have a very pleasant interview with her.

Naturally it wasn't all work and we did take a little rest and recuperation. We decided that we would have a ride on The Peak Tramway Funicular Railway since we were told that it was a must for all tourists in Hong Kong. We duly arrived by tram to Central District, the start of the railway, bought a ticket and settled down for the ride of about one mile rising nearly 1,500 feet. We got out at the Peak to see the magnificent view of the harbour, and, incidentally, all the high rise skyscrapers as well. Now we knew very well that for every 1,000 feet you ascend from sea level the temperature drops by about 3°C and at 1,500 feet the drop in temperature was very noticeable.

BILL: *The Chinese are very entrepreneurial, so that when we saw there was a trip around the bay to see the stricken China Airways plane from a few days earlier, we decided to go and have a look. I think what persuaded us was the fact, that on this particular boat, it advertised free gin and tonics! We caught a tram to the harbour which in itself was a novelty for us both, but the lasting memory I have of that journey was of a little Chinese boy of about 2 feet 6 inches standing next to John at 6 feet 6 inches and looking up at him thinking he was looking at a giant. So the stories his mother had told him to make him behave were true!*

We arrived at the harbour and went down the steps to the boat where the passengers from the previous tour were just getting off. We met three elderly ladies on the stairway as one of them shouted out "you're Bill Giles the weatherman on the BBC "so our fame had spread, but the problem then is you have to behave yourself.

On the boat trip across the bay I only had a small gin but John made up for me as we cruised around the one-time pride of Air China now a sinking hull in the muddy waters.

JOHN: *We then received an invitation from the Bahamas Hurricane Conference – it looked like a jolly, but on further reading it was being sponsored by the islands as they were concerned to ensure that any hurricane forecasts appearing on TV properly reflected the risk, rather than just a blanket comment that could well hopelessly affect the tourist trade – so vital to the islands economy.*

They wanted Bill and me to go and give a talk about how we dealt with this on BBC World News. The dates were a problem, as following a rather busy time for both of us, we had just booked a holiday with our wives in the Canaries. Following a bit of negotiation, it was arranged that we would leave our wives to finish the holiday, whilst we flew to Madrid and then caught a flight to Miami and then a local flight to Nassau. Lead balloon doesn't really describe the reaction from our wives, Suzanne and Maureen, who would have to pack up the rented villa and get themselves home.

We got to Madrid, no problem and onto a TWA flight. Whenever travelling we always flew the flag, but as the tickets had been provided, we found the experience of an American airline rather novel. Due to unionisation, the airhostesses were the oldest I have ever seen. Apparently the more senior you were, the more you did transatlantic flights. As we climbed up to cruising height, two 'very old ladies' were trying to push their trolleys 'up hill', up the aisle. I suggested to Bill that perhaps we should get up and help them!

The flight had been delayed taking off, so by the time we had arrived and cleared customs our flight to Nassau had gone. TWA didn't want to accept any liability for the missed connection. So, then we tried to get our luggage back, but as it was checked through to Nassau, it then proved that they were liable.

Several hours later they announced that they were unable to get our luggage out of the system and it would automatically go on the flight the next morning. However, they were prepared to fund a hotel and taxied us to it. Of course we had nothing other than the clothes we stood in. I remembered my wife Suzanne telling me that if I ever got stuck like this just to wash my pants and socks in the basin and hang them up to dry overnight.

The next morning they were as wet as when I washed them. So I had no choice but to go commando and sockless. With new stiff jeans I had to walk rather like John Wayne to avoid chafing myself. Finally at Nassau airport we were met off the plane, escorted through customs to the luggage collection hall. Bill's case soon arrived, so that was a good sign that the luggage had been loaded on our plane. However, after half an hour, and everyone else had collected their luggage, there was no sign of mine as we stood in the now empty luggage hall. A lady told me I would have to fill in forms for lost luggage, but in the meantime would I like to look in the lost luggage store. This space was larger than the whole of the collection area. It was filled with the most amazing collection of items, from bicycles to a writing desk, a rack of surfboards to a pile of hats. The most extraordinary sight was eight pairs of snow skis - in the Bahamas! Just as I sat down to fill in the form, the carousel started again, and there lonely and forlorn was my case. Where had it been and how it got there I didn't care!

Outside waiting was our transport to the hotel - an eight seat, white stretch limousine. We fell in the back, as like visiting rock stars we arrived at the hotel, a spacious lush and flowered monument to unbridled luxury. Eventually we found our rooms.

A Climate of Change

After the 36-hour journey, we pulled back the curtains to see an expanse of golden beach leading into an azure coloured sea. Wow! Forgotten was the farce of getting there – we were in the sea within 5 minutes. It was like a warm bath. Bliss! Later we met up with the organisers. We hadn't missed much and our talk was not until the next day. We were given our badges and documentation and told that the coach would leave at 6.00pm.

The coach took us to the Sandals Resort that looked fabulous and we walked to the jetty where a fast launch took us across the sea to the private island. By now we were both a bit shell-shocked and thought we had landed in heaven. Standing on the beach, we compared how much money we had between us. I was sent off to see what the bar prices were. But there wasn't a price list to be seen. I reported back to Bill and he, like me, was concerned that they were fancy prices that you only found out when you got the tab.

I was sent off again to ask what the prices were. "There are no prices Sir because here at Sandals everything is included." God, did we get drunk that night! The island had its own restaurant, and when we sat down to eat, we realised that we knew most of the other guests from meeting them at AMS conferences. What a party we had that night!

The next day, we dragged ourselves on stage and delivered, what we were told later, was an excellent presentation. In some ways it is much easier to do talks as a double act and of course we represented two different disciplines. Bill could talk about the meteorology and I could talk about the broadcaster's responsibility, especially when broadcasting worldwide.

One curious thing we did find was that not only did we have badges for ourselves, but also for a guest. On enquiry we found that we could have brought our wives rather than leaving them in the Canaries. But then we would have had to buy their tickets! We went a couple more times to the conference in other years and did pay to take Suzanne and Maureen.

On one occasion we woke up to find the outside of the hotel littered with broken furniture and uprooted trees. Apparently most of the guests had been up all night watching a tropical storm rip the place apart.

We had slept through it all!

Both John and Bill realised the importance of supporting and reinforcing National Met Services, if it was to provide global TV forecasts. The quality, timeliness and breadth of coverage of observations of the atmosphere from each of the 186 National Met Services were vital to the success of computer models run by the UK Met Office. To do anything to jeopardise this would compromise the BBC's ability to provide authoritative weather broadcasts.

In one particular situation, where a monsoon had been poorly forecast by the Pakistan Met Service, but accurately forecast on the BBC, questions were asked in their parliament as to why that particular country needed their own Met Service "when you only have to watch the BBC". So high were the concerns, that the World Meteorological Organisation (WMO) based in Geneva, contacted us to discuss data attribution and agree a framework for the authority of issuing official warnings.

Data attribution meant that the BBC would always credit the WMO as the source of data representing 183 Met Services around the world. Official warnings were a more sensitive issue, as in many countries the local Met service had a statutory obligation to issue formal weather warnings.

The concern was that international broadcasters did not do their own, and if they did broadcast a warning it was clear that it had been issued by the local Met Service. The real concern was that a situation could arise where the BBC or CNN gave warnings that were at odds with local warnings and put lives and property at risk in the process.

We held a series of meetings together with them and CNN to try and ensure that our exposure in other countries was sensitively handled. John was never sure that his colleagues in CNN ever understood what all the fuss was about! But, that's the difference in attitude between a commercial channel and a public service broadcaster.

As a leading player in world broadcast meteorology, we became more involved with international meetings called by the WMO and the American Meteorological Society (AMS). There was also growing concerns over moves to commercialise weather data, which would make it increasingly difficult to provide weather services in other countries. In particular, the annual meetings of the Broadcast section of the AMS provided a valuable resource with its programme of lectures and the opportunity to meet with others in the broadcast meteorology field.

JOHN: *At a conference held in Boston, the home of the AMS, we were standing in a large group talking to the then Director of the AMS Ron McPherson about the world of weather forecasting, when he excused us from the group and hustled us into his large office. Sat us down opposite him and said "right, tell me everything that's going on". He like many Americans was growing increasingly concerned over what was happening with data commercialisation and how it was going to affect the world of meteorology. We made good friends with him, so much so, that later at a WMO conference we were standing on a paddle steamer sailing down Lake Geneva, which had been hired by the Swedish Met Service for a reception. Glasses in hand, we were discussing the forthcoming election of the new Secretary General of WMO as Patrick Obassi was stepping down. I had the idea that the two front runners, a Russian and our old friend Evans Mukolwe from Kenya, would split the vote and the Deputy Secretary General, Michel Jarraud, from France, would get in.*

He had been a very good friend to the IABM and helped us a great deal to interface with the WMO. As I was saying this, up came Michel to say hello. I repeated my own prediction and we had a good laugh and he shrugged his shoulders a lot, as the French do, and we had another glass of wine.

A few days later he was elected Secretary-General.

One of the main reasons we were able to make the progress we did and expand the BBC Weather Centre so quickly, was due to an internal accounting change in the BBC, known as 'Producer Choice'. Up until that point there was really no internal market. Once a project or programme had been agreed by the channel controllers, then a project number was issued with a total value applied.

The internal departments of studios, design, costume, make-up, video editing etc would then agree their rate and charge against the project number. To create an internal market, Producer Choice effectively gave the cash to the producer and they were then able to spend it wherever they wished, and if they could get the services cheaper from suppliers outside the BBC, then so be it!

JOHN: *My opinion is that this policy caused the downfall of the BBC more than any other of the many hair brain ideas to which we were subjected. Margaret Thatcher had already forced the BBC to put a third of its programming making to outside companies and that had caused huge problems for the internal suppliers, but this new idea really marked the end of the golden days of the BBC. I am sure that the accountants would not agree, but then they had never made a programme, so how would they know? Up until this point, the BBC was an entirely self-contained centre of expertise. We only existed for one purpose and that was to make the best possible programmes we could for the least amount of money. Economy of scale really did work in this case. But more importantly, the BBC had harnessed the best craft talent in the world. So when a programme was made, it used the best artists, carpenters, painters, cameramen, film and VT editors, directors and producers. Everyone was a member of staff and fully committed to the shared vision. Due to the unique method of funding, there were no commercial masters to serve. It was just one big co-operative system, where the public funded the BBC and in turn received the best radio and TV in the world. Indeed, we were the envy of the world.*

But as Producer Choice took hold, the internal craft departments were unable to compete. Small, back street enterprises with tiny overheads could easily undercut the BBC's own resources on every front. This led in turn to whole departments either closing or being sold off. The concept of staff positions and the BBC's commitment to it's staff soon disappeared as more and more short-term contracts were used.

A relaxing dip in the sea for John and Bill at the Bahamas Hurricane Forecasting Conference

A treat for us both visiting the famous Sandals Resort for dinner

A Climate of Change

The commitment to the shared vision also waned as more production staff, now on contract, were more concerned about where there next job was coming from than the show they were working on. Next came a wholesale pensioning-off of any producer or director over 50 years old. A whole generation of skills, judgement and expertise disappeared forever almost overnight.

JOHN: *But these massive changes also meant a complete change to the internal accounting system and mistakes were inevitable. One year I got a phone call from the accounts office to say that I had underspent by £50k, and could I spend it by the end of the financial year in a week's time?*

Part of Producer Choice allowed me to spend up to £2,500 on any single capital item. Up to this point you were not allowed to spend on capital items and had to go through a lengthy process to make a case and get it approved. This new system meant that so long as I had money in my budget, I could, for example, buy DV cameras for the Weather Show. I called a meeting with my Producers and Vince Vesey, the systems engineer permanently attached to the Weather Centre. I always kept a running 'wish-list' of equipment we needed, so we worked our way through it.

However, nearly all of it was over £2,500. But we had developed a technique, where we would ask a supplier if they could break down their piece of equipment into separate bits that did not each cost more than our limit. It was a loophole in the system that nobody had really noticed. So, within a day, we had done the negotiations, and issued all the purchase orders on the understanding that invoices must be marked as due on the 31st March.

So all of our goodies arrived and made a big difference to our operation. The following week I received a phone call from the same accountant "you know that £50k underspend, well we made a mistake and it is a £50k overspend". I explained that he was just too late as I had already spent the money!

So, Producer Choice did work to my advantage, however, so much did I dislike the concept that I continued to use internal departments such as graphic design, engineering, computer graphics workshop etc. Sure there was a bit of horse-trading over price, but I really wanted to keep their skills working on Weather.

The annual negotiation became a Kafkaesque event, where the supplier would take me to lunch and we would talk about our families and holidays, then after the second bottle of wine we would have a quick negotiation and then we went back to work. Whichever way you analyse this enjoyable diversion, it was all about relationships and trust – those vital factors that make good TV.

There were many anomalies in the system, when for instance the Pronunciation Unit was closed. This had been a vital service for the whole of the BBC and not just Weather. If you had any doubt over how to pronounce a name or a place or even a country, then a quick phone call to the unit and you would get the official way to pronounce it.

But this was a centrally funded unit, and when Producer Choice arrived the funding went. Luckily when there was a barrage of complaints from all over the BBC, and central funding was found.

One other important part of the AMS conferences was that there was always an exhibition demonstrating the latest techniques in computer graphics. There was no equivalent meeting anywhere else in the world, and it quickly became a 'Mecca' for broadcast meteorologists from countries outside the USA. Seeing how other people broadcast weather was particularly important. You are never too big to learn.

Our first excursion across the pond was to Chicago. To say it was like two schoolboys on a day out would be an understatement. We were on a very tight budget and it was almost as if we only had limited pocket money. The hotel was jaw dropping in both size and grandeur. Because the 'windy city' goes from baking summers to freezing winters, the architects had fashioned a huge internal atrium with a lake in the middle. On one side there was a raised bar area with a grand piano, all suspended over the edge of the lake, and connected up to the next level by two gold escalators.

On the other side of the lake were two restaurants. We would save our pocket money for a drink of an evening, to sit by the piano played by someone with white gloves, as we watched the great, the good and the downright gorgeous people of Chicago go up and down these suspended escalators.

JOHN: *When it came to settle our bill at the end of the conference there was a long queue and I could sense that Bill wanted to tell me something.*

He was concerned that he had been watching those notorious premium channels on his hotel television and he had just calculated that it had cost over $150. I was not much pleased. However, at the desk, his charge was nothing and I had to pay. It transpired that he just channel hopped and never registered anything, where I had watched the entire programme, just to check the lighting and quality of acting!

At the exhibitions we were rather taken by the Doppler radar rain coverage in the States. They were building a network of 350 stations, which rather palled into insignificance the total of 15 for the UK, but then the USA is a big country. I was particularly interested in the fact that they updated the image every 3 minutes, whilst in the UK it was every 30 minutes. This allowed for very smooth animations and I was keen to show the displays on BBC World.

The main difference with Doppler is that the scan not only looks through the rain, but also up into the cloud that helped with tornado forecasting. We needed to see if this was something we should also be using. For one conference we were able to adjust our itinerary to go via Houston where my brother lives, as he knew the chap who ran the brand new Doppler radar just around the corner from where he lived.

When we arrived it was a bright sunny morning, but soon the clouds developed and the heavens opened. Following this on the Doppler was a very excited station boss. As Bill and I looked out of the window at the 10-inch an hour rainfall, I noticed that a large convertible had left the roof off.

Bill was sure if we enquired it would belong to the senior forecaster. We asked and he was correct. But when it came to take him for lunch we had to go in our car as his was completely ruined with water pouring from the doors.

But the States produced its own problems as when BBC World finally started broadcasting there, we realised that the temperatures would have to be shown in Fahrenheit where the rest of the world were using Celsius. But the BBC Computer Graphics Workshop came up with a software fix that allowed you to save a chart in °F and the software would do the conversion from °C. But that did cause a problem for Canada who used Celsius. One day the USA will catch up with the rest of the world!

It is a tribute to the BBC Weather Centre that both Bill and John were invariably asked to do a presentation at the conferences, as they were very interested in "how we did things the other side of the pond".

One of the constant complaints from broadcasters in the USA, was about the crassness of their colleagues in the Newsroom. The way in which TV is organised in the States means that there are really no National Weather reports. Each city has one or more TV stations, each with their own weather presenter. These stations were basically for news reports and so all the presenters were owned and managed by news people.

Happily the BBC Weather Centre was owned and operated by the central Presentation Department, who really only had one remit – and that was to serve our viewers. It wasn't there to feed the egos of hyped-up, self-serving news journalists. We were the envy of the world! Sad to say, that BBC Weather was transferred to News Division in 2001.

It will never be the same again.

CHAPTER 11

FIM, IABM & WMO

During the late 80s and early 90s, there was an explosion in broadcast meteorology across the world, in particular in Europe, where the demise of the old Soviet States, had led to TV stations being started with new ideas and lots of enthusiasm. More channels were being developed and there was an ever increasing demand for weather broadcasts.

This in turn led to the launch of an International Weather Festival started in Paris in 1991. François Fandeux had been a presenter on France's first TV channel TF1 and his father Michael worked as a meteorologist for Météo France, the state Met Office. He had a vision for a 'Festival international de météo', which would celebrate the business of weather broadcasters. The main attraction to participants was that it was fully-funded, with flights, hotels and food all paid for by the organisers. For many from developing countries, it was the first time they had left their countries. For most of us, this was the first time that people who broadcast meteorology both in Europe and other parts of the world had got together to exchange views and ideas.

JOHN: *We met so many wonderful people, that there are just too many to mention, many are still our friends. Certainly the late Jean Francois-Leroux had a big influence on the conference. He was part of the organising committee and became a good friend to us all, and latterly becoming involved in setting up the International Association of Broadcast Meteorology (IABM). One particular person who stands out above all was Australian Ray Wilkie who was one of life's true eccentrics. A big rugged man, with a tiny wife called Joanie. Ray was a true meteorologist in the classic way.*

He didn't believe in computers, just good observations and common sense. He had been a navigator during the war on Coastal Command, rose up the ranks to become a Regional Director in the Australian Met Service, before going into broadcasting.

He was also an accomplished saxophone player. Ray was no fool, but his larger than life, 'Dame Edna Everage' accent and a voice that was as loud as a shout, made him stand out above the crowd. He first came to our attention at the first Paris Conference, when a video showing a white Australian, blacked-up as an Aborigine weather presenter, got Ray to his feet and with his fog-horn voice started with a phase that became his signature "I would just like to say" and then proceeded to demolish our French hosts as if the 100 years war was still current. The clip was from a comedy show, but Ray was having none of it!

At another conference we were all assembled in the huge gothic reception room of Hotel de Ville in Toulouse. Ray asked Bill if it was a hotel chain as he had noticed the same name in other towns!

We had come to Toulouse to visit Météo France and their new super computer, although Bill and I thought it looked more like a BBC Micro. A well briefed Mayor, welcomed us all and in particular Ray and Joanie celebrating their 50th wedding anniversary that day. Before the Mayor could draw breath, the inbuilt loud-hailer turned on in Ray's chest as he started "I would just like to say". And he did for the next 15 minutes. At dinner that night, we got onto the subject of UFOs - as you do. Ray went very serious and white-faced. He told the story that once driving in the outback; a very bright light appeared in the sky moving at great speed. It landed on the road a way in front of him, and then it shot upwards, sideward and backwards at enormous speed. It couldn't have been a helicopter as it moved too fast and in very straight lines. After a while it shot back into the sky and disappeared. We all sat there spellbound waiting for the punch-line, but Ray was silent and look detached. He had really seen what he had described. Spooky eh!

The conferences were lavish affairs, with formal dinners, and receptions. We marvelled at how it could all be funded with people from all over the world. There would be over 120 broadcasters at each conference. The event was held in the Paris district of Issy-Les-Moulineaux, and the Mayor André Santini was very much part of how the festival was able to take place. He was an ambitious politician with his eye on government. He realised that the international publicity that would result from this, let alone in France, would help his ambitions. We later learnt that it was common practice in France, for developers, having been given planning permission, to make a 'charitable gift' to the Mayor's favourite project.

But then France has always been different to the rest of the world and to the French, style comes before content. The three day event would culminate at a 'Hollywood style' awards ceremony held in a big theatre and televised in France. Part of the requirement for going to the Festival was that everyone had to submit a tape of a recent weather broadcast. We were then forced to sit through them all and give them a score. This was then used to decide on the winners at the awards ceremony. Suspicions were raised at the 1st Festival, when at the reception after the awards, we all compared notes and decided that none of us had given sufficient votes for the winner to come first. But it was a great event, and we made many new friends, discussed our favourite subject and had a great time.

JOHN: *Bill and I had long discussed whether a weather presenter's star sign was relevant to their ability to broadcast successfully. Bill is a Scorpio and one of their traits is that if they make a mistake – they just shrug it off and move on. Important in broadcasting, because if you dwell on your mistakes, they can eat you up. In the BBC Weather Centre there were more Scorpios than would normally be expected statistically.*

1991 and the 1st Festival de Meteo in Paris and one of the many presentations

Some new colleagues that we met and are still friends in particular through the International Association of Broadcast Meteorology (IABM) that was later formed out of the Paris Festivals

A Climate of Change

At one Festival, after the awards, we were in a group of 25 presenters discussing the results and complaining about how they had been rigged again!

I told them our ideas about star signs and asked for a show of hands of who were Scorpios and out of the 25 there were 15 and the other 10 wished they were. Rather strange eh?

There were always film crews and photographers in droves at these 'after awards' receptions. At one evening there was a young female Canadian reporter with her crew filming the contestants. Unusually by this time we had managed to consume a couple of glasses of wine when she accosted us. She explained that she was doing a piece for her newsroom about the use of language in weather forecasts. Being a pet subject of ours we were soon into 'double-act' mode talking about those words that were onomatopoeic such as 'drizzle' or 'splash'. I said that I was particularly fond of 'frost' to which Bill said, "you mean David Frost". I replied "it's Sir David Frost now as he has been done by the Queen". To which Bill replied, "he isn't a queen – he's married!" "No! I said The Queen". Bill said "But he's an interviewer not a rock star!" So this nonsense went on and at the end of the interview she seemed delighted with us. Some months later we heard from a colleague who lived in Canada that the interview, when broadcast, had caused a sensation, because the TV station had never had so many complaints that we had insulted the Queen. The moral of this story is to never drink and speak – at least not on camera!

We were surprised to hear that the Festival was going to take place the following year and indeed ran every year until 2002, when it was greatly scaled down following the untimely death of François at only 45 years old. We sat through the tapes again, made our votes only to find that again the winner bore no relationship to who we voted for. Finally we realised that the whole voting process was just a smoke screen, and the organisers decided who was going to win, based on their own political agenda. So, when one year, English weather presenter Fred Talbot was invited, he duly submitted his tape.

Granada Television, his employers, decided to do a programme about the Festival and asked the French organisers to send a tape with some sample broadcasts.

On viewing it they found that the tape actually was a compilation of the winners, which included Fred. This was three weeks before the festival! But the French way of running competitions was reinforced when John's Assistant Producer, Andrew Lane came to one Festival. We were told that there was to be a prize of a holiday, all expenses paid on an exotic island. The winner would be whoever had attended the most talks and receptions. Andrew fancying his chances religiously attended everything and ensured that it was all duly recorded.

At the presentation evening, they announced that the prize had been won by a rather pretty Russian Weather lady, who had actually arrived halfway through the festival. Poor Andrew - shame he wasn't prettier.

At the very first festival on presentation night all the broadcasters and their producers duly arrived and we were ushered up onto the stage looking out across the theatre packed to capacity with worthy citizens of northern Paris. We waited with bated breath to find out the winners of the competitions from the tapes we had supplied but before any of that could take place we were to watch the entertainment for the evening, this time it was to be a magician, who as well as the normal tricks with playing cards and scarves also had some caged animals which he made disappear and re-appear.

All went well although it was more than a little crowded on the stage as we sat next to our colleagues from RTE in Dublin. Rhoda Draper, who was the weather producer for RTE, was seen to lean across during the proceedings, put her hand into one of the cages saying "what a pretty cat" not realising it was a black panther!

The following year we were all allowed to sit in the audience and watch the show before being called up on to the stage to receive our prizes. Of the assembled throng from all parts of the Globe very few spoke French so most of us were at a loss when the entertainment started and we realised it was to be a French-speaking comedian. Unfortunately for him he had little response from the audience but the French liked it.

BILL: *The hospitality at these Paris conferences was unsurpassed. Had it been held in the UK my department of the Ministry of Defence would have been hard pushed to give everyone a cup of coffee but in Paris things were very different. We were always entertained to a gala evening where the food was magnificent and the wine flowed freely. During the second conference we were all dressed up and bussed into the centre of Paris to the Officer's Club. Standing in the entrance none of us could be accused of being underwhelmed. It was magnificent and the thought that in the past Napoleon himself strutted around these beautiful rooms. We were led into the banqueting hall and ushered to our seats for dinner. What followed was a culinary feast that was enjoyed by all of us.*

The Mayor of Issy-les-Molineaux, Andre Santini, sat at the top table surrounded by his selected group of French speaking broadcasters when it was decided by the people on our table, that we needed to thank him for all his hospitality and in the hope that we would all be invited back again next year.

It was agreed to ask him to become President of the newly formed Weatherman's Association and I was asked to offer him the position. The speeches went on for a while and then it was my turn. All through the dinner I was wracking my brain to get some link between weather broadcasters and politicians and as I stood up to speak it suddenly came to me. " Monsieur Santini" I said "it would give us great pleasure if you would consider being the first President of the Weatherman's Association" I went on "Politicians and Meteorologists have a great deal in common. We both lie but we both get paid at the end of the month" It was well received by all attending the dinner although the mayor did not seem to enter into the ensuing laughter.

A Climate of Change

As the conference out-grew the hotel in the area, we moved to a bigger venue on the Périphérique (ring road) and the Parisian equivalent of Earls Court. This was a big hotel with a central atrium of lounge, bar and restaurant, with the bedrooms hanging from the walls like a bee-hive. It was ideal as all of the participants were in one place and here outside of conference business we could meet and greet.

JOHN: *One particular year we managed to take our wives Suzanne and Maureen with us, as the organisers were happy for them to share our facilities so long as we paid for the fares to Paris. This in itself was very unusual, as it was not considered appropriate by the BBC for wives to accompany their husbands on trips. So, it was always just Bill and John throughout the world. Bill's equivalent on CNN was Valerie Voss. A superb performer, with all the talents that make a good broadcaster. She had shown us around their Atlanta facility the previous year and we had become very good friends.*

We were sitting having lunch in the atrium and in the distance we saw Valerie and beckoned her across to join us. We noticed her look quizzically at Suzanne and Maureen, so we introduced them. Valerie looked both surprised and shocked and drawing herself up remarked in her powerful voice that echoed through the atrium "You have Wives?" She later explained that at all the times we had met her in the past it was only the two of us and she was convinced we were an 'item'.

The name 'Kavouras' crops up time and again, no less than in Paris. Kavouras was an American Company that made a clever graphics system. It was not suited for BBC use, but we always went to their stand at any exhibition to see what new tricks they had and got to know them very well. They were very keen to get me to buy their system, as the prestige of it being used by the BBC would be immense.

They had tried every way to persuade me, but I was having none of it. One night in the hotel's atrium bar, they tried a different method. Pete Sapponas, their very clever software expert was playing the piano, Ted McGowan a salesman was chatting up some woman and Greg Slater, the larger than life, cowboy Sales Director was sitting alone at a table. I had planned to meet Bill for a drink, but he was running late, so I went down, only for Greg to ask me to join him. He looked me in the eye, paused and then loudly slapped the table saying "why won't you buy my f***ing machine?"

I patiently explained that with our complex hybrid system it wasn't appropriate. Louder he slapped the table and louder said "why won't you buy my f***ing machine?" By now the other people in the bar were sitting up and looking. "Look Greg" I said "without repeating myself it's not for us."

Even louder he slapped the table and now at a shout said "why won't you buy my f***ing machine?" The whole bar was silent, Pete had stopped playing and everyone else was silent. Even Ted had stopped his chat up line. Greg repeated the process at an even higher volume.

On stage for the Festival Show with L-R Rhoda Draper and Gerald Fleming (Ireland), Inge Niedek and Dieter Walch (Germany) and next to Bill, his boss Roger Hunt of the Met Office

Bill wins an award presented by the Mayor Andre Santini on the left

A Climate of Change

People in the restaurant had paused to listen; others came out of their rooms to see what the commotion was all about. Again I said no. Again Greg got louder still. He had one final shout, I said no. Then in a normal voice "Ok, it was a worth a try – fancy a drink?"

BILL: *Kavouras' hospitality was on a par with Andre Santini's and whenever and wherever we met them they entertained us royally, I believe for two reasons; firstly because they never gave up on trying to get John to buy their system and secondly because I think they genuinely liked us and our company. But on one occasion things didn't quite go to plan and we had one or two very embarrassing moments.*

The evening started well enough with us all having a couple of drinks in a local bar but then Greg decided it was time to move on to something more exciting. We stood outside this nightclub facing a huge Russian doorman whilst Greg went to discuss us all going in. The conversation between them started quietly enough but as was Greg's want it became louder and louder. The rest of us were cowering close by but not attempting to intervene between the American and this giant of a Russian.

As the conversation between the two started to get to around 100 decibels Greg was heard to shout at him "I'm an American why can't I come into your club? I've got plenty of US dollars to spend" We all waited wondering what the outcome would be when it all went very quiet. Greg came back to us and muttered something about moving on somewhere else. He was reluctant to discuss his rapid change of heart but eventually told us that the night club he was insisting we were allowed to join, was for the Gay community.

And move on we did. I do not know how we ended up in the next club, but as we mounted the stairs, which took us into a large well, decorated room both John and I were feeling more than a little uneasy. The room was tastefully furnished with many prints of well-known artists hanging from the walls. We were invited to sit on the sofas dotted around the room, the lights were dimmed and hostesses brought us some drinks. At this stage I thought we were about to see a video or something and, I found out afterwards John thought much the same, when a door opened at the far end of the room and in came a bevvy of beautiful girls. When I say beautiful I really mean it, they were all shades from white with blonde hair and blue eyes to those with shining brown skin and dark hair and as we watched they slowly paraded around the room. Greg sidled up to us and whispered in our ears "they are all yours and the charge is on me." John and I quickly realised that we were in a very high-class brothel and it was at this point that our background of staid Anglo-Saxon upbringing and lack of experience in these establishments took hold.

We were rooted to the spot not daring to move or even glance around the room because by catching the eye of one of these beautiful girls meant that they would come and sit next to you and start discussing business.

A very proud Bill with his award for services to TV Weather Broadcasting

John gets the consolation prize!

A Climate of Change

We knew this because some of the other people who had come along with us were already chatting away with them. As the room slowly emptied we had to make a decision to stay and go with the flow or make a rapid exit. I think we both spotted the toilet sign at the same time and made a dash for it racing out and down the stairs. As we gulped in the cool night air we signalled for a taxi and rode back to our hotel and a very large brandy.

But many of us thought the Festival too shallow. To give up three days in busy schedules, it needed a bit more meat. We asked that there should be some lectures about meteorology and its broadcast. However, again it proved to be style over content. But, something useful did come out of it, as at one of these events they produced a membership card for everyone saying that we were now members of the World Weatherman's Association (WWA).

There was much curiosity over what this all meant and our German colleagues called for a copy of the constitution. First there was denial. Then they said that there was one and would we wait a couple of hours so they could run off sufficient copies. When they arrived they were in French. We were convinced that in those two hours they had written it from scratch! Later at the awards, the WWA made a presentation of a weather station to the chap from the French Cameroons, who the following year won the scientific prize although none of us had voted for him!!

But still, for many of us at the conference, we felt that there was an urgent need for an international organisation to represent the views of all of us involved in the growing industry of broadcast meteorology. So, at the Festival held in the Paris district of Issy-Les-Moulineax in 1993 a large group of the participants met in a local cafe and agreed that an organisation should be formed. This idea culminated in November 1994 at a conference held in Gran Canaria where we were guests of the Spanish Met Service. 25 founder members met and resolved to form the International Association of Broadcast Meteorology (IABM).

JOHN: *The Canaries conference was designed to offer a better understanding about its unique weather and interest European weather presenters in mentioning it in their forecasts. The conference hotel was one side of a main road and the restaurants and nightlife the other. There was fencing along the road to stop people jay-walking into fast traffic. The only way to get to the other side was via a footbridge some half a mile down the road. Gerald Fleming from Irish TV announced he had found a sub-way. So, that night a group of us were led in the dark (strange there was no lighting) through the bushes to the entrance to this tunnel. Some refused to carry on. But us intrepid ones crouched as we walked through this 5 ft high concrete tube (Bill didn't need to crouch!) As we emerged to the brightly lit restaurants, we realised that we had been through nothing more than a storm drain, known for evermore after Gerald Fleming who discovered it, as the 'Irish Storm Drain'.*

Bill and I had already been to the Canaries in October 1990. By chance a letter had arrived on my desk that had done the rounds of the BBC asking if anyone involved in broadcasting the weather on the BBC would be interested in attending a conference in the Canary Islands. After much soul searching and personal sacrifice, we decided to go!

There was no expense involved to the licence payer and we were aware how many UK citizens were now taking holidays on the islands. On arrival at Las Palmas airport on Gran Canaria we were whisked away by coach to the military side of the airport. The place was empty other than a lonely private jet sitting shimmering in the blistering sun. Surely not for us! But it was. Inside we met our hosts, two from the local met office led by the boss, a charming lovely man, Giuillermo Rivero and his assistant, there was Jose Antonio Maldonado – the Bill Giles of Spain's first channel TVE, and a chap from Bulgaria who did not speak any English. Other than that there was a very pretty lady from the tourist office (not that I noticed) who served drinks. In the coming couple of days we learnt that they had written to all the European TV stations, but only TVE, BBC and Bulgarian TV had replied. On further investigation they had obviously written to the wrong departments!

So this small, but beautifully formed group, flew round the islands, stayed at posh hotels, ate too much, certainly drank too much and were generally treated like royalty. The final day we were wheeled into a room with cameras and lights and sat at a big table with an important local person and asked to sign a protocol before the press and the TV expressing friendship between the Canary Islands and the BBC. We still do not know to this day exactly what we signed as the whole document was in Spanish!

At the second conference in 1994, Francis Wilson from Sky Television had a few too many Sangrias over lunch and passed out on a sun bed. The next morning when he arrived for breakfast he was a pale white down exactly one half of his face and bright red on the other! Francis liked his tipple, and one evening in Paris we were all having dinner at a long table when he came up to me to have a chat about coming back to the BBC and working at the Weather Centre. About an hour later I noticed that he was missing from the table, concerned about him I asked my producer Andrew Lane to go on a hunt. Sometime later he returned to say that he had found him in the toilets fast asleep! To be fair to Francis, all weather broadcasters work a crazy schedule of antisocial hours and probably had not had sufficient sleep. However, after that I never continued our conversation about working for me.

The founders of this new association, which included Bill and John, understood the simple truth that weather broadcasters straddle the worlds of meteorology and the media, depending on both for the resources to do their job properly, but belonging fully to neither. Their responsibility was first and foremost to their audience, who expected them to be informative, educational, entertaining, witty …and above all - right! Weather presenters needed a strong and united voice that would make it heard on their behalf.

At the founding meeting it was realised that there was some urgency in forming the Association as one of the biggest challenges facing the industry was actively being discussed by the World Meteorological Organisation. The job of the WMO is to represent the 183 Met Services all over the world and coordinate their activities including the collection of observations taken by each service. The resolution was scheduled for discussion at the WMO Congress in Geneva in June the following year. The resolution reflected a growing move by some National Met Services to restrict the free exchange of weather data and commercialise its access.

Those who were tabling the resolution saw it as an attempt to put some order into the method by which meteorological data was exchanged between National Met Services (NMSs). The reality was that many European governments were trying to reduce their spending on meteorological services and make up the difference with commercial activities.

So, on one side of the argument was the USA, where the basic data was freely exchanged but the value added by enhancement and distribution. This was because under the Freedom of Information Act, data generated by government was free to use. On the other side were the Europeans, led in particular by the British, French and German NMSs who wanted the data placed in tiers and priced accordingly. Then in the middle were small NMSs, in particular the developing countries who were facing increasing threats of reductions and even closures from their governments, who thought that local services were no longer needed with the availability of international broadcasts from the likes of the BBC and CNN. There was certainly a moral issue here. Why should British taxpayers pay again for something that they had already paid for? Should any government deny its people information that may prevent the loss of life and property or aid them in their daily lives and business?

There was obviously a clear risk of anarchy, and the founder members were concerned that in the final analysis they had a clear responsibility to their viewers and listeners to provide the most comprehensive service and that any change in data charges would affect the content of their broadcasts and any increase in costs would have to be met by the broadcasting companies. If the broadcasters could not or would not pay for the data then the service to viewers and listeners would suffer.

But it didn't just stop at data, as we were getting concerned over noises from EUMETSAT who operated the Meteosat geostationary satellite 26,000 miles up above the Earth's surface. They were funded by 26 European states on the basis of their GDP and were working on how to pay for the next generation of Meteosat by suggesting that they were going to start to charge for some of the images. On news of this in States, who provided free images from the GOES-East and GOES-West satellites, they retorted by saying that if Europe started charging – then they would.

A private plane was provided for our tour of all the islands of the 'Canaries'.

We were taken to see all the stunning sights in the Canaries.

A Climate of Change

The IABM was very concerned over this development, in particular for emerging nations such as Africa who would be caught in the middle and unable to afford the fees. We really needed to argue for some joined up world government. The simple fact was that by denying any weather data to poor countries, they would be unable to advise their farmers properly, leading to crop failure and the World Bank having to step in with funding that had come from the rich west who were restricting the data in the first place. A no brainer if ever there was one! So, in our humble way we started to try and sway the argument. So a delegation from the IABM went to the EUMETSAT headquarters in Darmstadt Germany (Germany was the largest contributor) to meet the then Director Tillman Mohr.

As they walking into the building Bill was joking about the bit from the BBC programme 'Fawlty Towers' about "whatever you do don't mention the war". Tillman was well known to our colleagues Inge Niedek and Dieter Walch both of ZDF TV as he had been the boss of the German Met Service, Deutscher Wetterdienst. With his clipped moustache, traditional jacket and formal manner, he was every inch a German. John opened the conversation with "we are very concerned about the data wars". If he saw John colour-up, he was too much a gentleman to comment!

Out of these discussions came a wider vision of not only providing a voice for the industry in these international debates, but also providing a framework to develop and encourage broadcast meteorological skills, by sharing and distributing information. It was noted that the vast bulk of those involved in the industry worked in an environment where they were isolated and starved of information. It was important that the Association was truly representative of the industry, and so membership would be open to anyone in the world, and would include both journalists and meteorologists.

There was no doubt of the need for an association, and the founder members then resolved to form one as soon as possible, mindful of the fast approaching WMO Congress. Draft objectives were agreed and a small working party was formed from those already attending the 75th Anniversary Meeting of the American Meteorological Society (AMS) held in Dallas in January 1995.

The working party worked on the objects and organisational structure of the association, and discussed the membership and financial arrangements. Also important contacts were established with the AMS, the Director of the American NMS and officers of the WMO, to inform them of the emergence of the Association. Founder members met again in March 1995 to formally agree to set up a Limited Company registered in Ireland under the title of the International Association of Broadcast Meteorology (IABM).

One of the core tasks of the IABM was to represent the views of weather broadcasters worldwide, to communicate those views to other bodies, and to ensure a voice for weather broadcasters in discussions concerning the supply of weather information. To ensure this the IABM immediately entered into dialogue with bodies such as the WMO, European Organisation for the Exploitation of Meteorological Satellites (EUMETSAT), and The Economic Interest Grouping of the National Meteorological Services of the European Economic Area (ECOMET).

In 1998, the IABM was granted consultative status with WMO, a position that allowed it to forge contacts at the highest levels within Meteorology. Members of the IABM began to participate actively in expert teams and task forces reporting to WMO, keeping the concerns of broadcasters always to the forefront. Their headquarters in Geneva provided a convenient place to hold committee meetings. These were always held at weekends, as most of the committee were broadcasters and it was easier for them to fit it round their rotas. The normal pattern was to fly in on a Friday, meet all day Saturday and again on Sunday morning ready to fly out on Sunday afternoon to be in the office on Monday. After Bill and John left the BBC in 2001 they decided to continue their involvement with the IABM. One major piece of work culminated in 2004 when the IABM presented the 1st World Conference on Broadcast Meteorology held in Barcelona.

The ability of broadcasters, through the IABM, to directly communicate with Heads of NMSs at the highest level through the WMO has dramatically changed the way in which Broadcast Meteorology has developed throughout the world. Through dialogue, training sessions, meetings and conferences the aspirations of both broadcasters and meteorologists have been realised. Some of this has been fuelled through the dramatic increase in the availability of web based weather services, but much more through the dialogue between those who produce the forecasts and those who broadcast them. Two very different cultures that were traditionally reluctant to understand what was after all was their shared needs.

On one hand, there was the ultra conservative meteorological community who were looking to broadcast 'scientific lectures' and the 'trendy' broadcasters who wanted to 'sex-up' weather broadcasts. What the dialogue has produced is a mutual respect, and a shared vision that both parties have a vital role to play.

JOHN: *We worked hard to make contacts within the WMO as we knew they would help with the data issues in particular with our broadcasts for BBC World. Once at an AMS conference in San Francisco there was an Hawaiian themed evening and we were all asked to dress in an appropriate shirt. When we came down to the room, seated in one corner at a table all by himself, was the then Secretary General of the WMO Patrick Obasi. This was the most senior meteorologist in the world. An inscrutable Nigerian in a floral shirt.*

So, rather than go and join other tables with people we knew, I suggested to Bill we should join Patrick.

We were soon joined by others and we had an excellent evening, he relaxed and talked about his family and laughed with the rest of us.

Next time when we were in Geneva he made a special point of saying hello to his friends Bill and John. When later we wanted to interview him for the Weather Show, he did not hesitate, although he was known for not granting interviews.

Strange to say, Climate Change has also helped this process of dialogue. There has been a realisation by the scientific community that it needed the media to communicate the message. In particular, it was identified that one of the most trusted people on TV and Radio was the weather broadcaster.

This led directly to the formation of the Climate Broadcasters Network – Europe (CBN-E) by the European Commission. At the Third World Climate Conference (WCC-3) held in Geneva in August 2009, not only was CBN-E there in force, but officers of the IABM were part of the organising committee working side by side with WMO on events designed to focus media attention on the role that Broadcast Meteorology is playing in communicating climate change.

'A coming of Age?' No, not yet – there is still a great deal to be done. But it is worth noting that at the Annual General Meeting of the IABM held in Geneva during WCC-3, there was general agreement that in the 15 years since its formation, the basic objects had been accomplished and that now, the next phase was to further develop and encourage personal development for those involved in our industry.

More colleagues from around the world preparing for a conference (with a few beers)

John Teather, Gerald Fleming (Ireland), Claire Martin (Canada), Tomas Molina (Spain) and Bill Giles representing the world of Broadcast Meteorology at a WMO Conference

A Climate of Change

CHAPTER 12

GETTING IT RIGHT AND WRONG

Weather forecasting is a difficult art, some say close to a black art at times, but throughout the last century great strides have been made. The Met Office statement is that the 'three day' forecast today is as good as the 'one day' one was 20 years ago and that the present 'five day' forecast is as good as the old three day one. That assumes the old one day and three day forecasts were any good. Seriously thugh, weather forecasting by the UK Met Office is as good as anywhere in the world. That is not true of the 1987 storm which crops up time and time again. But what really did happen on that fateful night of the 15th - 16th October so many years ago?

BILL: *The previous Sunday in the Farming forecast, and in those days we actually did the forecast for the whole week of seven days rather than just the five they do today, John Kettley, on the advice of the Senior Forecaster at Bracknell, did say that we expected some severe weather later in the week. We continued this theme on subsequent days, but when it came to Wednesday it wasn't good enough just to talk about bad weather we had to put the details on it. Would the strong winds and rain reach London or East Anglia or would it be only along the south coast of England?*

We all knew that the strongest winds of all would be over northern France, and it turned out that way, with the strongest wind gusts on the Brittany coast. As the week progressed the weather model we were all following started to downplay the storm to the extent that it now gave the advice that it would more likely just skim along the south coast and that the main problem would be the heavy rain over southeast England, and that was what was in the briefing, I had before broadcasting on television that evening.

The bottom line was we got it wrong, as did the French and Belgium Met Offices, as the very strong winds pushed into the southeast and East Anglia blowing trees down and causing general mayhem. Very sadly eighteen people were killed that night but it could have been much worse. We forecasters had had some bad luck and some good luck that night. Bad luck since there had been a lot of rain over the previous week or so and the ground was sodden. This meant that the tree roots were somewhat shallower and easy moved and at this time in October there were still a lot of leaves on the trees. Had it been a fortnight later the trees would have been largely devoid of leaves and wouldn't have shown such resistance to the wind. The good news, if indeed there was any good news, was that the storm happened at night.

Had it been during the day when people were out and about there would have been very many more casualties. In a comparable storm, because this was a once in a 200 year event, in the great storm of 1703 over 4,000 people lost their lives, mainly at sea but this certainly doesn't belittle the fact that we got this one horribly wrong.

Michael Fish has taken a lot of criticism about his comment, and rightly so. He said that a lady had phoned him saying she had heard that there was a hurricane on the way to which he replied that there wasn't. He actually made up the story using it as a link after the one o'clock news but one of the newspapers found and interviewed "the lady". Whatever was the case, it was a rather silly statement to make, knowing that severe weather was forecast for that evening. I understand that it was to be put in the Guinness Book of Records as the worst forecast in the history of the Universe, and if it wasn't it should have been. In fact Michael has always put the blame on me for the storm since I did the 9.30pm forecast that evening and said that it would be" breezy up the channel" To get him back I always tell the story that I have tried to get Michael to write a book. It would have two pictures on the front, one of Michael and one of a hurricane showing a beautiful eye of the storm. The title of the book? 'Hurricane forecasting by Michael Fish MBE' and on opening the book all the pages would be blank!!

I had a further briefing with the senior forecaster after the 9.30pm broadcast to check and see that he was happy with the latest model run of the computer and having no further update from him, allowed the late recorded BBC2 forecast to go out at about eleven o'clock.

I left the BBC Television Centre at around ten o'clock that evening and by the time I arrived in Buckinghamshire noticed that the winds were really starting to blow with some strong gusts. In fact the wind was so strong I had to make a decision as to whether I went the short way for the last couple of miles down through an avenue of trees and risk branches coming off, or the longer way without trees. I settled on the short way and made a dash for it.

Strictly speaking I should have been off duty the next day but after watching the early morning news I realised all hell had been let loose overnight so I immediately got in my car and drove to the Television Centre. Ian McCaskill had been the senior forecaster at London Weather Centre overnight and was still there half way through the morning. As his line manager I rang him up and told him to go home and let the day shift deal with the aftermath and the fact that his warnings had gone out at a very late stage overnight. Without my knowledge, or agreement, he appeared as the lead story on the one o'clock news. What we saw was a dishevelled man, without a tie, who looked as though he had been up all night, which indeed he had. Michael Buerk's opening remarks were true but very cruel when he said to Ian "Well a fat lot of use you were last night".

Ian had no answer to that apart from some stumbling reply. When I questioned him sometime later on his performance he said that his was going for the sympathy vote. My retort was "Well you did that all right". I was very cross that he had stayed on to do the interview when it would have been much more sensible if I had done it. I had a long standing arrangement to give a talk at Hastings on the Saturday following the great storm and was very fearful as I picked my way south to the small town on the south coast of England where there had been two fatalities during the storm two days previously.

The room, which had a balcony, was crammed with people just waiting to hear what I had to say. During my talk it was fine because I held the stage but when it came to question time I was more than a little worried. It was immediately apparent that there were many journalists there baying for my blood, and for that of the Met Office as well, and I was coping with the answers reasonably well when a stocky man in the audience stood up and addressed the newspaper men. He said "I am the coxswain of the Hastings lifeboat. What would you all have done if Bill Giles had told you that there was going to be 100 miles per hour winds last Thursday night? There was nothing or very little you could have done" and with that he sat down. I am very grateful to that man because he saved me from a mauling by the gentlemen of the press.

Two weeks later winds were forecast to reach the same levels of 100 miles per hour over the Cairngorm Mountains in Scotland, which is not uncommon. The following day on my broadcast I mentioned that I had scoured the newspapers that morning to see what the press reaction was, only to find no mention of the strong winds and I am sure that, damaging as it was, the main reason there were so many column inches written in the press about the October 1987 storm was because it happened in the southeast of England and in particular London, the centre of the universe!

The Burns' Day storm of the 25th January 1990 covered a much greater area than the 1987 one, virtually the whole of England and Wales, and because it happened during daylight hours more people were killed, some 47 which made it the greatest weather tragedy in the UK since the great storm and sea surge down the east coast in 1953.

It certainly didn't get the coverage of the one fifteen months earlier mainly, in my opinion, because it wasn't centred on London and the southeast and the Met Office forecast it correctly in severity and area it covered.

Forecasting severe weather events is very difficult, but for the weather observer and forecaster it is one of the more exciting aspects of our daily routine. I have often thought that it would be nice to be a weather forecaster somewhere in the dry, sunny heat of the Sahara desert, or perhaps Singapore where they almost invariably have sunshine every morning and a thunderstorm at three o'clock in the afternoon.

In all reality forecasting the weather in the UK on the eastern side of a great ocean and on the western side of a large continent is much more exciting even though we don't get the extremes, as happens in the centre of large land masses. Ours is a much more varied climate, although we do have some exciting moments. Take 1976 for instance, this year is etched on the British psyche as is 1947, 1963 and, of course 1987. It was the summer of all summers. The previous summer and autumn were very dry as was the following winter; the grounds were parched and as the dry weather continued Dennis Howell MP was made the Minister for Droughts and it is said, although I'm sure not at all true, that he was seen doing a rain dance every morning before breakfast.

In fact, water in the reservoirs was at an all time low and many people across the country had to use standpipes to collect their drinking and washing water and I do remember an advert for saving water that went "Save water, shower with a friend".

When the summer sun started it beat down relentlessly, there was little moisture in the ground for the sunshine to evaporate so it was all used in heating up the ground and the air above it. The temperature reached at least 26.7°C (80°F) somewhere over England between 22nd June and 16thJuly and 32.2°C (90°F) between 23rd June and 7thJuly. Five days in that period it exceeded 35°C (95°F) with the record temperature going to Cheltenham of 35.9°C (96.6°F) on the 3rd July. Because of the drought as well as the heat, forest fires started to rage in the countryside and on the national radio and television forecasts we also gave fire danger risks.

There was another problem for us on the television broadcasts because at that time we were slowly changing from giving the temperatures in Fahrenheit to one in Centigrade and on most broadcasts would convert so we would have on the maps centigrade and orally convert to Fahrenheit. That led to a problem during this very hot summer of 1976. We, as meteorologists, always worked in centigrade and could convert into Fahrenheit within the normal range of temperatures without even thinking about it, but now the higher temperatures were causing us to have to think a little harder rather than it being automatic. Jack Scott, a very experienced broadcaster, came on one day and announced during the broadcast that the temperature would reach 31° centigrade but he had forgotten the Fahrenheit conversion so his explanation went something like this. "Tomorrow's temperature will reach 31° centigrade and that's very hot!"

The hot summer weather continued through August and people were getting more than a little fed up with it. It is the nature of the British that they do not like one type of weather to continue for more than a week, in fact the old definition of a British summer is three fine days and a thunderstorm.

So that towards the end of August it was such a talking point on the national news that I was taken out to the entrance of BBC Television Centre to do a piece to camera about when the fine weather would break. I remember looking up into the sky and seeing some wispy high cirrus cloud and saying to the interviewer that if that cloud thickened then rain would be on its way.

That is precisely what happened. The clouds thickened and lowered, large thunder clouds gathered and the heavens opened and we had a wet September and October and Mr. Howell was out of a job, actually I think he took credit for the rain arriving

We've had hot summers since then of course but it was in 2003 that the heat was felt right across Europe when it was considered to be the hottest summer since at least 1540. Heat stress killed some 70,000 people with 15,000 dying in France alone. A lot of these extra deaths were among older people because of the very hot nights and no air conditioning in their homes.

Ian McCaskill and Michael Fish

Suzanne Charlton and Bernard Davey

On the 9th August 2003 Scotland recorded their highest temperature at Greycrook in the Borders with 32.9°C and on the following day the record for England fell at Faversham in Kent who recorded a temperature of 38.5° Celsius that's 101.3° Fahrenheit.

Not long after this time the Met Office, in accordance with the WMO, decided that they should give credence to Anders Celsius the Swedish astronomer who developed the centigrade scale so we changed from calling it Centigrade to calling it Celsius. In actual fact Mr. Celsius's original scale was the other way around with the melting point of ice at 100 degrees and the boiling point of water at 0 and it was only in 1744, at the time of his death, that the scale was reversed to what we know today. I remember the day we changed from Centigrade to Celsius because we often showed the temperature of different towns and cities as a league table with the heading Centigrade. I mentioned that from that day onwards we would be calling it Celsius and as I said it, I changed the graphic with the only difference being the title at the top.

Of course we've had our share of miserable wet and cold winters to counteract the warm summers and the winters of 1947 and 1962 come to mind. However, the spring of 2013 was also notable, March 2013 especially. In that month the average UK temperature was 3.3°C below the long term average and it was the second coldest March in the past 100 years, equalling March 1947 and only losing out to March 1963 by 0.3°C. So what is the reason that every now and again we get some very cold winters when you would expect the mild winds from the Atlantic would predominate, especially with the continued talk of "global warming".

Generally we have low pressure near Iceland and high pressure somewhere near the Azores referred to as the North Atlantic Oscillation (NAO) and this combination brings in our temperate mild and sometimes wet weather.

However, this can change as it did in the early spring of 2013, and indeed in all our previous cold winters, with the high pressure over Scandinavia taking over, blocking any weather systems from the Atlantic and bringing to the UK very cold continental air from Russia.

The Jetstream, which is a band of very strong winds at about 30,000 feet above the Atlantic, sometimes reaching 200 miles an hour in winter, moved much further south than normal and instead of guiding the windy, wet and mild weather across our shores sent it much further south into the Mediterranean. So the pattern over the Atlantic has changed the low pressure in the south and higher pressure in the north giving a negative North Atlantic Oscillation and those perishingly cold easterly winds. There are three main reasons for this happening. Firstly, early melting of the Arctic sea ice allowed relatively warm waters to move down off Newfoundland helping to push the Jetstream southwards. Secondly the research meteorologists and climatologists have discovered that if sudden warming takes place in the stratosphere by the ultra violet from the Sun being absorbed by the Ozone layer between 10 and 50 kilometres above the Earth's surface, as it did in 2013, then some two to three weeks later it can influence the weather patterns in the Atlantic.

A Climate of Change

And thirdly, although I am sure those clever research boffins will find more correlations, if the Madden-Julian Oscillation, which shows itself as increased and decreased amounts of tropical rain as it travels eastwards across the Indian and Pacific Oceans is active, as it was during February and March 2013, it also shows trends of creating a negative North Atlantic Oscillation some two or three weeks later. All three of these events, evident in early 2013, conspired to allow the cold Scandinavian high pressure to develop and give northwest Europe a very cold Spring.

A year later it was all change. despite the headlines on the front of the Daily Express by Natham Rao on 13th November 2013 that the UK was in for the coldest winter in modern times with copious amounts of snow, the winter of 2013-2014 turned out to be the wettest over England and Wales since at least 1766 with barely a flake of snow falling and temperatures 1.5°C above the long term average.

There were at least 12 major storms, extreme flooding, especially over the Somerset Levels and through the Thames Valley with tidal surges adding to large parts of the coastline disappearing into the sea. It was all blamed on the Jetstream being stronger than normal and further south than is normally the case allowing a succession of very deep depressions to develop over the Atlantic and move continuously across the country.

Taking into account all the good work produced by the modellers and forecasters in the Met Office, John and I had always agreed that the weather forecast for the general public should give the answers to all their concerns at any point in time. We had already made sure that the language that was used on the broadcasts was one that everyone understood and told the weather story.

The job of the person delivering the message was to translate from the meteorological jargon that we used when talking to our peers into a language anyone without a scientific background would understand.

In my opinion, it is no use doing the best broadcast in the history of the universe if your listeners or viewers don't understand it. I have often been asked which I would prefer - the forecast to be correct or the broadcast to be wonderful. It has to be the broadcast because if that was unintelligible no one would understand the forecast at any rate. You have to decide what is the story of the day, what do people want answers to and that is what you should lead with because anything else using a routine of graphics every broadcast, no matter how good they are, soon becomes very boring to watch and often irrelevant.

After spending a great deal of time in the 1980s and early 1990s in adding to and perfecting the electronic graphics we started to look at better ways to talk about the effect of the weather on people and their daily lives. We had meetings at the Department of Health to discuss how we could portray pollen counts and sunburn in our forecasts. The meetings involved not just Civil Servants but Doctors, representatives of companies that manufactured sun creams and others.

The meetings were very formal and conducted by a senior civil servant who was always speaking on behalf of their Minister and often objecting to the way we wanted to move forward.

BILL: *I remember one day getting exasperated about the minute details holding up the discussion as a civil servant said once again that she wasn't sure her Minister would agree. My remark fell on stony ground when I dared to suggest that we get the Minister in for the next session so he could speak to us direct. This apparently was tantamount to asking God to come down from the mountain and talk to us and it never happened.*

On the subject of sunburn, the committee couldn't agree on the scale to use and in the end John told them we would use a scale from 1 to 10 where 1 was no problem with the ultra-violet light on any type of skin to 10 which was extreme danger of burning. We did find a slight problem with the scale, simple as it was, because of the various skin types from the very light skinned northern Europeans to the dark skin of people from the tropics. It went on air when relevant during the summer months, using model output from the Met Office and became an instant hit with viewers. At the same time that we were starting to show the sunburn graphics that the Ministry of Health were running as a campaign to show the potential dangers of getting burnt.

This didn't go down too well with the lads on building sites who invariably stripped off at the first sign of summer, so it was decided to target young teenage girls, the mothers of the future, not with necessarily getting burnt but by showing them if they went out uncovered too much in the hot sunshine at 30 years old they might look like 40 and when they reached 40, someone may guess their age as 55. It worked and now when the sun is shining brightly many of the youngsters playing are either covered up or have sun cream applied.

John purchased the 'pollen count' from the National Pollen Research Unit, which not only gave us the pollen count for the day but, using the weather forecast, the count for the next day too. These again we put on a scale from 1 to 10 enabling people who suffered when the forecast was high, to take their medication or stay indoors with the doors and windows shut.

This was quite a sophisticated forecast, as it didn't only show grass pollen but many others including counts from different trees.

We were not only looking at indices for sunburn and pollen counts but also toying around with windchill. The windchill is the perceived drop in temperature felt on exposed skin owing to the combination of temperature and wind. In other words if you are out in a strong wind, especially in winter, how much colder it feels compared with the same temperature on a calm day.

There are several mathematical formulae to describe windchill which we looked at and settled on the one Bill thought most relevant for temperatures we were likely to face in a UK winter rather than arctic conditions. By using this table we could calculate the windchill for any given temperature and wind speed but, as with all our graphics, they were not to be used until the temperature got close to or below freezing and the difference between the apparent temperature and the actual one shown by a thermometer was large enough to be significant. We would then, as now, talk about the temperature, say tomorrow, followed by the windchill temperatures, which by definition would be lower. This again proved a great hit with the viewers who then knew they had to wrap up well when they saw the maps. The reverse of windchill is heat index when the actual feel of the temperature is higher than that shown by the mercury. We had more of a problem with this one since the effect really didn't kick in until the temperature was in the high 20s or 30s, which doesn't happen too often in the UK.

BILL: *The weather presenter at the BBC Television Centre has to split themselves in two. In the office they have to be weather forecasters analysing the data, considering advice from the computers doing the numerical forecasting, and also rely on their own experience. After weighing up all that information they then come to an understanding of what is the most likely forecast.*

Then, as they walk into the studio to tell the story, they leave the forecaster behind and become a broadcaster. Experience, as a weather forecaster, in my opinion, is extremely important, and a background in forecasting for the Royal Air Force for a few years before coming to work on national radio or television should be the norm. After all forecasting at a fast jet station deciding whether the cloud base would be high enough for the jets to return to base in the middle of the night is real forecasting and you certainly get a feel for the weather very quickly.

When I started broadcasting in the 70s we all had a background of 5 to 10 years weather forecasting before going on to radio and subsequently on television. Nowadays the broadcasters are very young and inexperienced so have to follow the computer output blindly. This is the fault of the accountants who now run things and since a 23 year old forecaster is much cheaper that a 40 year old with experience, they prefer the younger person.

I had to fight my corner very hard in the last few years in charge of the forecasters at BBC Weather Centre because of that. As, had I got rid of Michael Fish or Ian McCaskill, I could have had two young forecasters for the price of one from the salary point of view. I steadfastly refused to do this, perhaps I was wrong in the light of their involvement with me later on, but I was not prepared to lose their experience at both forecasting and broadcasting.

Leading the team of broadcast meteorologists was not the easiest job in the world. I really had two bosses; one looking at the meteorology and the other at the broadcasts and sometimes it was difficult satisfying both. The Met Office was the more difficult of the two because, apart from my boss Roger Hunt, very few others understood the way we had to craft the story of the weather to make it understandable and interesting to our viewers. Not only that, we had to push the boundaries of meteorological thinking on subjects such as climate change but also the way we told the general public about it.

CHAPTER 13

THE WEATHER CHANNEL

The Weather Channel (TWC) in the USA launched in May 1982 to a sceptical world. How on earth would it be possible to fill 24/7 with weather and who would watch it anyway? But the sceptics were wrong; it soon established itself as an essential and iconic part of the American culture.

It was cheap to produce, and sold advertising well. Using specially developed software, the channel could also be easily adapted to provide local services. It quickly became a phenomenon in the industry and certainly played a major part in the development of broadcast meteorology. There were envious eyes from this side of the pond. But there were two major facts that made it successful. USA already had a well developed cable service, with most homes having upwards of 50 channels. Also it is a big country with extremes of weather. There was always something going on of interest somewhere.

Whilst visiting his brother Roy who lives in Houston, John had observed that cable ownership produced a very different viewing culture. Roy constantly channel hopped. So, if watching Star Trek, as soon as the adverts appeared he would switch to The Weather Channel, watch an update or two, then with some miraculous in-built timing, switch back to Star Trek just in time. For TWC it was a business model made in heaven, as this channel hopping was copied all over the country. They were getting visits, albeit short ones, but where they could advertise. They were very good at sponsorship opportunities, so everything was a 'something' forecast. The Wal-Mart Weather or the Ford Forecast or the MacDonald's Moment. Also it was being used as a sort of background wallpaper, as viewers simply left their TVs on the TWC as company. Other than News it was the only live programme.

The owners of TWC, Landmark Communications, thought that they could spin their product into the UK and The Weather Channel launched in the UK on the Sky Satellite on the 1st October 1996. The story was that they were prepared to invest $12 million and if the money ran out before they turned a profit – then they would cut their losses and pull out. The channel shared a transponder with The Racing Channel on Sky and transmitted from 6am until 11am. It was really designed for cable as it had specific local weather, in some cable areas it was on 24 hours a day. But at this time, the cable service in the UK was very patchy and there was no culture to watch it. Also the viewing habits were so different, the Americans had just not done their homework.

Cable was a fledgling and the changes in weather conditions in the UK were too small to fill the time. The channel ceased transmission in April 1998 due to poor viewing figures.

But John was convinced that another model could work and be successful. With all of the contacts that they had made on the international stage, he began to formulate ideas for a World Weather Channel. The BBC Weather Centre and the very high degree of automation meant that the unit cost of each broadcast was very low. The concept was based on an hourly wheel, part of which was generated in London but with several opt-out points at which local services would do their own weather. One of the big issues at WMO was 'capacity building' which literally meant helping emerging nations to develop their own high-quality weather services. The plan was to provide training and graphics at the local station. The hourly wheel also allowed for opting out for local commercials, which would pay for the link from London and a contribution to the BBC's central costs. The back half of the wheel would consist of more feature based material drawing on the already increasing library of film being made by the Weather Show.

John felt it vital, that in building this concept, WMO should be fully involved. They alone could help develop the relationships with individual National Met Services, who would need to be fully motivated, as they would be providing the staff and forecasts for their local opt-outs.

JOHN: *By chance Bill and I were in Singapore training on behalf of WMO and two of their key players were there as part of the course. Eirah Gorre-Dale was the public relations expert and close to the Secretary General and Haleh Kootval of the Public Services Division. Both were very committed to improving the range and quality of meteorological broadcasting throughout the world. They had jointly arranged this particular training course as part of their outreach programme. So, I hosted a dinner for them at the famous Raffles (where else?) together with Tom Hartwell from the BBC Computer Graphics Workshop who was also there providing a graphics system for the training. Over dinner I explained the ideas that I was developing and discussed any sensitivity that there might be in WMO and the NMSs.*

It was a jolly affair and we were enjoying the occasion in our private dining area with four white-gloved waiters seeing to our every need. Bill was in good form and had just cracked a joke as we were being served with a sorbet as an amuse-bouche between courses. The joke just struck Tom as so funny that he hit the table with his fist and the sorbet jumped from the plate and onto his shoulder. Instantly the waiters rushed to his aid and cleaned the offending article of his jacket. But what really demonstrated the style of the world famous Raffles was that the headwaiter then apologised to Tom for any inconvenience!

As the number of channels available was increasing due to the change from analogue to digital TV coupled with a change in viewing habits, the BBC was already working with commercial partners to develop new channels.

The big challenge for everyone in the industry was finding good content to put on these new channels and John was trying to get into the debate with his ideas for a Weather Channel.

JOHN: *One of my greatest problems in the BBC, that there was only me to champion weather. Pam Masters my Head of Department was very supportive, but her attention was on another agenda, and that was who was going to actually transmit all these new services. She was firmly of the view that this was exactly what the Presentation Department was there for. Indeed, later on that is precisely what happened, however, in the scramble for the BBC to sell off its assets, the whole Presentation Department was sold off, and effectively became a huge transmission machine for the BBC and all its new partners. The down side was that Weather was thrown to the wolves in News as it was felt that Weather was "not a fit" in the new privatised business.*

But, that said, Pam was prepared to put some limited funding into researching the potential. I had previously received some correspondence from Thailand, as they had wanted to buy our weather graphics system for the King as a birthday present. He was very keen on weather forecasts and had been very concerned for his farming subjects as there had been a disastrous crop the year before because of bad weather. As a young man, he had worked on the land and had a special affinity with the people, and wanted to improve their lot. I wrote back saying that a graphics system was not the answer, but we would like to talk to them about a special Weather Channel that we were developing.

Alan Bancroft, the departmental Business Development Manager and I flew to Bangkok and on arrival were treated like royalty. People often do not realise the high regard in which the BBC is held overseas, and this was no exception as our host was a fan of BBC World and the Weather in particular. We gave a presentation of our suggestions to considerable interest from our host who it transpired was part of the Royal family. He said it was exactly the sort of initiative they were seeking and with partners like Thai Telecoms, who were looking for content for their growing TV service, funding would not be an issue.

Very helpful in finding Asian contacts was Hugh Sheppard, my old boss, who had moved on and was now the BBC's representative in that region based in Sydney.

He arranged for us to go to Singapore to meet with Singapore Telecoms who like the Thais needed new content for their services. A very good meeting and considerable interest was shown. I had also been in conversation with SRG the German speaking part of Swiss Television as they were looking to expand their channels and were very keen on the concept I was developing.

On our return to the UK, little progress was being made with commercial partners and so Pam was investigating whether the BBC might do it itself using BBC Worldwide, the commercial arm of the BBC. She was also of the mind that we should make contact with The Weather Channel in the USA to see if they might be interested in investing in the concept, as they were the experts.

I was not convinced this was the right way forward, however, Alan and I flew to Atlanta to have a meeting with the Senior Vice President, Ray Bann. I knew Ray through AMS Conferences, and he had also visited the BBC Weather Centre for a tour and lunch. We had a very amicable meeting, although I didn't go into too much detail, as I didn't want them to know our concept in full. It was an interesting visit and I enjoyed the guided tour of their facilities, though I was struck how much of the staff and technical resources were applied to getting the commercials out, in comparison to the rather meagre weather production facilities. But then, that is commercial television. Anyway, Ray said that he would raise it at the next board meeting and get back to us. But then it all went very quiet.

Back in the UK I was busy with some pilots (test programmes) and trying to get a realistic budget. That year he family holiday was in Disney Florida and on our return, we were met by my brother-in-law to say that whilst we had been away, our house had been burgled. But he said it was all very odd. All the exterior cables had been systematically cut. The alarm had been disabled. Little had been stolen other than my BBC laptop.

But the oddest thing was that all my private papers and files had been taken out of the filing cabinets and arranged in fan shape on the floor as if someone was trying to find something. Other than a vintage barometer in the hall, a bit of costume jewellery and a TV found in the garden – nothing else had been taken. It all looked as if professionals had done it. The police didn't have a clue although they agreed it was odd.

Later that year, we were still getting no sense out of TWC, and we needed to either count them in or eliminate them. So, with still no reply from Ray, Alan and I flew to Atlanta and forced a meeting on him. He was very deadpan and non-committal, citing that other problems had kept them occupied. He wasn't the Ray that I had known and shared a beer with. We asked to speak to the CEO who we had briefly met at the earlier visit. We were told that it was not possible as he was out of town for the rest of the week. That evening, to drown our sorrows, we went to a random restaurant for dinner and there sitting on the far side was the CEO and a guest. We had been shafted. It was as much as I could do to stop Alan going over and thumping him!

On my stolen laptop were all the plans, descriptions and contacts for the BBC Weather Channel. So perhaps they really didn't need to meet us after all!

Back in the UK winds were changing. The plan to privatise Presentation was in full swing and so my master's attention was elsewhere. Then in early 2001 I was summoned to my line-manager's office, who at that time was Sandy Maeer, and told that Weather did not have a part in the new 'BBC Broadcast' company and from 1st April, Weather would move to News. I knew then that both my future and that of a World Weather Channel was coming to an end.

Too often, you can complain that your bosses missed a chance, but I honestly believe they did in not pursuing a Weather Channel. It exactly fitted the glove of public service broadcasting.

It would have reinforced the leadership position that the BBC had taken in broadcast meteorology throughout the world and more importantly – would have made money.

CHAPTER 14

PROGRAMME MAKING

The BBC often made programmes about the weather, and for many years made an 'end of the year' review that was shown on New Year's Day. It provided a chance to look back over the previous year at notable weather events and how they had affected lives and property. John directed many of these and Bill invariably presented them.

BILL: *For me, one of the more enjoyable parts of being a television weatherman at the BBC in the 1970s and 80s was that at times we were allowed out of the studio to make films.*

I remember my first time as though it was yesterday. I was standing on the beach at Slapton Sands in my home county of Devon, a place I knew well since I grew up just a few miles away near Dartmouth. I was to interview a person called Laurie Emberson on the huge waves which had pounded the little seaside village that Autumn. Everyone assumed that I was an experienced broadcaster, but I knew nothing of the techniques involved with filming. For a start I kept forgetting Laurie's name and didn't realise that I had to remember the questions I had put to him, so that we could film the cut-aways of me asking the questions to camera afterwards. The BBC Production Assistant, Shirley Edwards, was also new to filming and she didn't take note of the questions I had asked, so it was a shambles, which had some interesting scary moments in the cutting room at a later date.

During the couple of days spent filming for this particular show, we stayed at the Castle Hotel in Dartmouth - a very old and charming place. The head waiter, who had a very ill fitting wig, recognised me for being on TV, mainly because I was a local lad from Dittisham, a village just a few miles up the river Dart from Dartmouth.

John thought up a great idea with him to have some fun at Jack Scott's expense. Jack, who had been broadcasting for many years and was extremely well known, was coming down to meet us to do some filming the next day and the stage was set. The arrangement John made was for the headwaiter to come to our table and ask me for my autograph while totally ignoring Jack. It worked very well, much to Jack's annoyance and disbelief, and to the day Jack retired neither of us had the nerve to tell him it was a set up.

There were many other mishaps during the making of this particular annual review of the weather. I remember we all went to a house in Blackawton where Jack Scott was to interview a vicar's daughter about some large hailstones that had fallen and which she had conveniently placed in her freezer for us to study.

Jack was the doyen of weather broadcasters at that time, very experienced, and one to which we newcomers looked to for guidance. On this particular occasion, though, Jack had obviously infatuated with the lady in question because his interview with her about the hailstones was like a young puppy talking to its master. He was all dew-eyed and stuttering and it took us a lot longer than it should have done.

Another time, also down in Dartmouth, we spoke to the Navy helicopter crew about their rescue mission on the ill fated 1979 Fastnet race, when a sudden worsening of the weather, with storm force winds, devastated the sailing race. John and I together with Shirley Edwards had duly arrived at the helicopter pad at the top of Dartmouth. The large Sea King was waiting for us to start the filming. I was to be winched up 100 feet from the ground and then walk through to interview the captain who had taken part in the earlier rescues. We waited and waited for the BBC camera and sound crews to arrive only to find one lot had gone to the Royal Naval Air Station Culdrose in Cornwall and the other nearby at Helston.

After much phoning around John eventually got them all back in the right place and we were about to start filming, when the cameraman, a very strong union official, stated that it was lunchtime so he and his crew we going to take their lunch break.

The navy fliers, as well as us, just couldn't believe what we had just heard, since we had been there hanging around all morning unable to film as we were waiting for them to arrive. Nonetheless he was adamant, the camera was packed away and we just had to wait for another hour. Such was the strength of the broadcasting unions at that time, but Margaret Thatcher brought some semblance of order in the next few years.

After lunch we eventually got going the Sea King helicopter started up and hovered above me as I was very jerkily lifted up into the open bay. The winchman apologised for the poor lift by saying that the main winch was out of commission and they had pulled me up with the emergency one. I clambered aboard the body of the helicopter and made my way forward to speak with the captain. We had throat microphones on which, at the best of times, are not the easiest devices with which to understand a conversation. The noise of the engines drowned my footsteps as I moved forward, I reached the Captain and greeted him. His answer was an enormous shock to the BBC crew and me because, unbeknown to any of us, he had a stutter that made him difficult to understand even without the noise of the aircraft. Needless to say I went through the whole of the interview not understanding a word of his reply and it took a great deal of expertise in the editing suite in the days to come - but it was all worth it in the end."

John felt strongly that it was vital for the weather presenters to be provided with other opportunities to broadcast. The BBC was rather strict about personal appearances, as it wanted to protect its brand and would not allow weather presenters to be figures of fun. However, with the 'end of the year show' we could have a bit of fun.

JOHN: *So in 1978 I made 'That Was the Weather That Was'. Each year we would think of ideas to illustrate a particular weather event. That year there had been severe floods. I had been told that Ian McCaskill was a very good swimmer. So I arranged to take him to an indoor pool at Ruislip in north-west London.*

We arrived on time only to find the cameraman complaining that the camera had misted up and we would have to wait at least an hour for it to acclimatise. You wondered if they ever read the filming sheet and might have noticed we were filming in a swimming pool!!!! Finally all was ready, the shot set up and Ian briefed. He was to swim to the middle of the pool, then on cue, swim to the steps and say his piece. I called "Ready, take one, action".

Ian got to the steps and breathlessly delivered his piece. It was unintelligible. "Right take two". "Take your time Ian, there is no hurry." The same happened again. I began to wonder if the 'very good swimmer' wasn't true – or he was having a heart attack. "Right, take three". The same happened yet gain. So worried was I by now, that I took him to one side to see if he was all right. He just laughed and said "oh sorry, I thought you wanted me to do it that way!" Aaaahhh!

In 1979 there had been a particularly chilling wind from Siberia, and I had read that the east face of Big Ben had actually frozen up with ice and snow. There were other stories that year that centred around the cold, so I came up with programme the title 'There's No Business Like Snow Business'. After prolonged negotiations with the Palace of Westminster and signing all manner of waivers and contracts, we arrived to film it. However, that week all film sound recordists went on strike! I had a presenter, Jim Bacon, and a cameraman, but only with the prospect of filming with no sound. So, after 334 steps up to the bell tower and clock mechanism, the best we could do were shots of Jim looking at clocks, looking at bells and generally looking.

When it came to editing the sequence we added Jim's commentary and some sound effects and it really did not look too bad. He told the story that for a time in that blizzard the hands on the east face froze. Oh dear, the letter that subsequently arrived from the Palace of Westminster was written in blood. At one point I thought that I was for the Tower. It refuted our statement; the clock had not frozen and never would. Naughty, naughty me!

In the same show, we had included the story of an abandoned football match in Scotland, where every time they tried to play, they got snowed off. The Scottish Cup 2nd Round tie between Inverness Thistle and Falkirk was scheduled for 6th January 1979. However, after 29 postponements it was finally played on February 22nd 1979. Falkirk won 4-0 in the 30th attempt to stage the match. Afterwards on the commentary recorded by Jim he said that Inverness Thistle had won. We were in a videotape edit suite doing the final bits, when a face appeared around the door to say "are you sure you have got that the right way round?" After frantic phone calls and some clever sound editing, the show went out with the correct score! Whoops!

A Climate of Change

John is on camera and Bill doing a forecast in Presentation Studio 'A' known as Pres A

A rare screen credit for John - a long time ago

One programme I made in 1980 was about the Greenwich Observatory. Although it had been built in 1675 by King Charles II to observe the transit of Venus, it had for many years been a meteorological observing station. I had this idea of doing a flash back 200 years with Jack Scott appearing in a costume of the time. The naff title I came up with was '200 Years of a King's Rain'. Part of the story would show Jack arriving in a horse and trap of the period, however, filming never goes according to plan. When the company, we were hiring this from, arrived, they delivered a cart horse and old farm cart. After a meaningful discussion and the admission they had got it wrong they agreed to supply what we wanted. By the time it arrived it was getting dark, and I remember the cameraman saying "if there's an image on the film it will be a bloody miracle".

In 1996 the BBC decided to commission a weekday six minute programme that became "The Weather Show". It would be great if this was a result of the BBC showing any commitment to weather. Sadly not. It was simply that the then Controller of BBC daytime had scheduled an American drama before the lunchtime news. These programmes always ran short because, although they were for an hour long slot, once the advert breaks were removed for a BBC audience they only ran about 47 minutes.

You can fill some of the time by running a bit late and putting in a few trailers – but it still left 6 minutes. So someone had the bright idea of doing something about weather.

John was invited to a series of meetings to discuss money and staffing as there was little time with only about two months before it was due to go on air. The reality was that we were going to produce a 30-minute programme a week. But as luck would have it, a producer had just returned to the department from an attachment and was available to work on the show. We decided to try and keep it as much as possible 'in house' to drive efficiencies. A production office opposite the Weather Centre had just become vacant, so we were able to grab that. Two researchers and a production assistant were added bringing the team to four.

Inside the Weather Centre John had a small technical store that could easily be converted into an offline-editing suite. He did a deal with an outside company to supply all the editing equipment and an editor - all on a rental basis. There was also another spare area where we could store all the tapes.

The luck also continued as far as the filming was concerned. Technology was just coming on the market in the shape of DV (Digital Video) cameras. Although really made for the up-market amateur consumer, they were just about of broadcast quality if used sensibly. It was a digital format and so made the use of digital editing that much easier. The advent of Producer Choice, also allowed John to spend up to £2,500 of capital expenditure on any single item, so he was able to equip the team with cameras, tripods and lights. They were all set and ready to go.

A Climate of Change

Bill was down in Devon, in a little village near Kingsbridge, enjoying a well-earned holiday with his wife, stepdaughter and her two children when out of the blue he got a phone call from John.

BILL: *"I need you in London tomorrow" John said "for the launch of a new programme". Needless to say I wasn't very happy about it but nonetheless got on a train and went. The following day when I arrived at the BBC Television Centre I was met by Ann Mills from the Press and Publicity department, who proceeded to act as my minder and advisor.*

We duly went to a press conference where it was announced that we had been commissioned to do a daily six-minute programme on the weather. This was the first I had heard of it but John swears that he had discussed it before I had gone on holiday. I knew he hadn't and just put it down to forgetfulness on his part, but over the years I came to the conclusion it was just deviousness!

But this was the start of something magical and I am indebted to him to have got this off the ground in such a successful and cost effective manner. It was so different to our normal day-to-day routine in the studio and although, it was recorded and edited, it wasn't quite so tense, but there were other stresses and strains to cope with.

Because filming the Weather Shows was such a different technique not everyone at the weather centre was suitable and it did surprise me that some of the more experienced broadcasters were not too happy to do them, but others were in their element and as time went by the Weather Show producer found her favourites and tended to use them most of the time. We had to keep the costs down for making the programmes so much to the annoyance of the accountants at Bracknell, then the headquarters of the Met Office, so I agreed that all the staff would have to do was sign the hours for the time they spent on the show.

By this time the BBC Weather Centre was making an international name for itself as the premier weather-broadcasting centre and we were invited to many conferences worldwide, notably in the USA. Whilst at them John would bring along a small digital camera and during the course of the conference the two of them would make anything up to three six minute weather shows to be edited and played when we got back to the UK.

BILL: *I well remember one which we did near St Louis on the Mississippi at the Stone Hill Winery. Before we left the UK our BBC researcher Meg Harries had done the groundwork about the winery, with stories about using sophisticated electronics to predict when the weather was right for spraying.*

However, she had failed to notice that it was some 100 miles away from the city and we spent the first two hours trying to find it within 10 miles of St. Louis. No change there with our usual ability to get lost! On Later trips we tried to hire cars with Sat. Nav. Once in Los Angeles it had a Japanese voice that kept telling us to turn "reft".

Luckily we had two German colleagues with us, Dieter Walch and Inge Niedek, both weather broadcasters with the state broadcaster ZDF, who realised where we had to go. They had come along because the wine-growing region where we were headed was an area populated by descendants who came from Germany and who still spoke to each other in an old German dialect.

We duly arrived and were greeted by "Poppa" a large man with his trousers held up with braces. He introduced us to the rest of the family business including his very much smaller and very shy wife. We weren't surprised about that since "Poppa" was very over bearing and loud but equally very charming.

After filming in the vineyard and being told all about pests and spraying as well as the destructive element of humidity, we went into the bottling plant and after a long session there we were duly invited to join all of the family for lunch.

This consisted of lots and lots of bread, meat and cheese and, needless to say, what appeared to be gallons of wine, starting with white going on to rosé and finally to some superb red. It was at this point that John announced that we had not finished filming, as we had not done the introduction to the Weather Show programme on the winery, so we all went outside to do it.

What I had to do was walk down some steps talking to the camera and saying "Welcome to the Stone Hill Winery" and then carry on and explain where we were in the USA and so on. Now walking down some deep stone steps in bifocals, looking and talking to a camera whilst remembering your words is not the easiest thing in the world to do, but to have to do it after such a sumptuous winey lunch was near impossible.

We had about 6 takes at doing it but they were totally unsuccessful. I would either stumble down the steps or when I got that right would come out with the worlds "Here we are at the Hill Stone Winery or Wine Stone Distillery" and it was a nightmare. Eventually I got it all together and came down the steps like a gazelle, looking straight at the camera and issuing the immortal words "Here we are at the Stone Hill Winery" only to discover that on that particular take the camera had gone out of focus!

Our German friends still laugh about it to this day as broadcast meteorologists they knew exactly what was going on. That was a very tiring day for me having to do quite a lot of filming on all aspects of wine making. From the growing and nurturing the grapes to making and bottling the wine and then marketing the produce, so I looked forward to a nice peaceful ride back to St. Louis, but that was not to be because as we clambered into the people carrier, John reminded me that I was the only one licensed to drive it, so I ended up in the driving seat whilst the other three slept and snored all the way back."

That evening they had dinner with other colleagues in a restaurant on the roof of a hotel in St Louis. This provided a stunning 360° view across the city as it slowly travelled round on its giant turntable. It was a bit odd though, as if they went to the toilet, when you came back their table it had gone.

But it was one of those rare magical evenings where they could see amazing thunderstorms forming to the east that was filling our German colleague Dieter with so much excitement. The huge St Louis Gateway Arch towered above us, and down below was a packed stadium as the local team, the St Louis Cardinals fought their way to the baseball league playoffs.

BILL: *The next morning John had arranged for us to film at the top of the Arch. This 8th wonder of the World reaches up into the sky to a height of 192m. But John doesn't have a head for heights, which is odd when you think how tall he is. Over breakfast he admitted that he had not really slept that night in fear of having to go so high. Access to the observation is in a tram that travels up through each leg. As the door opened to reveal this windowless car, he admitted that unless he had not been carrying a camera – then he would never have got in it.*

Two-man filming is certainly a very efficient way of making programmes but it does have its problems. Being able to film at conferences meant that we were able to offer viewers reports from around the world without costing a fortune, as our conference costs came out of another budget and not that of the Weather Show.

You often wonder why film crews have so many people involved. In the case of Bill and John they could have certainly done with more help at times.

JOHN: *My job was principally as director, so I would work out the storyline with Bill and how we would then cover it. Bill would then go off and rehearse what he was going to say to camera whilst I got the camera out, set it up on the tripod and sorted out the microphone.*

On one occasion we were high up overlooking one of the great salt lakes of Salt Lake City. The story line was about global warming and the over use by agriculture that could turn many lakes around the world to look like this Great Salt Lake in the background. I had to arrange the shot so that Bill was in the foreground and the lake behind him. The sun was off to one side of him leaving a shadow on his face. No problem I had brought up one those pop-up reflectors you see on fashion shoots. But who was going to hold it? There was just the two of us and nobody else in sight. In the end we developed a scheme where, if I got in tight enough to Bill, we could rest one end on his stomach and I held the other end just below the camera lens with one hand whilst the other hand operated the camera. It was a good job we were on our own!

After this set-up shot, the next bit I needed to film was of Bill actually at the edge of the little bit of water that still remains right in the centre of the lake. We had seen other vehicles driving over the salt so were sure it was safe for us to drive on to it.

Bill on the balcony preparing for yet another take with John, head in viewfinder, on the RH

Surrounded by bottles Bill and John get ready for an interview with the Manager

A Climate of Change

As we approached the start of the salt lake, we could see groups of vehicles very far off in the distance, shimmering in the heat. It is difficult to describe the sheer size of the lake, and we seemed to drive for miles before we were anywhere near these other vehicles. As we got closer I could see that people appeared to be sunbathing. Strange we thought. Then we noticed that there weren't any women. Strange we thought if people were sunbathing.

Then I saw a man standing by his car completely naked and by his demeanour – proud of his manhood!

By mistake we had fallen across the local gay meeting place! It was the fastest filming we ever did. We noticed that a couple of the cars were moving towards us. Too late to turn back. We sped on to the edge of the water, jumped out, put the camera on the tripod, the microphone on Bill, and I said "quick only one take!" He did it. We threw the kit on the back seat and sped off as fast as we could before the cars moving towards us could catch us up. They obviously thought we were trying to film them as some sort of police bust!

The very small size of the DV Camera also had its own problems. It wasn't always obvious to people that we were filming. Often people would walk through shot whilst we were doing a take. Bill would be spouting away, and a few yards back I would have my eye to the camera. But still they were oblivious to us. I am sure it was simply that they were used to seeing filming with lots of people and big cameras. Once we were filming up in the hills above Los Angeles doing a piece about urban smog and temperature inversion. True we were filming in a car park, but a camper van drove between me and Bill in mid take, stopped between us, the family got out, unloaded the picnic table and chairs and proceeded to have their lunch. We were so flabbergasted that rather than remonstrate with them, we simply moved to another position.

The budget for the show was so tight, that we had to be inventive and never miss an opportunity. So, when we went on holiday on a cruise together with our wives, I took the camera equipment. We weren't always sure how it would all fit together, but with my film editing experience I was able to work out in my head how it might all work.

So, arriving at Venice we did a piece about sea-level rise and how that was causing more incidents of severe flooding. In Cairo against the backdrop of the pyramids we examined how the deserts were getting bigger and moving further north. Also in Cairo we examined how air pollution caused by too many vehicles and more incidents of temperature inversions was leading to the authorities banning cars from the centre for whole days at a time. In Ephesus in Turkey, we looked at a primitive method of air-conditioning used 2,000 years ago to protect books in a library. The good news is that we had a crew in the shape of Suzanne Teather and Maureen Giles, so we had someone to hold the reflector and keep people from walking through shot!

We returned from holiday with all these little gems, but at that point I was not sure how to link them together. Later that year we were at a conference in Geneva and during a break we went up into the mountains and the snow.

Between us we worked out how to put it all together, with a piece about heavier snowfall as a result of climate change ending up with Bill linking from the cold of the snow to the heat of the desert......the show was made!

Climate change was very much on our agenda for these shows, and at a conference in Phoenix, Arizona we took the car into the desert. We had been given a free upgrade to a huge Lincoln Continental. I can't remember why, but I wanted a shot of a car speeding away from the camera. So we found a dirt track off road, and set the camera up with the lens tight into the trunk (it was an American car!) Bill was then to drive off at speed as fast as the car would go. My cue to him was "hit it!" We did a couple of dummy runs, and then he would reverse the car back ready. After the final rehearsal, he backed it up and I made sure the camera was in the right position. Set the camera to run, and was just about to shout the cue, and I don't know to this day why, as I was about to open my mouth, I noticed that the reversing lights were still on!

I jumped out from behind the camera and shouted at Bill "you're still in bloody reverse!" Had I given the cue, he would have hit the gas and taken me and my camera into oblivion. I'm not sure who was more shaken up!

At the same conference we met a senior forecaster from the Met Office (he was famous for using the 'BBQ summer' term for a long range forecast and then it rained the whole summer). Each morning as we walked up to the Conference Centre we would exchange pleasantries.

On Monday he told us he had met this girl in a bar. Tuesday he told us he had met her again and they were getting on fine. On Wednesday he was besotted. On Thursday he was in love. On Friday he told us he had put his hand on her lap – and found that she was a bloke!

Considering the amount of travelling we were fortunate enough to do, we really didn't have any major catastrophes. The closest was when we lost a tripod at an airport. As usual we were on cheap tickets and arrived at the 'hub' in the States to collect our luggage, go through immigration and customs before re-checking the baggage for our onward flight. It was a strange airport as there were two main terminals, International and Domestic linked by an underground railway. When we eventually got to the gate where you had to re-check-in your luggage I noticed that the tripod bag was missing. Bill said, "I thought you had picked it up. No, I said, I thought you had picked it up".

The tripod wasn't the problem, but the bag contained all the batteries and charger for the camera. Without that there would be no filming. So, I left Bill and told him to check us in, whilst I would try and get back to the International Arrivals. Well, we have all had those dreams where you are lost and nobody wants to help and you are running out of time.

But this was no dream. I had to get back to the train. Once on the train I found I was going the wrong way. Changed trains and eventually got back to Arrivals. But all the doors were designed for exit and not for anyone to get back in.

A Climate of Change

I found myself running down a long dark corridor when suddenly a door opened and I breathlessly explained to an official my problem. I was lucky, a charming lady took me through all of the security into the baggage claim area and there was the tripod case lonely on the carousel.

I then had to get back to the other side of the airport and the departure board was showing that the gate was closing on my flight. I ran and ran. Got to the gate, the area was deserted, explained to the lone attendant who rushed me through the gate onto the plane as they closed the door. There sipping a drink was Bill who could only comment "thought you had missed the flight". The nightmare ended.

BILL: *On a long flight back from one of the conferences in the United States John casually said to me that he had arranged for me to go the next day to the Thames Barrier to record a Weather Show. My reaction was 'you must be joking' there is no way I'm going to do it. I used to find that flying from west to east overnight across the Atlantic was very tiring and I wouldn't be in a fit state to do justice to the six minute programme. He was insistent saying that he had already booked the camera team and that I really had to go. Eventually, and very reluctantly, I agreed to do it.*

Next day I arrived at the barrier, I would like to say bright eyed and bushy tailed, but in all fairness I was jet lagged and grumpy. Nonetheless the filming had to be done and so we started. Actually it went surprisingly well and I thought I would be able to wrap this one up quickly and go home to my bed by lunchtime. Not a bit of it - that's not the way the BBC operates, "got to give the licence payers value for money" they would keep saying to justify long hours filming.

It was no different that day as we set sail up the Thames, filming as we went along and eventually ended up with not one six minute weather show but three! At last the time came to stop and we wearily wended our way back to the Thames Barrier once again." One last thing before we finish" the director said to me "we want you do a trailer advertising the programme." We trudged up to the main reception, the cameraman got ready, sound too, and away I went.

I thought the "take" went well but the director wanted one more. I started again only to be interrupted by Suzanne Charlton and John Kettley with another person, whom I vaguely recognised, trailing behind. I wondered what on earth they were doing there and especially interrupting me whilst I was in full flow. Then I recognised the third person it was Michael Aspel with his little red book tucked under his arm.

As he got closer to me he uttered the immortal words "Bill Giles OBE. This is your life." To say I was surprised is an understatement and parts of my reply to him had to be bleeped out, but Michael was very relieved when I agreed that I would do the programme for him.

Afterwards he did tell Suzanne Charlton that his greatest fear in fronting the programme was that the subject of it would refuse to go ahead, and I can understand why.

A quick bit of filming for the 'Weather Show' in Cairo in Egypt and in Ephesus in Turkey

A Climate of Change

Venice provided some very useful material

Filming at sea also provided a lot of very nice pictures

As he got closer to me he uttered the immortal words "Bill Giles OBE. This is your life." To say I was surprised is an understatement and parts of my reply to him had to be bleeped out, but Michael was very relieved when I agreed that I would do the programme for him.

Afterwards he did tell Suzanne Charlton that his greatest fear in fronting the programme was that the subject of it would refuse to go ahead, and I can understand why.

The planning of any of these shows must have been a nightmare. Whilst I was away in the United States my wife, Maureen, had been involved with the researchers in deciding who would be on the show. She had many a heated discussion with members of my family who didn't want so and so to be there or could they walk on rather than just be seated. There was a great debate as to what part the grandchildren would play in it because she knew they were a major part of my life, and although they were Maureen's rather than mine, I adored them, and still do, and she was adamant that I would insist they were there taking an active part.

My poor wife also had a big problem concerning my parents who had broken up and divorced when I was eight years old but it proved no problem at all because they met up on the programme and got on like a house on fire. They had not seen each other for nearly 50 years!

After agreeing to do the programme that evening I was whisked away to the television studios and deposited in a very comfortable dressing room. A clean set of clothes was already there, courtesy of my wife. I dressed and got ready to record the show.

There was mayhem going on behind the scenes as all the audience and participants gathered and were seated. The grand children were nervously excited because it was only that morning they were told that they didn't have to go to school but were going to do a television programme instead. In fact that day, in the afternoon, they had recorded a little piece that was shown later. Elise and Charlotte stood on chairs and at the appropriate time tipped water on Carly who was dressed in waterproofs doing a piece to camera and ending with my immortal words "Bye for now" and giving the camera a wicked wink.

The time had come to record the programme and I entered with Michael Aspel to start the show. The first guest was Maureen, my wife, which went well because on that occasion she actually remembered when we had got married, although never has since.

We then went through the usual procedure of everyone saying what a wonderful chap you were, with most of them keeping their fingers crossed behind their backs as they said it. I think my mother was the only honest one when she said that in my early years I was "devious" and that nothing had changed. Alan Titchmarsh, Geoffrey Boycott and Dickie Bird said their pieces, the programme ended, I was presented with the big red book and we all adjourned for a party.

That was very pleasant talking with many people that I hadn't seen for many a long year and watching whilst Dickie consumed his fair quota of lager whilst chasing my mother around the table. But it all had to end. It had been a very long day for everyone including Carly, Elise and Charlotte and they sank into the comfortable seats in the large chauffeur driven car and were soon fast asleep.

The 'Weather Show' proved to be a great success with viewers and it was commissioned for another two series with a new Producer Sue Walton. With her small team, and even smaller budget she produced some really excellent work. Audiences averaged at about 3 million, which was double what you would expect at that time of the day.

But then the daytime schedule and the controller changed and we had to make way for the 'Vanessa Phelps Show', which in turn was also axed. We never managed to get The Weather Show re-commissioned again. It would be a cheap swipe to say that the BBC never really showed much interest in weather on TV. But we all knew that the controllers saw it as a necessary evil, that they felt they had to do it, but would much rather not have bothered.

The interesting thing was that there was never any shortage of ideas. You would think that there would be a limit to the number of stories connected to the weather, but by the end of the show there were still over 150 shows that were researched and never made.

Michael Aspel presents Bill with his 'This is Your Life' book whilst he was filming at the Thames Barrier for the 'Weather Show'

Bill Giles O.B.E

A Climate of Change

CHAPTER 15

OVERSEAS TRAINING

One of the reasons for the BBC Weather Centre becoming the premier broadcasting office in the world was because Bill and John had the ability to spot raw talent and train them up to be competent broadcasters both on radio and television.

The Met Office was very keen to help weather forecasters from the Commonwealth countries to become weather broadcasters but it was not an easy task. Because of the funding it was easier to bring forecasters from Kenya to Television Centre in London than to fund us going to Nairobi. They duly arrived at television centre to be put through their paces using the magnetic symbols on the metal boards. It wasn't easy to get them to understand that they had to change their approach from being scientists speaking a scientific language to television presenters speaking in the language of the man in the street. I am sure they learned from us but their main preoccupation was trying to get afternoons off to go shopping.

BILL: *Once we had gone into computer graphics it seemed to me to be pointless to bring the east Africans to London to do their training on equipment they would not have available on their return, so I suggested, with tongue in cheek, that I go out to Nairobi instead. After lengthy discussions going as far up the line as the Treasury it was agreed and after having all the necessary jabs I caught a Kenyan Airways flight to east Africa. I was met on arrival and escorted to my hotel, not the New Stanley, which most people stayed in but one run by a local Indian family right in the middle of town. I had asked for that wanting to get the flavour of the city rather than a westernised hotel and by and large it was very pleasant, there was one night I wished to forget however.*

I was taken by car everyday to the college where I was teaching, returning to the hotel for lunch with a return journey for the afternoon session. The students were not really all that interested except for one, Philip, who beavered away quietly on his own. After a few days of this I said to the class that they would never get to the standard that we had in the UK for television weather broadcasts because they didn't work hard enough. Their reply shattered me when they said that no matter how hard Philip worked he would never get on because he wasn't related to anybody high up in the service.

I felt more than a little embarrassed when I was taken to and from lunch and decided one day to stay with the course members and have lunch in their canteen. On arrival there was a great choice of meats to eat and being unsure I asked what they were and then settled for the liver dish.

That was fine and the afternoon passed off peacefully and I do believe I got them to work harder than they had done before. At the end of the day, waiting for my transport to take me to my hotel, I spied a person I knew.

Albert was a very cultured West African forecaster with the Kenyan Met Service whom I had met in England while he was studying for his MSc in East Anglia. We arranged to meet that evening in my hotel to chat about old times and bring each other up to date on what had happened since last we met.

To put you in the picture, when anyone from a Commonwealth country was selected to come to England to study, they were paid for by the UK Met office out of a fund held at Bracknell. All the college fees were paid and they were given a living allowance but at the same time they also received their monthly salary from their own Met Service that they were able to save. So when I asked Albert that evening what he did with all the money he made on the deal he sheepishly looked at me and said that on his return to Kenya he married another wife. I could hardly believe it and told him I thought that was foolish because he now had two mothers-in-law. We drank all evening, which fermented on the elephant liver that I had eaten at lunchtime and I spent a very uncomfortable night sitting on the toilet.

I felt so bad in the morning but knew I had to go to work, so I asked my driver to stop at a chemist on the way. I don't know what the chemist gave me to take but it certainly did the trick, I think it must have been quick drying cement - much stronger than today's Imodium!

The time had come to fly back to the UK and I was duly taken back to the airport to wait for my Kenyan Airways plane, and boy did I have to wait. I waited hour upon hour but to no avail and then finally some six hours late it arrived at our departure bay. What transpired was that the Kenyan President, Daniel arap Moi, had commandeered the aircraft to take him on a trip to Mombassa and we had to wait until he got back.

I used to get more than a little embarrassed that wherever John and I went to promote the BBC Weather Centre and the UK Met Office that the BBC paid all the bills. So I managed to persuade my office to fund a trip for us to Kenya where we were to train forecasters from all over East Africa to broadcast on radio and television. Our British Airways plane touched down and we waited patiently to clear customs. Sitting on a raised podium the man checking our passports stared down at us all until John presented his papers. John, at a height of 6' 6", looked down on the official seated in his lofty perch, flustered him so much he forgot to look at John's documents!

As a celebration of our arrival, the Kenyan Met Service threw a party that evening in our honour with all the food lovingly prepared by their wives. We duly arrived to be greeted by the Director of the Kenyan Met Service, Evans Mukolwe, whom we were to meet regularly over the next few years at the World Meteorological Organisation offices in Geneva.

The building was typical civil service with the paint trying desperately to stay on the walls and the air conditioning struggling to get out. As we stood there being introduced in came, in very formal style, the ladies who proceeded to bring in trays full of food. I looked at John and he looked at me because we had no idea what was on these plates, but everything looked brown. There were plates with big brown things on, plates with little brown objects and even plates with medium size brown fare.

Now for both of us, as it turned out, brown was not our favourite colour so we passed on it all although I must admit, I suppose because I'd been to Boarding School, I did sample a couple of pieces and to this day, I know not what.

JOHN: *We stayed at The New Stanley Hotel which was very comfortable and settled in for a fortnight. The next day we were taken to the place of work, which turned out to be at The Voice of Kenya Broadcasting Centre, their equivalent of the BBC. We were shown into the studio and met the course students. They were all experienced weather forecasters, many of whom had already done some broadcasting so we made them do the "one minute test". This was a technique we employed as the first introduction of the students to us the trainers, really so we could judge how they reacted. They were told that they had to talk to the camera for exactly one minute on any subject of their choice but the story had to have a beginning, middle and an end and they had to finish exactly after one minute and look at the camera. This was a very good test and one that we have used over and over again at the beginning of any training course.*

One of the first issues we had to tackle was to find out how each country presented the forecast to their audience and so we asked each of them in turn to tell us about it. It varied from country to country, but by and large they were very similar in their approach except for the forecaster from Uganda. At that time Uganda was a very backward country, which had suffered greatly for several decades of instability and civil war under Milton Obote and Idi Amin. We asked their forecaster how he presented the forecast to his television audience.

It was heart breaking to us as he described how they drew paper weather symbols styled on our magnetic ones and coloured them in. When I asked how they displayed them he said that there were pins jutting out from the weather maps onto which they placed the symbols. Bill remarked that it must have hurt as you place them on during a live broadcast.

It was then that the forecaster turned his hands over to show massive numbers of pin marks on his palms. He must have been very dedicated!

We have always stressed that for anyone to do a good weather broadcast they need to know the complete weather story and its evolution over the next few days. To enable this course to do that, we commissioned a forecaster from the headquarters of the Kenyan Met Service to come with their synoptic charts. They were slightly different than what we see at home since isobars don't really work in the tropics, so streamline charts are used instead, but they amount to the same thing.

BILL: *Albert, my friend with the two wives, was the duty forecaster and came into do the weather briefing for us. He started, as we always do when briefing other meteorologists, with the overall picture using his streamline chart. After that he went onto the detailed forecast for the whole of East Africa before finally ending with Nairobi. On the third day he did the same thing and told us that it would be fine in Nairobi that day with a temperature of 26°C.*

John looked out of the window as Albert was speaking and noticed the rain lashing down. Albert hadn't obviously seen it and when John asked him to repeat what the weather was to be that day, Albert repeated that it would be fine, dry and warm. When John asked him why it was raining at the present moment Albert looked at his charts and said "No rain on my charts so it will be fine and dry and warm."

That did present a few problems to us training all around the world because forecasters are reluctant to change from the weather they first forecast even when later evidence proves them wrong.

We then needed to get all the students, in turn, to present a weather forecast in the studio. John was up in the gallery directing the recordings and I was acting as his floor manager giving directions to the presenter with hand signals as to when to start, how much longer they had to go and to count them out at the end of the minute.

When the first weatherman started it seemed to me fine but after about 20 seconds I heard John bellowing down my earpiece "What the hell is going on?" Apparently the camera was shaking like mad. It got worse and John, with the patience of a hungry lion eyeing a snoozing wildebeest screamed in my ear "What the f***ing hell is going on. See what the cameraman is doing." I moved across only to see the cameraman and the camera shaking up and down at an amazing pace. Afterwards we found out that he was so nervous of having to work with a BBC Weatherman and a BBC Producer the nerves had got the better of him.

We had a few more small problems at the beginning of this course. The studio that was built and given to The Voice of Kenya, by the German government, was magnificent. However, the studio air conditioning unit had failed 18 months previously and there were no funds to repair it. It became so oppressively hot in the studio that we had to stop every half an hour to open the doors and let some fresh air in.

Soon after that the batteries in the clip-on radio microphones worn by the presenters started to fail. John, who by this time, was getting more than a little ratty, turned to the engineer in charge and asked for some fresh AA batteries to replace them, only to be told they didn't have any. "Well then" said John "why don't you send someone down to the local chemist shop and buy some?" After a lot of shuffling about he was told that there was no money in the budget to buy them.

I thought at this stage we were close to a diplomatic incident but it all calmed down and some lanyard microphones were found, and so they had to do the rest of the course with them strapped around their necks.

JOHN: To me, this studio summed up everything that was wrong with overseas aid. It was in usual German style beautifully built and equipped. Certainly capable of high quality recordings, it was complete with five cameras and a fully equipped gallery.

However, there were two vital factors missing. There was really no trained staff capable of running it and no funds to maintain this very complex facility. I had reservations about coming to Africa with Bill in the first place after having suffered the numerous injections administered by the BBC's medical unit, mostly in my backside. Then after receiving lectures about AIDS and being provided with an HIV plasma pack and dehydration pack – I had really gone off the idea. The hotel was just about adequate, but we were warned not to venture outside at night without an escort. Bill had told me that this was one of the more civilised parts of Africa, but on the first morning as we drove to the studio there was a dead body on the roadside- it was still there when we drove home in the evening!

BILL: *At the end of each day a car would take us back to The New Stanley Hotel where we would arrive at nearly 6 o'clock giving us exactly 20 minutes in the swimming pool since we were just over one degree south of the equator we always had 12 hours of sunshine and 12 hours of darkness at exactly the same time each day.*

At the weekend we decided to treat ourselves to a trip into the bush and I booked up with 'Wilson's Tours' that were advertised in the hotel. Expecting executive luxury travel we were surprised when Mr Wilson himself turned up in what I could only describe as an old jalopy. Against our better judgement we got in and told him to take us where we could see some wildlife. As we drove off he turned on the air conditioning, which consisted of opening all the windows and we settled down to be entertained.

Actually it was pretty good especially when we stopped for a long while at Lake Nakuru, which boasts over 400 species of birds recorded there, with the most famous of them the pink flamingos. There were thousands of them walking in this shallow soda lake with their long pink necks thrust under the waters looking for food.

They were so delicately coloured we could have sworn that a group of artists had been there in the morning painting them. We moved on and stopped by a small clearing where Mr Wilson pointed out a family of warthogs snuffling in the undergrowth. I got out to take a picture but was warned that these pigs were amongst some of the most dangerous animals in the bush. After saying that I didn't manage to photograph them because as I turned towards them they grunted and ran off in the opposite direction.

We were on our way back to Nairobi driving through what looked like a frontier town with poor roads sending up a plume of dust wherever we went, when Mr Wilson suddenly pulled over on the side of the road and asked us to get out. Reluctantly we did and found ourselves stranded in a strange town, the only Europeans. By the looks we got it was the first time many of the locals had seen a white man. It was eerie and frightening and we dare not go into the local shop for a beer in case people saw how much money we had on us - not really a lot by our standards but a great deal by theirs.

So we remained outside trying to find some shade against the piercing sun and hoping that we were nearly invisible. It seemed a long time before Mr Wilson's 'tour bus' arrived back in town. He told us as we started off again for the safety of Nairobi and The New Stanley that he had received a message that one of his colleagues that had broken down. Kind-hearted Mr Wilson, after dumping us in the middle of nowhere, went to his rescue. Apparently his friend's car had broken down with his engine seized up, so the pair of them had to go to the local scrap yard to get a replacement.

On returning to our hotel we went for a swim when John noticed he had been bitten by something on our trip into the countryside and it was starting to swell up. John, with his very fair skin, is susceptible to insect bites so this was nothing new - or so we thought but by the next morning it had really swollen and looked very yellow.

I think he must also have eaten something strange on our visit to the bush because his stomach wasn't too great either. On reflection, though, we have since come to the conclusion that it was the wine we drank in another restaurant that evening whilst celebrating our safe return from Mr Wilson's tour. We were well known for our ability to shift red wine by the bottle but on this occasion, and only ever this one occasion, the wine was so dreadful that we couldn't even finish the first bottle. Perhaps John should have put some on his wound rather than drink it!

He decided to take to his bed for the day and I went on my own to continue the course work. On my return in the evening I popped my head into his room to see how he was. He was no better so, being a President of St John Ambulance at that time I prescribed plenty of orange juice and sat there while he drank it only to find out later that it was the worst thing he could have had, since it was a powerful laxative, and made his bowels far more uncomfortable.

This continued over the next few days as we moved towards the end of the course and our thoughts of going home. On the final Friday I attended to the "graduation" ceremony and returned to the hotel for the final time only to find John sitting up in bed looking rather pale. When I enquired if anything was the matter he told me the houseboy, looking after his room, had taken a shine to him and had asked John to take him to London when we went back.

Needless to say the next day we checked out rather quietly and headed towards the airport. It was with great relief on John's face when he saw the British Airways jumbo jet sitting on the tarmac to take us home. Not long after we took off the airhostess came around asking what we would like for dinner. John, who had not eaten for three or four days, was doubtful about having anything but I persuaded him to try the fillet steak.

When it arrived he pulled the tin foil back to reveal a delicious meal. He turned to me and said, in a rather pathetic voice, "Do you think this steak came from England or was it bought in Nairobi?" My reply was that of course it was bought in England. Without a moment's hesitation he attacked his meal as though he hadn't eaten for a week - but there again, he probably hadn't.

A Climate of Change

Because this was a trip funded by my Met Office there were very strict rules on how much we could spend and in my report to Roger Hunt I concluded that "At one point we were spending well in excess of the subsistence level but fortunately the BBC Producer became ill and didn't eat or drink wine for four days which brought us back to the correct spending level again".

Both John and I enjoyed training meteorologists to become competent broadcasters and, indeed, still do. It is a skill we have developed over the years and the rewards we have seeing some of our students broadcasting on television channels in many countries across the world made it all worthwhile.

This was one of the reasons why we were very active in helping to set up the International Association of Broadcast Meteorology (IABM) whose two main aims were to improve the standard of weather broadcasts around the world and to make sure that weather data was free and freely available to them.

In 1987 John received a letter from Liam Miller, the programme director responsible for weather at RTE, the Southern Ireland equivalent of the BBC, asking if we would consider going to Dublin to look at the weather set up for them. They were planning to change to computer graphics but were not quite sure what route to take and since we had been doing it for some time thought that they would like some advice. Bill sought permission to go from the Met Office, who were to be paid £1,000 for each day he was there, this was agreed and a date set to start.

They climbed into an Air Lingus jet at Heathrow early one morning and were treated to tremendous hospitality as they crossed the Irish Sea. Champagne breakfast was more than they could have expected at that time of the day so as they descended the aircraft steps in Dublin, rather a little worse for wear. There was an air of cautious optimism as they moved to passport control.

BILL: *We were duly met by Liam, ushered into his car and headed to RTE. The political sensitivities at that time between the UK and Eire made it such that we had to keep our visits low key and that continued throughout the following months as we made our trips back and forth. At RTE we had coffee and sat around to find out the way the weather broadcasts were done at that time and how the television company sought to change it, if change was needed in the future. These talks extended into the evening while we were entertained to a delightful meal by Liam's wife and family.*

The training course in Kenya was only weekdays, so at the weekend it was time for filming

We also had time to visit the Bush and some museums

A Climate of Change

They climbed into an Air Lingus jet at Heathrow early one morning and were treated to tremendous hospitality as they crossed the Irish Sea. Champagne breakfast was more than they could have expected at that time of the day so as they descended the aircraft steps in Dublin, rather a little worse for wear. There was an air of cautious optimism as they moved to passport control.

BILL: *We were duly met by Liam, ushered into his car and headed to RTE. The political sensitivities at that time between the UK and Eire made it such that we had to keep our visits low key and that continued throughout the following months as we made our trips back and forth. At RTE we had coffee and sat around to find out the way the weather broadcasts were done at that time and how the television company sought to change it, if change was needed in the future. These talks extended into the evening while we were entertained to a delightful meal by Liam's wife and family.*

At that time there was one main evening broadcast Monday to Friday after the nine o'clock news. Paddy McHugh was the senior forecaster in charge of the forecast office of Met Eireann, the equivalent of the UK Met Office, and after a day's work would take his maps and go to the television centre to do the evening broadcast. Paddy had been doing this routine for the past 25 years and was very well known and liked across the whole nation.

It was decided to have a complete change following the pattern we had established at the BBC and RTE would use forecasters from the State Met Office as we did across the water. Instead of just the one broadcaster, as in the past, they would use many more as the new schedules would involve an increase in the number of broadcasts through the day and also weekend work.

This meant complete changes to the working practices of both the Irish Met Office and RTE staff, which appeared insurmountable, but with John's knowledge of television scheduling and Bill's expertise in rostering weather forecasters we managed to produce a timetable acceptable to both parties.

We had to decide who should broadcast and train them to an acceptable level. John also advised RTE in establishing the method of putting the graphics on air as they were not able to go down the chroma-key route at that point.

A Dublin based company, Lendac, was chosen to develop the new weather graphics and over the months its owner, Danny Lendac, became good friends with us. So the graphics were being sorted out and now we had the difficult task of deciding who should appear on the television weather forecast to show them night after night.

After talking to all the forecasters at Met Eireann who were interested and ensuring they understood the need to translate from the jargonistic phraseology all meteorologists spoke, to the less scientific vocabulary used in everyday conversations by their potential viewers. We set down a timetable to interview them that consisted of Bill talking to each of them in turn and asking a mixture of meteorological questions and general banter, all the time being filmed by John. Afterwards we reviewed the tapes and came to our conclusions.

BILL: *We interviewed what appeared to be the whole of the forecast division and selected John Doyle, Aidan Nulty, Evelyn Cusack, Joan Blackburn and a young part timer Gerald Fleming. Gerald was the obvious choice to be the leading broadcaster in charge of the team but at that time he was only working part time, but by some cunning manipulation, we persuaded him to go full time. The training continued over many weeks with both John and I spending a few days in Dublin and then returning to London.*

As the same time Danny Lendac was developing suitable graphics and we continued our weekly trips on Air Lingus. On one occasion we were not the only group on the flight from the BBC. Malcolm Walker (the previous Head of the BBC Presentation Department that owned the weather), was also there with colleagues going over to view the arrangements for the forthcoming Eurovision Song Contest which the Irish seemed to win every year.

Sitting a few seats in front of us Malcolm beckoned the stewardess over and said that she should speak to the man in seat 15C, thinking it was John, and tell him that he was not allowed any champagne on this flight.

We watched as she came down the aircraft not really knowing what Malcolm had said, but she stopped just in front of us, woke the man up from his slumbers, and told him the message. Malcolm had got the wrong seat number, John was in seat 16C! Afterwards we found out that the poor man was petrified of flying and the only way he could survive a flight was to get to sleep as fast as he could before the plane took off and stay that way until we landed.

We had a greater shock when RTE changed from Air Lingus to Ryan Air because as we sat waiting for our champagne breakfast all they came up with was a coffee in a plastic cup and a biscuit, and I'm not sure that we didn't have to pay for that as well.

Our routine was established by this time. After arriving in Dublin we would get a taxi to our hotel then go on down to the Met Office headquarters for a weather briefing and on to RTE where we continued training the broadcasters. We'd return to the hotel late afternoon before retracing our steps to RTE to watch the late weather broadcast. Finally we returned to the hotel for our late evening meal, which included a bottle of red wine. Our ambition was to go through the hotel's red wine list before the contracts came to an end - and we very nearly did!

Before RTE launched its new flagship weather broadcasts we had a very delicate task to perform and it fell on Bill to do the dirty. Paddy McHugh, who had done such sterling work for over half a century had to step down, and Bill had to tell him.

BILL: *John had disappeared off somewhere with Liam and said that he would meet me at the airport ready to fly back to England. I told Paddy the news as he drove me to the airport, that after 25 years it was time for him to retire, take things easy and let the youngsters get on with the new system.*

I thought he was a little quiet after that but decided it must have come as a big shock and nothing more was said on that journey. The next time we arrived in Dublin, Paddy, who was his own delightful self again, announced that to celebrate his retiring from the TV, he and his wife would treat us to a night at the theatre. That evening we met his wife, who was so excited to meet us, because, as she said "thanks to you two I now see my husband every evening because for the past 25 years he has always been at the television studios". Paddy had booked seats for us all to see a Sean O'Casey play who was well known for his anti-British sentiments. We can't say we were enjoying it all that much and we reckoned that Paddy had got his own back in a very clever and subtle way. At the interval the lights came up and just in front of us was a large crowd of middle-aged ladies who made a beeline for me asking for my autograph and totally ignoring Paddy, their own television icon. After that, the rest of the play didn't seem too bad.

The time was drawing close to when the first of the new broadcasts would take place. The system was very similar to the one John had come up with at the BBC with the self-operate office studio. It consisted of the weather broadcaster sitting at a desk with a box on the desk, which had a switch enabling the presenter to change from them being on-air to the graphics shown in full frame.

The aim was to start the broadcast with the presenter in shot to set the scene, then they would cut to the graphics sequence before finally coming back in shot at the end to say goodnight. Obviously we had in mind that Gerald, the leader, would do the first few broadcasts before taking in turn with the others, however, RTE had other ideas and insisted that a woman was first, and it was going to be Evelyn Cusack!

BILL: *The two ladies came into the team later than the men so had had far less experience on the new system, so it was with some trepidation that we prepared Evelyn for that evening's premier.*

During the evening we had several rehearsals, but because she was very new to the job, Evelyn sometimes forgot to press the switch to change from her to the graphics so, for some reason, that I can no longer remember, I was to squat under the table to prompt her if needed during the live broadcast.

So the scene was set. Evelyn at the desk, me underneath, and Danny Lendac with fingers crossed that the graphics worked as we went live on air. After a lovely smiling introduction, Evelyn forgot to press the button to move to the graphics. It appeared to me, squashed underneath out of sight, that she was getting a little agitated. I thought what could I do to move the graphics on for her? I realised apart from shaking her legs and whispering to her all I could do was to change it myself. What the viewers saw on-air was my hand appearing from below the table, move along the desk, and push the switch. After that everything went to plan.

After the broadcast was over I uncoiled myself from under the desk to hear John saying, "What the hell was all that – I can't believe you just did that" to which Liam answered "Well that was a good one - well done everybody". Evelyn has gone from strength to strength and I wonder if she still remembers the evening I sat under the table looking at her knees? Incidentally, Evelyn is still broadcasting after over a quarter of a century later, so we made a very good choice. That evening in the hotel John and I polished of a bottle of Chateau Neuf de Pape 1966 - each!

Since the Met Office were being paid £1,000 for each of my visits, I just signed the hours that I worked since they were obsessed with making sure everyone worked, on average, their 41 hours per week. The green eye of envy kicked in after a while and I was informed that I could no longer sign for the hours I worked in Dublin. My answer was straight forward, every time I went in future, I would take it as annual leave, do the work as normal, but it would be me that collected the money instead. Actually I decided that this was more than a little unfair on John since he would get none of it.

So when at the end of our involvement, Liam said he wished to thank us for all our hard work and suggested that since RTE had a lot of contacts with the tourist industry around the country that we might like to take our wives on a short tour to visit some of the beautiful sights his country had to offer.

We felt it would be ungracious of us had we refused. It was a wonderful period for both of us and we are more than a little proud of the fact that we helped to get it all off the ground and that it is now a very professional weather programme to rival anywhere in the world.

The World Meteorological Organisation in Geneva is the UN system's authoritative voice on the state and behaviour of the Earth's atmosphere, its interaction with the oceans, the climate it produces and the resulting distribution of water resources.

There are 183 countries and 6 territories in the association all speaking the same international meteorological language of mathematics so that weather data from around the world is accessible to all and understandable by all.

Both of us would go as Directors of The International Association of Broadcast Meteorology with observer status at all the major conferences there and discussed at length the need for broadcasters around the world, especially in the emerging nations, to have adequate training in getting the weather message across on radio, television and in the newspapers.

Gerald Fleming with his new team after launching the 'new look' for the Irish TV service RTE

The full team that helped put together a significant change in the way weather was presented on RTE

It was also important, in our view, that the Heads of the Met Departments across the Globe also had training on how to react to hostile interviews on weather related subjects. Unfortunately that course never materialised since the Heads of the Met Services thought they could cope, not realising that a poor interview makes their department look amateurish and lacking in scientific knowledge.

BILL: *We, in the UK Met Office, found that out after the 1987 storm when senior members of the Office had to attend a course in "Speaking to the media". I remember I went along with The Director General, Sir John Houghton and his brother David. We were interviewed by John Humphrys, who gave us a savaging time, but with a lot of sound advice from him, we left more confident that we could all give a good account of ourselves and our office when called upon to do so.*

Bill and John were asked if they would run a course for potential broadcasters in the Far East. After a little persuading they agreed and soon found themselves on a flight to Singapore. Driving from the international airport they were very impressed by the wide avenues with their beautifully manicured trees and flowers in bloom and were still in awe as they arrived at the hotel.

JOHN: *Our first impressions were of a very well organised country, well run and clean, but I suppose it is relatively easy to do that with a population of fewer than 4 million in the mid 1990s compared to a country with 55 million inhabitants. After saying that, we always felt very safe day or night wherever we were in the country.*
The training course was held at the airport where most of the Met Office staff worked and such is the nature of aviation meteorology worldwide that Bill reckoned he could have gone on shift there right away and it would be little different to London, Heathrow.
Still we were there to train aviation meteorologists in the art of broadcasting and changing their attitudes towards the general public, but first we had to meet the people that WMO had assembled for the course.
They came from many countries, South Korea, Malaysia, Singapore and Vietnam and although most of them spoke very good English the man from Vietnam had no knowledge of the language at all.
BILL: *One of the problems we have found over the years and in many different countries, when running training courses, is that we do not always get the correct people on them. These courses are designed to train forecasters who are going to broadcast or who have already started to broadcast but so often the Heads of the Met Departments send the wrong people. . You can sometimes find that a person has been sent on a course as a reward for hard work but with no chance whatsoever of going on air and this was the case of the man from Vietnam.*

A lovely man who tried very hard to learn, and was partially successful, but he worked in the climatological section of his Met Office as a librarian and it was never intended that he would ever broadcast. He was sent on the course as a reward for his many years of hard work. Actually we felt very sorry for him because he checked out of the hotel we were booked into and moved into a doss house down the road thereby saving the subsistence he was given which, we understand, amounted to at least six month's salary.

The course started with the normal briefing from the senior forecaster on duty at the airport and we settled into the routine of the one-minute tests and the need to translate the jargon of aviation meteorology to the language spoken by the listeners and viewers. Incidentally we always allowed the trainees to do the broadcast in their own language if they wished especially if they struggled a little in English.

BILL: *The senior forecaster at the airport sat in on much of the course work since he was very interested in what we had to say. He was a lovely man of Chinese extraction and I christened him "Uncle Wong" which he took as a great compliment.*

We actually got "Uncle Wong" to stand in front of the camera to do a weather forecast just to show him how difficult it was and so that he could sympathise a little when his junior staff went on air.

There was one young forecaster from Singapore who was a natural with an outward going personality who on some days was actually on duty in the airport and did the morning briefing. As usual in Singapore heavy showers and thunderstorms occur from mid afternoon onwards.

I asked him when the thunderstorms would start and he told me three o'clock in the afternoon. Exactly at three they started and he was overjoyed until I asked when they would stop. He hadn't thought about that at all and the point was made that his public would want to know.

On these overseas trips we had little chance to explore the country that we were in so if the opportunity arose for a day off we took it. It happened to be a public holiday and we all, John, myself and Tom Hartwell, our graphics expert, decided to take a trip to Sentosa Island known for its peace and tranquillity. We were to take the cable car across the water separating the mainland to the other island. We arrived at the cable car station at Mount Faber that was to take us across Keppel Harbour to the island. John dislikes heights. I found this out when crossing the famous Golden Gate Bridge in San Francisco so the thought of 'flying high' over the water was a nightmare to him. We had got about half way across, hundreds of feet above the water, when I jokingly said that it would be terrible if we stopped now. And with that the same it happened. We stayed suspended for what seemed like an age before jerkily moving on to our destination and on arriving there a brandy was called for before I remarked we had to do it all again on the return.

The course went from strength to strength and the improvement of the trainees was truly remarkable and a delight for us to see. Even the man from Vietnam was starting to enjoy it and speaking a little English. Our hosts, the Singapore Met Office, were so pleased with the progress of their staff that the Director hosted a meal for all of us on the last but one night. We got all spruced up and duly arrived at the Chinese restaurant for the meal.

BILL: *Sitting in the foyer laughing and discussing all manner of things I noticed that the Vietnamese chap was having an intense discussion with another one of the course members. Intrigued, I ask what they were getting so animated about. Apparently they were discussing the merits of whether brown dog tasted better than black ones.*

That was to set the tone for the evening because in the Foyer was a fish tank with many large and beautiful fish swimming in it. Casually talking to the Director of the Met Office I said how good they looked upon which he ask which was my favourite.

I pointed it out and the next time I saw it was on a platter brought in by the waiter, cooked, and ready for us to eat. I felt dreadful about it - but worse was yet to come.

We had a mixed hors d'oeuvre, many of which neither John nor I recognised, but nonetheless we ate it, apart from one slimy greeny black thing we were told was sea slug. John hadn't gone to Boarding School like me, so steadfastly refused it but I thought I would at least give it a try. I did manage to eat small portions but only when washed down with copious amounts of red wine.

And then the fish arrived.

Apart from feeling guilty at picking it out in the tank it did look good enough to eat and I was looking forward to this part of the meal, when they dropped the bombshell. Apparently we two, being the honoured guests, were to have the choicest part of the fish - its eyes. Most of the people around the table looked at us in envy. I looked at John, he looked at me in utter disbelief until we found the solution. We gave the eyes to the gentleman of Malaysia for his sterling work on the course. He beamed with delight at the honour that had been bestowed on him and the meal continued. I must say it was a wonderful evening and we thanked our Hosts as we caught our taxi back to the Hotel to get ready for the long flight home.

The World Meteorological Organisation (WMO) were pleased with the success of that course and were gradually listening to our arguments that broadcasting the weather message to the general public was very important but even more important was the means of issuing the severe weather warnings that occur with regularity around the globe.

A celebratory dinner at the Raffles Hotel with Haleh Kootval and Eirah Gore Dale of WMO and Tom Hartwell from BBC Computer Graphics Department

Tom Hartwell helps the trainees make up weather graphics for their 'broadcast'

One such warning is where the typhoons were especially destructive in the western Pacific where these tropical storms cause havoc to the large and small Islands alike. WMO were also conscious that there was a need to help the smaller nations, who had only very small meteorological budgets, to be able to transmit weather information correctly and on time.

We were asked to go to Fiji where we would help run a course for many of the small Islands in the western and southern Pacific. No way, we decided, would we take up this offer unless we flew British Airways business class. This caused a bit of a stir in Geneva but they came up with a wonderful solution. If you flew from Geneva to Fiji via Australia they had an arrangement called 'grey business'.

This arrangement is basically a discount, between the airlines and the United Nations because their staff flew so many times a year. We settled for that, but it meant picking up a flight from Heathrow to Geneva, getting our tickets there, to then fly back to Heathrow to get our plane to fly to Sydney!

This time the flight went without a hitch and, because of the extra comfort and leg room, arrived at Sydney airport quite refreshed. The trouble started there because we had quite a long wait to pick up our flight to Fiji, so we set off for the business class lounge to wait. But they told us that we were not allowed in because as there was no class distinction on the small aircraft taking us on to Fiji, our business class tickets had ended as we touched down in Sydney. After some very meaningful conversations with various officials we were allowed into the lounge on a temporary basis that, thankfully, lasted until our flight was ready.

As we boarded the plane to take us to Fiji something appeared to be wrong as technicians came and went. It transpired that the crew could not shut the door properly and that we might be off loaded and wait until the following day.

That would have presented a problem to us because we hadn't got a visa to enter Australia so we would have to wait overnight in the airport, but in which lounge? Fortunately at the last attempt they managed to slam the door shut and off we set for the island of Fiji.

This course, held amid tropical lushness, was different from any other we had participated in. On the first day, with all the course members assembled, John asked by what means of communication their forecasts were open to them. Each island appeared to be different and varied tremendously from advanced communications in Fiji, much the same as they had in the UK, to the Cook Islands who still used telex. This was going to be difficult because one of the more important jobs we had to do here was to enable them to write scripts and warnings for others to read. That in itself wasn't too bad since all the Islanders spoke English but many used words and phrases that had long gone out of fashion at home.

BILL: *We conducted the radio and television training in a local radio station that also did a little television. They had a small video camera which John adapted and with a crude arrangement of a studio and weather graphics managed to complete their training. John and I paid a visit to the main Met Office on the Island who was responsible for issuing Typhoon warnings for the whole of the western pacific. I was questioned in quite a harsh manner by the Officer in Charge, as to why we did not use their forecasts of Typhoon movements when doing the BBC World Service broadcasts.*

My reply was that we used the American forecasts from Guam because we never received any from Fiji as we should have done. From then on the data from Fiji was received direct at the BBC as soon as it was issued.

To celebrate the end of the course we all went out for an evening meal. Sitting under the swaying palms and looking out on the beautiful Pacific Ocean you would think this was heaven and surely nothing could spoil the evening, but it very nearly was.

I was asked in a very casual and friendly way if I had ever been to the southern Pacific before. I nearly answered "Yes." Luckily I hesitated before replying "No" because the last time I was here some 40 odd years before was at Christmas Island, now renamed Kiribati, where we were testing Hydrogen Bombs a mere 1,300 miles away!

Not only did we go around the world training broadcast meteorologists, but many visitors came to BBC Television Centre. They were primarily interested into two aspects, firstly to discover how the State Met Office interfaced so successfully with the State Broadcaster because this was the main problem that we had found in almost all countries, apart from the USA. Secondly, they all wanted to know about the system John had got developed which enabled scientific weather maps to be automatically redrawn and suitable for television.

On this particular occasion a gentleman from Cameroon had come to talk to John about buying the BBC Weather System. We took him to lunch in the BBC waitress service restaurant, to which we always took our guests and were normally served by Margaret who gave us a bit of special attention. After studying the menu he announced that all he wanted was langoustine, mashed potato and a pint of lager, which Margaret had to get from another restaurant. They duly arrived but before we could say anything he took hold of one of the langoustine and put it in his mouth complete with the shell. We were so surprised that we didn't dare say anything as the poor man gradually emptied his plate asking from time to time for more lager. He didn't buy the system.

We are rather passionate about training. There have been great strides made by WMO to do more, but it is not enough. The WMO is at the centre of a huge training programme for meteorologists and invests in this in an institutional way. It is part of how they see their role. But not when it comes to disseminating the forecast to the public and emergency services, they seem to have a mental block. It's probably because it is more of an art than a science. It's not empirical, it requires judgement and style and you can't quantify that. We will continue through the IABM to encourage the WMO to do more weather broadcaster training and just hope that one day they see the light.

Training in Fiji for students from the surrounding South Sea Islands

Bill preparing the course notes ready for the next training session

CHAPTER 16

BULLYING

The BBC Weather Centre was a unique organisation in that there were two separate parts. John, as Producer and later Editor, was in charge of the Centre for the BBC and was line manager to all the producers, assistant producers and graphics artists, and held the budget. His responsibility was to give the best value to the licence payers and to decide how the Weather Centre would develop over the next few years. Bill's responsibility was towards the weather presenters who all worked for the Met Office and to make sure that whatever the BBC and John wanted with regard to services and output, that the broadcasting staff were there and trained up ready to do the job. The two parts came together at that level with John's secretary co-ordinating everything between the two groups.

From the outset in 1954 when George Cowling did the first television broadcast the presenters came under London Weather Centre right up until 1 September 1991 when BBC Weather Centre became a Met Office in its own right with Bill promoted to Principal Scientific Officer in charge of the team and later in 1998 to a Senior Principal or Grade 1. Prior to that only people at Higher Scientific level could work there and on promotion, were posted away. As the BBC Weather Centre grew from 3 broadcasts a day to 143 in a 24 hour period, so the numbers of broadcasters that were needed grew from 5 to over 25 and since it was impossible to recruit them directly from the Met Office other ways of finding them were used.

BILL: *John and I then had a great dilemma, how to get staff and train them quickly to go on air as we could only use about 1% of the forecasters in the Met Office who were suitable for broadcasting at the national level. So we had to initiate a different approach.*

John and I decided that if we couldn't recruit fully trained meteorologists then we would take people who had a science background and Suzanne Charlton and I would teach them the meteorology that the BBC demanded they needed at the BBC Weather Centre. I had quite a meaningful discussion about this with three very senior members of my team who vehemently opposed this view until I pointed out that if we didn't, since we had contracted to increase the number of broadcasts, they would be working 7 days a week.

Luckily for us the European version of the US Weather Channel had got into difficulties by believing they could operate in a similar way to that in the United States, not realising that we did not have a United States of Europe but a collection of fiercely independent countries all with their own language.

We recruited Louise Lear and Carol Kirkwood from there, Victoria Graham from a shopping channel and two people, David Braine and later Philip Avery from the Royal Navy. Then in 1997 to cover the increasing number of broadcasts we started pulling people in from the regions and they included Peter Gibbs, Helen Willets and Darren Bett. With this large influx of Met Office staff, I decided that I would put in a tier of management to better cover our varied customers. There would be person to deputise for me, a manager for BBC National output as well as the new Breakfast Time, World Service, and one to co-ordinate Training. I believed that the senior members of my team, Ian McCaskill, Michael Fish and John Kettley would automatically apply. But none of them wanted to bother. I suppose it meant extra work with no financial reward. I did find this unbelievable since my attitude has always been get as high in the organisation as you can because you then have a chance to influence the route it would go down. But I was singularly unsuccessful with this trio, but did warn them that the outcome would be that I would appoint people who were very much junior to them in both the Met Office and broadcasting and that I wouldn't countenance them moaning and bitching about decisions that were made by the management team. Bernard Davey became my deputy and was splendid in that post although it was only a year or two later he developed MS and had to take early retirement. It wasn't long after he had gone when I got a plaintiff call from him saying that the pension they paid him was very much less than he thought he would get and would I be kind enough to look into it. It had been agreed when we settled the allowances for broadcasting that they, apart from the clothing allowance of £3 a broadcast shift, would be pensionable, but these were missing on his pension cheque. I searched my files but could find no reference to it and assumed it would be at London Weather Centre. No luck there and nothing could be found at Headquarters. Luckily Treasury never throw anything away and his rightful pension was restored.

Suzanne Charlton took on the task as Training Manager and she and I complimented each other well as we were both of the star sign Scorpio, and neither of us would take prisoners easily, since our main task was to make sure that both the meteorology and the broadcasting was at a high standard. In fact we had a difficult task as we had two masters. On the one hand we had the Met Office always watching to see if what had been said on the broadcasts was meteorologically correct and the BBC who were interested in the presentational style and understandability of the broadcasts. In the early days that was very much a problem because there were words and phrases that, from the Met Office point of view, we couldn't use.

We were not allowed to talk about flooding because as far as the Met Office was concerned, we forecast the rain falling out of the cloud and their argument was that it was the Local Authority's, and later The Environment Agency's, responsibility for what happened to it when it hit the ground.

This seemed very stupid to me so we thought hard as to how we could get around it and then came up with the phrase "excess surface water on the roads and fields." Another one was thunderstorms, which are now mentioned often as a throwaway.

Some people are frightened when you talk about thunderstorms so you have to be very careful when you use them and my advice was only forecast them when you are pretty certain they would occur.

There was one dear old lady who, whenever thunder was mentioned in the forecast, would ring up London Weather Centre and ask about them and then go under the stairs with a bottle of Gin. I answered the phone to her one day and she told me the story, but she said there was a sad ending because, although she still went under the stairs she had been diagnosed diabetic so couldn't take the gin anymore. Another lady, as soon as she heard even a chance of heavy showers would go down on the Central line of the Underground and go round and round until the threat of them was over.

Daniel Corbett arrived later in 1997 to look after News 24 and a very good job he did for us. It was a totally new concept where the forecaster was in the studio with the news team. Daniel was born in the UK and lived here in his early years before moving, with his parents in 1974 to New York where, later, he graduated in Meteorology. His television career started at Tuscaloosa, Alabama in 1995 before returning to the UK and the BBC Weather Centre in 1997 to start broadcasting on News 24. He was badly done by 'the powers that be' in that I was promised that once he had settled in as the manager in charge of 24, that he would be promoted within the Met Office to Senior Scientific Officer. As far as I remember, fight as I might at the Met Office Headquarters, it never happened. He, understandably, got somewhat disillusioned and left to try his hand again in the USA before returning back to the BBC. Like Ian McCaskill, Daniel had a different approach to broadcasting, more of an enthusiastic manner favoured by the Americans rather than the slower more laidback style most of us in the UK have, so was well suited to a faster pace adopted by News 24. It was a sad day, in my opinion, when he finally left the BBC Weather Centre in May 2011 for a new life weather broadcasting in New Zealand.

Suzanne Charlton also looked after domestic channels BBC1 and BBC2, but when she left to have a baby, Helen Young took over. Considering her lack of experience compared to some of the others, she was exactly the right choice and went on to replace Bill as the leader of the broadcast team on his retirement in 2000.

David Lee took over as the manager of World Service and broadcasting to the troops abroad through The Sound Services and Vision Corporation situated in Chalfont St Peter. David had worked for Bill during his time in the Public Relations branch at Bracknell and discovered that he was a dedicated meteorologist.

BILL: *So that when we found we were very short of broadcasters as we expanded quickly I persuaded John that we should take David on. Very much against his better judgement, which later proved to be totally correct. John reluctantly agreed and David Lee arrived.*

He settled in well at first but his broadcasts were very much in the style of a Met Office briefing to aircrew and he never developed the manner of talking to his audience in a way that made them feel as though he was just talking to them and this was to prove his downfall as far as broadcasting was concerned a few years later.

That was the team that was to guide us through the wonderfully dizzy days of leading the world in broadcast meteorology. Even with the introduction of the managers it was becoming an increasing task to administer my side of the operation especially when the presenters in Scotland, Northern Ireland, Wales and the English regions came under my wing and I was finding it increasingly difficult to do the job that I joined the team to do - broadcasting. What I found was that the administration took all week and so the only way I could broadcast was at weekends. There was a nasty rumour going around that I only did this to secure my allowances and consequently my pension but I would deny that entirely, although I must say it did help!

John and I shared the same large office (how on Earth he managed to get one that I size, I do not know to this day) and many a happy hour was spent discussing all aspects of the BBC Weather Centre. Most of the time it was amicable but sometimes it was not.

I remember one particularly bad argument, although now for the life of me I cannot remember what it was about, when I refused to speak and the only communications we had was by sitting back to back e-mailing each other. But on the whole we got on well and made the BBC Weather Centre the envy of the World.

At this time Peter Cockroft, Rob McElwee and Penny Tranter, all fully qualified independent forecasters from the Met Office, arrived to learn their trade on World Service and News 24. With so many new staff to train and assimilate, we decided, that for the sake of continuity we should limit the number of people who appeared at peak viewing time on BBC1, which in those days was after the six o'clock and 9 o'clock news. John wanted the same person Monday to Friday, but trying to schedule that was impossible, so he settled for the same person on Monday, Tuesday and Wednesday and then another on Thursday and Friday.

We then had to decide who would cover these shifts and then select them. They almost selected themselves with me, Ian McCaskill, Suzanne Charlton, Michael Fish, John Kettley and until he retired Bernard Davey.

This team, because they often appeared live and unscripted in front of audiences in excess of 12 million, had a somewhat larger performance allowance than those appearing on the other channels.

After all, World Service broadcasts were always recorded and the News 24 Channel audience was tiny compared BBC1 evening. Membership of the top team was not by right, but by merit and if it was felt that if someone on the team was having an off period they would be replaced by someone from News 24 or World, but this differential was accepted by most members of the team.

BILL: *The big problem I had was making sure that all the staff completed their 41 hours per week, averaged out over the month, as per Civil Service instructions. This started to become a problem when allowing certain people to go for long periods on Breakfast News. Naturally the programme had their favourites and one of those was a newly appointed forecaster who came to us via the Royal Navy Met Service, Thames television and as a forecaster working with the team doing the ITV weather. His name, Richard Edgar.*

I thought he was very good on that channel at that time of the day and that suited them well. But on Breakfast News the weather presenter only worked from four in the morning until nine five days a week adding up to 25 hours a week instead of 41 hours. After a month or two of this I found he was so many hours down that I had to do something about it as I was being pressured to sort it out by my superiors at Bracknell, and that was the basis of the harassment charge that Edgar brought against me a little while later.

The BBC deemed he was not ready to be part of the main national team at that time so I put him on the roster supporting World Service. Richard was always one for pushing the boundaries and sometimes didn't understand the need to get my permission as well as John's to take part in other programmes such as Blue Peter and the like.

Over the years I think I only said no on one occasion. I had a whisper that Richard was going up to the Midlands to possibly appear on 'Pebble Mill at One' so I did have a word with him about not doing it. At that time he was not in the BBC's or the Met Office good books after going onto a Blue Peter programme, quite legitimately, but then downgrading the forecasting skills of his colleagues by saying that we were just storytellers.

Switching on the television to watch 'Pebble Mill at One' who should we see but Richard Edgar? I forget what he was talking about but it absolutely incensed Pam Masters, the Head of our Department at the BBC who had already asked John to tighten up on these sort of appearances.

When he returned I called him in the office to seek an explanation. He said it happened by pure chance while he was there, on holiday with his family, but I did point out that that was unlikely and that it was premeditated against my wishes, since not only did he appear, but he had his own earpiece (for production talkback) with him.

So because Edgar was put onto the World Service shift to clear the deficit of his hours, and together with encouragement from some of the more senior members of my team, Richard brought a harassment charge against Bill. The Met Office took this seriously and the whole procedure started with John Bradford from Met Office Headquarters Bracknell, of a lower rank than Bill, interviewing everyone at the weather centre and gathering information regarding the charge against him.

BILL: *To do a job that we were doing, considering we were MOD Civil Servants (and thereby trained as introverts), was not easy since when appearing on air for that short time we had to be extroverts, because to get your message across you have to go over the top a little. The trick is then to come back to quiet normality once you were out of the studio. Managing more than twenty such people, all who thought they were God's gift to weather broadcasting, and rightly so, was not an easy task, because after listening to all their advice, as their manager, I had to make the final decision. This was not always straightforward, since I had to take into account not only what was correct for my employers, the Met Office, but more importantly, what was important for the BBC since after all we were just a lodger unit on their premises broadcasting under their name and being fully funded by them.*

The charge laid against me was that I harassed Edgar and made his life unbearable. I passed this on to my union, or association, the Institute of Professionals, Managers and Specialists, which now goes under the underwhelming name of Prospect.

They looked at the accusations and decided that it was so ridiculous, that it wasn't even worth compiling a defence since it would be thrown out completely. What I hadn't realised at that time was that the person accusing you didn't have to prove they were actually being harassed by you but only that they perceived they were.

This, after all the hard work I used to do on behalf of my staff at regular meetings with Headquarter staff many of whom had the "green eye" when it came to discussing national television. I must say that this was not the case with my immediate boss Roger Hunt who was very much in tune with and encouraging of what we were trying to do at the Centre and worked very hard on our behalf. I was astounded and disappointed at some of the remarks about me by the broadcasters many of whom, in my opinion, used Edgar as an excuse to get at me since they didn't have the courage to stand and say what they it to my face.

McCaskill was one, with his remark that "John and I were stalking the corridors of the BBC like prefects at a minor public school". That was a person whom I worked hard with to get back on to television when his wife had cancer and he was away all week at Birmingham Airport Weather Office so that he could be home with her every night.

Ian had a wonderful way of broadcasting and in the early days his one-liners grabbed the viewers and made them sit up and watch. But about two years before he retired those had gone, so we put him back to cover World Service, in which case his allowances and consequent lump sum and pension would be reduced. The accountants tried to make me drop his allowances down, but I refused right until he retired, saying that I thought in his early years he had brought a breath of fresh air to the broadcasts and taught us all how to do it. That was how he repaid me!

Michael Fish never did like me ever since I appeared on television a year after him, got promotion and in 1983 came back as his boss. I did, some years later, recommend him for promotion to Senior Scientific Officer and have always wondered since why I was so soft and kind.

Louise Lear was another that didn't come out of it too well either, since I had an opportunity of seeing all the comments made by her to the investigating officer. This was someone who was lucky to be employed when the Weather Channel collapsed and who, when expecting her first child came to John and me in tears. She was concerned whether we would we take her back after having the baby and if so she wouldn't be able to work full time. We told her not to worry and we would work it out when the time came. Which we did.

So there was a small group of my team itching to see me go and they wanted to make sure that David Lee took my place with the idea that he would be much easier to manipulate and they could then have a freer rein on what they wanted to happen at the BBC Weather Centre. This is why, in their plan, they wanted John to go as well. It didn't happen but it was a very close call.

After all the interviews of my staff were complete a member of the Met Office Board made an assessment and I was called to Bracknell. All the time this was happening I had no worry about the outcome, especially since my union were so convinced it was a ridiculous charge, although my wife Maureen did suffer badly from worrying about it. At Bracknell I was ushered into the Chief Scientist's Office and handed the judgement to me in a sealed envelope. Before I had chance to open it he departed. The conclusion was that I had been found guilty of misconduct and thus of harassing Richard Edgar. To say I was surprised was an understatement and when the Chief Scientist returned to the room he was subject to a tirade of expletives some of which I understand he had never heard before and I warrant ever since. I told him and Colin Flood, my boss's boss, much to their surprise and annoyance, there and then, that I would appeal and appeal with the utmost vigour against the decision.

All hell broke loose the next day with my picture, well just my head, appearing on the front page of the Sun newspaper with the headlines "Bully Bill" and journalists from all over the country wanting to speak with me.

The union machine, in the person of David Luxton, went into full steam ahead because I think they felt very guilty at giving me incorrect advice, as it turned out, on the initial charge. I am sure, that had we taken it up at that stage and put forward a vigorous defence, the guilty verdict would never have happened. Suffice to say, it had and so something had to be done about it. They worked very hard and represented me at the appeal hearing sometime later at Bracknell.

We all sat around the table and Peter Ewins, Chief Executive of the Met Office chaired the meeting. We gave our reasons as to why the guilty verdict should be overturned and then I found out the reason I had been found guilty. It transpired that the decision was made on the grounds that if I was found guilty I would be given the lightest of sentences, basically a slap on the wrist, told not to be such a naughty boy and since I was coming up to the end of my contract would retire and that would end the subject. Nice and neat but, of course, this all went by the board when I told them I was going to appeal against the decision. There was no way that I was going to leave the Met Office after starting at the lowest grade and ending up as a Grade 1 (one below the Board Level) under such a cloud!

I was told, off the record, that the Met Office was worried that if they had found me not guilty, as they surely should have done, with me still being in post, then Edgar could try to sue them. I then remarked that if the verdict stood then sure as hell I would. Meanwhile David Luxton had mentioned to the Press that the appeal was taking place at Bracknell and the press duly migrated down there.

JOHN: *As Bill's appeal was going on, Roger Hunt rang me to tell me that there was a huge number of reporters and cameramen massing at the entrance to the Met. Office. My reply was "what do you bloody well expect?"*

BILL: *The press were also noticed by people in authority in the building and as we were sitting at the appeal which was virtually over by that time, a Tannoy announcement boomed out loud and clear which said something along the lines of " Under Defence Council Instructions number so and so, I would like to remind all members of the office that they are not allowed to speak to the press without due permission which at this time will not be granted" As the message slowly died away Peter Ewins said to me " and that applies to you as well".*

I replied that that was not true. In the Met Office, at that time we had a list of so called experts who are the only ones that were permitted to talk on certain subjects. For instance, there was an expert on thunderstorms and another on climate change and if ever the media wished to know anything about those topics the expert would be approached to talk to them. I was the expert on the Press, so I told Peter that because that was the case I could speak to all of those massing at the gates.

I walked up to the besieging throng knowing I would never ever slag off my employers for the last forty years and who had given me such a varied and interesting career. On questioning I said that I had a fair hearing and was confident that the initial decision would be overturned and that far from being a bully I was a big softie that had fought tooth and nail for my staff over many years. I explained that this had all come about by a few egomaniacs always moaning and not knowing when they were well off. With that David Luxton and I went to our cars driving off and hoping that justice would finally be done.

I was in Geneva with John at the World Meteorological Organisation celebrating their 50th anniversary when I received a telephone call from Peter Ewins. He told me that after due consideration the earlier decision that had found me guilty of serious misconduct had been overturned and that I was shown to be not guilty. There was a rider, however, in which it was stated that there were some faults with my style of management at the BBC.

Even to this day I totally refute that. I had to manage over 21 broadcasters and it is not an easy task looking after that number of egos. As far as I am concerned this case should never have come to a charge of serious misconduct. It was brought about by a very small number of people at the BBC Weather Centre griping and moaning, as we all do from time to time, and then I believe it got out of hand with some senior members using Richard Edgar for their own agenda.

After it was all over I did express my views to certain people at Bracknell and concluded that if harassment charges are to be brought under these circumstances then it will be difficult in the future for managers to manage.

It was not only Edgar that had a go at me but also David Lee. The circumstances were somewhat similar to Edgar's in that Lee thought he should continue to appear on BBC1 at peak viewing time, but both John and I agreed that he should revert back to World Service as his style was becoming much more like a Met Office briefing to the RAF rather than a weather broadcast for the general public. After that decision was made it was my job to tell him. I remember asking him to come into the World Service studio and telling him of our decision.

I went on to say that in my opinion he was one of the best if not the best forecaster (as apart from broadcaster) at the BBC Weather Centre and that my advice to him was to go back into the forecasting division at Headquarters

I actually recommended him for promotion to Principal and suggested he would do a good job as a senior forecaster there. He obviously took umbrage at this and filed a harassment complaint against me. This was investigated and thrown out very quickly with the comment "that there was no case to answer and that he was just jumping onto the bandwagon." I did get "told off" by my pay department because I dropped David Lee's allowances down to the second tier too quickly and should have left them at the original level for one month.

The ironic thing about this whole episode was that Edgar should have made his complaint against his line manager and not me. His line manager's name? None other than David Lee.

I duly retired when my contract ended and, much to the annoyance of many in the Met Office, was employed directly by the BBC as a consultant with special responsibility for training.

However, during this time, John got dragged into the affair, as there was considerable press interest. His bosses suggested that he should be investigated by the BBC, to see if there had been any collusion with Bill. He strongly refuted such assertions, but with nothing to hide, agreed to cooperate fully.

JOHN: *I had been in the office that day, when Richard Edgar and David Lee came to confront Bill over the decision to put Richard on World News to 'burn-off' some of his outstanding hours. I got involved as Richard was claiming he was being punished, and why wasn't he allowed to be on BBC1. At this time, in order to be fair and open-handed over who broadcast on what channels, I held a quarterly meeting called 'Talent Review' consisting of the senior members of the BBC team, and the Producer of the Weather Show. We would look through tapes of the broadcasts of all the 'talent' (an industry term for those who perform) and decide who was performing well, and those who were not so good at that time. It is natural in broadcasting that everyone on camera has their ups and downs. It was clearly the job of the BBC to ensure that its best talent appeared at peak times.*

Bill also attended this review so that he was party to our thinking. I explained to Richard that currently he was not on the list for BBC1, but that perhaps he may be successful in the future. He then made some silly accusations that it was a fix and not fair, and at that point I left the meeting.

Later on, came a shock in the Teather household, when spread across a double-page Daily Mail article was the headline 'Bully Bill Giles and Climate of the BBC Weather Centre, behind the sunny smiles, a storm over staff claims of harassment and intimidation'. Not only was I misquoted and derided, but in the centre of the article was a picture of me, cigarette in hand, lounging at a table.

This picture had been taken at a BBC Weather Centre Christmas lunch, when I was relaxed and certainly inebriated. The photo had been pinned up on the centre notice board as a joke. The story was that Mike Fish had been seen taking it off the board and putting it in an envelope. I don't know whether journalist Joe Wood had been involved, but it was just his style.

A few days later, I answered a knock at our house front door to see our neighbour holding a large white envelope, from which she produced a photocopy of the Daily Mail article. She said that she didn't know what it was all about as it was nothing to do with her, but she knew that several people in our road had received them.

Later I found that several people in an Arts organisation, in which I was involved, had also received copies. This was obviously a crude attempt to intimidate me by trying to discredit me within my home community. I don't know who was responsible, but I can have a pretty good guess! But it didn't work. I had built up the BBC Weather Centre with Bill over many years. I knew him well. What was true was that he was a firm boss, but also very fair. On countless occasions, I had either witnessed or been part of many kindnesses shown to members of the team. I knew how he had fought their corner at the Met Office. I had witnessed the likes of Kettley, Fish, McCaskill, Lear, Lee and others as they asked for special help or favours and without exception Bill had helped them. The fact that they had now turned on him was a disgrace. It was clear that it was getting out of hand and the power of the pack had taken over. The animals were after blood.

But then it was really no surprise. To broadcast the weather needs a huge ego. You have to believe in yourself and have no doubt you are the best in the world. It was always a quality I encouraged and indeed sought in people I auditioned. So put together all those egos and you are bound to get a collection of people who really did believe they could walk on water. Add to this mixture a Met Office investigator who should have handled it more sensitively and Bill's bosses who had many axes to grind and you have a recipe for mayhem.

Eventually the BBC allocated Kevin Hosier to investigate me. He did it fairly and professionally. My simple position was that it was fundamental to a producer's responsibilities to decide on behalf of the BBC and viewers alike, who should appear on TV and on what channels. The 'talent review' process was fair as it involved just more than me. It should never be the choice of the talent.

After a few weeks I was summoned to my Head of Department's office to be told the result of the investigation. In this conclusion Kevin stated 'I have not found any evidence to support Richard Edgar's claim that John Teather's actions or behaviour amounted to deliberate harassment and bullying and I am therefore unable to uphold the complaint'.

However, mud does stick. At my first meeting with my new News boss, Roger Mosey, he enquired, "are there were any more skeletons in the cupboard"?

CHAPTER 17

THE PRESS

The BBC Weather Centre's relationship with the press over the years was a curious one. Certainly the notion that the British were obsessed with the weather was borne out by the number of column inches that newspapers gave over to it.

At a press launch in 1988, where we were announcing the use of radar rain for the first time together with a suite of other changes, we were introduced by Ann Mills of the Press Office to Joe Wood. Joe would have made the Hutton Press enquiry squirm. He was old-school gutter press, with a childlike conviction that he was exposing "those bastards" on behalf of the nation. He often referred to himself as "part of her Majesty's Press!" He had an interesting dual personality of speaking by turn in a posh voice, and then in a stream of vulgar abuse that brought water to your eyes. A big man, with the girth of someone who liked his food. He really had no sense of morality – anyone was fair game and he was happy to use any method to get his story. It was very obvious that we needed to be very careful with Joe, and over the years we were exactly that. On slow news days, you could bet that Joe would be on the phone sniffing out a weather story.

The BBC had an interesting symbiotic relationship with the press. Each fed of the other. The BBC needed to promote its programmes and services to drive viewing figures so that it could continue to justify the licence fee. The press needed personality based stories that it knew its readership had an endless capacity for. The weather presenters were national treasures and there was a big appetite for stories about them, from what they were wearing to where they went on holiday. We held many press conferences for weather, as the press office knew that it would result in many articles and pictures spread across all the papers. For one press launch we had combined with News Division.

The next morning weather was slashed across every paper, and in small type in some of the heavier publications, was a small paragraph about News. We never did make any friends in News – I wonder why?

Through Joe we were introduced to Nick Hellen at the Sunday Times and that led to many more worthy pieces rather than just personality led ones. They were more 'behind the scenes' looks at how the Weather Centre worked, and in later years a growing interest in the operation of the Met Office as it moved from a public service to a business under the Labour Government's privatisation of parts of the Civil Service.

Ann's job in the BBC Press Office was to act as a filter for requests from the press and to offer advice as to whether they were worthy or not of our attention. The balance was to provide access, but ensure that the result would be positive.

The press had a love-hate relationship with Mike Fish and he was subject to many less than positive stories.

JOHN: *Once on holiday in America standing in a supermarket, I had a call from my Producer, Andrew Lane. Had I seen the British newspapers that morning? Fish was spread across the front pages. By chance the supermarket has just had a delivery of papers, and there, splashed across the front pages was a picture of Michael with his supposed mistress. I phoned Andrew back as he was concerned what the BBC's position should be. I told him that whatever Mike did in his private life was of no concern to the BBC, but that we should take him off the rota for any BBC1 or BBC2 broadcasts until all this had blown over.*

BILL: *In the meantime Michael had come to me, being his line manager, to find out what was my reaction and what would be that of the Board Members of the Met Office. I was quite sympathetic and took the same view as John in that what he did in his spare time was his own affair but I was quite concerned that it might be considered to be putting the Met Office in a very awkward position.*

At any rate my boss and I managed to smooth things over and after talking to Michael nothing more was said about the incident - or at least not in the office!

Years later talking to Joe Woods, the journalist from the gutter-press, who was extremely good company when eating in his favourite Chinese restaurant, we found out that on quiet news days they would often put a tail on some of us to see if we were misbehaving - it's a pity Michael didn't realise it at the time for it would have saved him a lot of aggravation. But it just goes to show how devious some of the press could be just to get a story - all in the public interest of course!

BILL: *Michael seemed to court problems of his own making. I remember reading in the Daily Mail, long after I had retired, a wonderful story about him. It transpired that at an airport check in Michael was trying to get an upgrade. Now there is no problem with that and I, for one, have tried many times in the past and often been successful. However, on this occasion, he wasn't getting anywhere with the Ground Hostess and uttered the immortal words "Don't you know who I am?" The hostess than asked him to wait a moment and she proceeded to get her supervisor. As the pair of them approached Michael she was heard to say to him "Could you help this gentleman please, he doesn't know who he is?"*

Michael, Ian McCaskill, John Kettley and Suzanne Charlton and I all became well known. In the early days, there was no rival channel that produced a nationwide weather forecast and since we were small in number appeared at peak viewing times regularly but this made us interesting subjects to the press on quiet news days. It also made us vulnerable to receive mail from some of those watching who really wanted to strike up a pen-friend type of relationship.

I remember one young Dutch lady who kept writing to me and also sending some photographs. This was a long time ago, soon after I started - so somewhere in the late 70s when we were just doing three broadcasts a day and had plenty of time on our hands between broadcasts.

She used to work both in Holland and the UK migrating from one to the other at about six month intervals. I was sitting in my office one Saturday afternoon when I received a phone call from reception to telling me I had a visitor. When I asked the name she said it was a Dutch lady with an almost unpronounceable name. I knew it was her, but before I went down to meet her I had a look at one of the photographs she had sent me. It was of a young, very pretty girl with flaxen hair and a cheery smile. But all the same I leapt off my chair and didn't bother with the slow lift but went racing down the stairs two at a time. I arrived at reception quite red faced and flustered but on looking around couldn't see anyone that resembled the photo I had been studying in the office. Thinking that perhaps she had just gone to the toilet I sidled up the receptionist and asked if she could tell me where she was. The receptionist looked rather blankly at me and pointed to a little old grey haired lady sitting in the corner. The photographs she had sent me must have been taken during World War II! She turned out to be a lovely lady but sad to say she had the very short tour of the BBC.

Over the years viewers have had their favourites but the one who mostly appealed to the ladies was John Kettley especially one lady who turned out to be a young nurse. She had obviously fallen for John and kept writing to him even though he never replied. In each of the letters she sent him a photograph of herself which, in itself was not an unusual event. However this pretty lady's photographs were different from most because in each successive letter she had less and less clothes on and, of course, both John Tether and I had to check each photo to see if it was interfering with the smooth running of the Weather Centre! It came to a crunch when she sent him one where she had divested herself of everything and was standing in the photograph smiling at the camera. Well, after studying it for some time, I realised this had to end so wrote a letter back to her suggesting that unless she stopped I would have to pass them on to the lawyers. What a killjoy I was, but someone had to do it!

Most of the letters we received from viewers were very pleasant and complimentary but there were also some that were very worrying. I received what was to be the most sinister of them all. My first wife and I had separated in January 1991 and this letter had come from Joanna, the daughter of her eldest sister - my niece by marriage.

I was Joanna's favourite uncle and my first wife, Eileen, and I helped her a lot to cope with her childhood which, to say the least, was unconventional. She started to skip school and fell in with a band of hippies and eventually ended up in Spain. There was a plaintiff cry from her for help and I told her Father to go over there and bring her back and that if he didn't, I would. She grew out of that rebellious stage, studied and became a State Registered Nurse.

She went to live at Sellafield, married and had two children. I think she found it increasingly difficult to cope with life and was very upset when my first wife and I decided to go our separate ways.

It was one day in Spring 1991 that the first letter from Joanna arrived at the Television Centre. Nothing too much to worry me, even when they started to arrive quite regularly. In rambling prose she talked about me being Hitler's right hand man. I could just about put up with that but when she then went on to accuse me of linking up the Met Office computer with those at the BBC and MOD I thought little did she know me since, at that time, I could barely open one up - and some say I'm not much better now! It then took a more sinister and ugly turn when she accused me of being her Father.

Her mother, who by Joanna's own admission was a severe alcoholic, sometime in the mid 80s, had told her that I was in fact her Father. Not satisfied with just telling me this astounding news she wrote to many of my staff at the BBC and the Met Office informing them as well. I naturally had to counter these accusations and sent a memo out to my staff saying that this was not true and if you had ever seen her mother you would realise why.

Counting back to the time when Joanna was conceived, I was in service with the Met Office in the heart of Germany at RAF Gutersloh. But when this was mentioned to her she just totally ignored it and demanded a DNA test. I was happy to do this but was advised by the police in Tiverton, Devon, that it would be a waste of time because had it come back negative, as it surely would have done, their advice is she would have said it had been tampered with or some other reason for doubting its authenticity.

Letters kept pouring in to me at home. I could have anything up to twelve a day, to my immediate neighbours and all the pubs in the village. She was very clever though because every time the police went to arrest her she referred herself to a psychiatric hospital as a voluntary patient where they couldn't touch her. When the time was right she would then leave and start all over again. Things came to a head in 1998 when she was jailed for 6 months for the harassment and writing my name in red paint on the Cenotaph in London.

Things went quiet again for a while even after she was released and we thought that she had learned her lesson but at the turn of the millennium it started again. I think that she was fine when taking her medication but not so good when she forgot for any length of time.

I used to sit pondering why on earth she was doing this, and apart from inheriting a defective gene from her mother I was at a loss, until one day it suddenly dawned on me. As I have already mentioned she had two children and lived very close to the Sellafield Nuclear Power Station in Cumbria and as far as I remember she let the children play on the beach close by. She was scared that they had been subjected to large doses of radiation but rather than blame herself, if I was in fact her Father then it could have come from me after being involved with the Nuclear testing in the Pacific all those years ago.

Things came to a head when she started to target the MOD and BBC. She even sent a parcel of dog excrement to the Director-General of the BBC and threatened the MOD with the IRA.

She was again summoned to court, found guilty and remanded in custody for psychiatric reports. All along I told the police and everyone involved (because it wasn't just me she was harassing) that she needed help and did not deserve to go to jail. I wanted her to be found not to be of sound mind or responsible for her actions and would have liked her to go into a suitable hospital to help her condition, but although she could appear quite unstable at times there was also a very sane side to her personality. When interviewed by psychologists to decide whether she should go to hospital or jail she would appear perfectly in control and lucid and that is why in 2002 she was sent to prison for two and a half years.

My new wife Maureen and I then had nearly ten years of peace and quiet and we mistakenly thought that the harassment was finally over but, probably by seeing me appearing in an advert on TV, she started again. By this time the harassment laws had tightened up and the police became more active right away and at the end of 2011 whilst I was away, my daughter phoned me and told me the news that Joanna had been found dead. It transpired that she had taken her own life.

The relief of knowing no more letters would arrive was far overshadowed by the sadness, that because she would not allow any of the professionals to help her, she died at a very young age.

So Mr Edgar and Mr Lee please don't ever talk to me about harassment - you don't know the meaning of it!

CHAPTER 18

NATIONS AND REGIONS

Towards the end of the 1990's there was another sea change when Bill and John became responsible for changing the way in which weather was delivered in the Nations and Regions. This is a rather pompous description, that basically describes Wales, Scotland and Northern Island as the nations, and the English regions of North East, North West, North, Midlands, East, West, South, South East and South West. It was a mixture in each area as to how they were doing local weather. The nations had their own meteorologists as weather presenters doing both TV and radio. The regions only had radio forecasts supplied from the local Met Office Weather Centre, either with the duty forecaster going into the BBC Station, or from a small studio at the Weather Centre.

Politically, within the BBC, there was a growing desire to make the BBC less London centred. The establishment of a Department for Nations and Regions was a manifestation of this. But really three factors came together that forced the change. A growing dissatisfaction by the BBC with the quality and lack of flexibility of the local Weather Centre forecasters, the plans to close some Weather Centres, and a growing concern over the lack of a 'one nation – same forecast' concept.

JOHN: *I had a visit at the Weather Centre from Andy Griffee, a senior manager in the BBC's English Regions. He said that many of his regional managers were concerned that the duty forecaster from their local Met Office Weather Centre were not up to the mark. They were also worried that they needed to be more flexible on transmission times, in particular during drive-time, which was a key broadcast period for local radio. He wanted to know if there was a solution.*

Coupled to this, John was growing increasingly concerned to ensure that wherever in the UK you listened to a radio forecast or watched on TV, Ceefax or the web, then it was the same forecast. He had already got to grips with Ceefax following numerous complaints that the temperatures shown often bore no relationship to reality. At times the minimum temperature was higher than the maximum one! He found that the Met Office was selling Ceefax a data stream direct out of the computer model with no human intervention employed. So he stopped that and took responsibility for inputting the data at the BBC Weather Centre.

BILL: *When I was promoted to Grade 1 in the Met Office (previously Senior Principal Scientific Officer) it was not just to look after the broadcasters at Television Centre but also those meteorologists broadcasting from other BBC Centres around the country. At that time the local weather broadcasters received written guidance from the senior forecaster at Bracknell and used that to compile their broadcasts and written forecasts, but John and I had, for a long time, been discussing the need for a roster of weather forecasters at the BBC Television Centre. The senior forecasters at headquarters of the Met Office were very good and with advice could interpret the computer models with great expertise but they were not trained in any way to understand the needs of the weather broadcaster and were much more inclined to discuss the forecast in meteorological terms or in the way an airline pilot would appreciate. The forecasters that we had in mind would be those with many years experience in weather forecasting rather than having a first class honours degree in mathematics. In fact such was the set up in the Met Office at that time that we were streamed into three levels. Stream one were the honours degree people with at least a 2/1 at a recognised university. These people invariably joined the Met Office in the research branches rather than forecasting and after a few years were promoted and put in a middle management position.*

Some of them at Principal level were made senior forecasters even though most of them had only completed short periods as forecasters, mainly dealing with the upper atmosphere. The story went that they had to be the senior people on duty because out of normal office hours they represented the Director General and it couldn't possibly be someone with a 2/2 degree or lower - could it?

You would think that the weather forecasters in the Met Office - the reason that the Office existed and our core business until the 21st century - would be the most important people in the firm but this is not true. Their qualifications ranged from Maths and Physics A-Levels to a 2/2 degree in the same subjects and were classified as stream two.

Stream threes were those with O-Level science and English subjects and were the weather observers and assistants to the forecasters.

Whilst I was posted to Headquarters for three years at a Senior Forecaster grade, I devised a not so well received test, to define who would be in which stream. The test would be, theoretically, to throw someone out of the window on the third floor. If they were a stream one, since they could do anything and had wings on their feet, they would just go into a hover and be fine. A stream two would plummet to the ground and really hurt themselves, but a stream three would also crash to the ground at great speed but not feel it. Of course it never happened, but there are a few I wouldn't have minded testing but most of those would have gone into the hover.

Had we been able to introduce a 24 hour roster of senior forecasters, and cost wasn't a problem, we would have sorted out a major obstacle to making sure that all weather broadcasters up and down the country, including the national, would be singing off the same hymn sheet and more importantly be having the correct emphasis on those broadcasts. We had decided that this shift, made up of people who had no wish whatsoever to perform on radio or television, would take advice from the senior forecaster at Bracknell but then put their own spin on it for the general public.

Conferences would be held with the other nations and regions on a regular basis throughout the day to inform and keep all broadcasters up to date and to make sure they were putting the correct emphasis on their forecasts. We put this to a meeting, showing how it could be funded, but it was rubbished by Stuart Wass, the BBC Account Manager, and was subsequently dropped. Needless to say it was resurrected in a slightly different form a few years later but instead of getting a new shift of senior forecasters from the Met Office, the BBC Weather Centre used some of the older broadcasters, which, I suppose, was one way of getting them off the air.

Following further discussions with Nigel Kay, the number two at Nations and Regions, Bill and John decided to tour all twelve areas to see if they could come up with a solution. They split it into two separate weeks, as it was a big undertaking. The first week, John's secretary Heather Narayan, had booked them into, what proved to be a collection of rather poor standard hotels, and after a long day of driving and meetings, all they wanted was a good meal and a comfortable bed. They were denied both, and at the end of the week on their return to TVC, told Heather of their tale of woe. On the next occasion she had done them proud, nothing less than 4-star and usually old country retreats with fine restaurants and four-poster beds!

Each visit to a region told basically the same story. They had to have the duty forecaster from the local Met Office Weather Centre, and although some were good, the rest were pretty poor. We were played recordings and they were certainly right. Training was suggested, but the reality was that it wouldn't make any difference for some. Their main issue, though, was availability, and those times were dictated by the other duties, in particular commercial ones at their Weather Centre.

What everyone wanted was their own dedicated weather forecasters, and in some regions they had gone part of the way by using journalists to read a weather report during drive time. But it was a stopgap and what they really wanted was proper weather presenters with the required technical knowledge.

In the nations it was slightly different, as they had a weekday meteorologist who did a local opt-out forecast. However, due to their shifts, the bulk of the radio was still broadcast from the local Weather Centre. We had one lucky break in Cardiff, when we met their weather forecaster, Helen Willetts.

We were sufficiently impressed to offer her a job in London. We were not popular with BBC Wales for that!

We also found an increasing wish for each area to have their local opt-out TV forecast, as part of the local news broadcast. The Nations were already doing this using a variety of non-standard and non-branded homemade graphics. They were pretty proud with what they were doing. John was appalled that so many different styles were being used. However, to provide a graphics system for each nation and region was a real task to solve. Computer Graphics Workshop came to the rescue, as they were able to provide a special PC, fitted with a Matrox graphics card. The onboard software would allow the local weather presenter to make non-data graphics such as symbol charts, league tables and summary charts. The PC would also have online access to a server in the BBC Weather Centre from which they could select a variety of charts such as pressure, temperature and rainfall. Both the local and remote graphics could be made into a bulletin and replayed in the local studio. Not only would they have access to a complete suite of graphics, but they would all look the same wherever you watched in the country.

But, we still needed to solve the staffing issue. The regional graphics system could be used without delay in the Nations as they were already doing a TV opt-out, but for the English regions it was much more difficult. So Bill and John came up with the concept of employing two weather presenters in each area – the number two would start the shift early and do drive-time radio, the number one would start later and do the late afternoon radio and then TV. The only problem would be how to recruit upwards of 20 people. They needed a science background, but perhaps not in meteorology at this time, as they could be trained in what they needed at a local level. The duty BBC1 forecaster at the BBC Weather Centre would do a special conference to ensure that everyone was on the same message. Certainly it was not going to be a trivial task as even if we could recruit that number we would have to provide training not only in meteorology, but in presentation and how to use the graphics system.

JOHN: *At the BBC Weather Centre I already had built a training room specifically for training weather presenters and after Bill retired from the Met Office I employed him direct to continue training. As each region was converted to the new system of a number one and two, they would start at the BBC Weather Centre for intense and extensive training ready to be released to each region to start broadcasting.*

In the Nations, the number ones were already there, and so it was only the number twos that needed training.

BILL: *I was always very keen that the weather presenters in both the national team at the BBC Weather Centre and in the other Nations and Regions should work for the Met Office.*

That way I could be assured of their meteorological training and that we would have some control over them. The fact that in 1998 I took them under my wing made it doubly important.

At that time there was only a broadcaster from eleven o'clock until after the early evening news but the BBC wanted to have local weather forecasts from the early morning through to lunchtime, meaning that there should be a local weather presenter on from six in the morning right through until mid evening.

I went, with my boss Roger Hunt, by car to Birmingham to a meeting chaired by Andy Griffee, to discuss the possibility of recruiting enough broadcasters to cover the proposed extended day. During the drive there I told Roger my thoughts on making them Met Office staff rather than just being on contract to the BBC. We talked through the fact that we made a great profit on the BBC contract for the existing shift that we could, and in my opinion should, offer the new people free of charge. That way the BBC would jump at it and we could make sure that the new recruits would have allegiance to the Met Office. It was all agreed but Roger got into a lot of trouble with the accountants for agreeing to it, but it worked, and worked well. We had the same system as at Television Centre in that the BBC obviously had all the say as to who would appear on air, but the Met Office had a lot of control over who they put forward.

Unfortunately after I retired and the Met Office accountants took over, the system fell down. They did not treat many of the regional broadcasters too well, many rang me to ask for advice, which was to get a contract direct with the local BBC Centre, which many of them have now done.

Recruitment was done by national advertising and a very long series of interviews and auditions. As they were to be Met Office staff, the recruitment policy would have to follow civil service frameworks, and during this period we auditioned someone who was blind, someone in a wheelchair and an undertaker.

These changes represented a considerable additional cost to the BBC and it took a great deal of negotiation to agree the funding. Computer Graphics Workshop would provide a bespoke machine for each area, which would contain the appropriate local maps designed at the BBC Weather Centre by Liz Varral, together with any special titles or graphics as requested.

This way we ensured that the design would be consistent. The package price also included them going to each nation and region and installing the machine, and helping local engineers with the wiring and communications, including a push button for the presenter in the studio.

JOHN: *To help with the process, I was joined by producer, the late Andrew Riley, from the Nations and Regions Division. Based at the Weather Centre, his job was to do the detailed negotiation for each Nation and Region as it became their turn to make the changes.*

He was ideally qualified for this as he had the amazing ability to come up with the goods whatever the problem. He was the sort of person you would want in a prisoner of war camp – a gofer who could rustle up a German passport or a map of the area. His help was invaluable.

In the end, what was a dream became a reality. Nowadays we take it for granted that in our viewing area, we will get a local TV forecast and that it all seamlessly integrates with the national forecast. Or if we take a car journey, the local radio station will be broadcasting the weather with presenters who sound as if they are actually enjoying what they are doing.

From humble acorns do mighty oaks trees grow.

CHAPTER 19

AFTER THE BBC

About two weeks before Bill finally left the BBC he had a phone call from a chap called Simon Strong offering him a job. As a Civil Servant he was forbidden to hold positions in a commercial company and his first reaction, as had always been the case in the past when offers had come his way, was to say thank you, but no thank you. But then he hesitated and mentioned that he had rung up at the right time as he was about to retire and would need something to occupy his mind. Bill arranged to meet Simon a few days later to talk over his proposition.

BILL: *I met him in an office in Warren Street to discuss what he had in mind, which, on the surface, seemed an interesting idea. Even to this day I do believe it has great potential when describing the weather forecast. After a very boozy lunch we sat down to discuss the details. His company started out in December 2000 as Weather Portal Index.com Ltd, changing its name to Weather Prophit Ltd a month later and it was trying to get into the market of selling weather data. I had seen over the years at the exhibitions I had organised for the Met Office how difficult that was, since most people quite rightly said that they had already paid for the Met office in their taxes, so why should they pay again for the forecast. There were already about twenty small independent weather companies in the UK, so to be successful we would have to find a new way of passing on the information.*

Already in the company with Simon was a young programmer Robert Watts, a very clever young man, who kept us at the forefront of technology. One day in the office Simon, as was quite usual, had turned his thoughts to things other than the weather and decided to go with three friends on a golfing weekend in Spain the following weekend.

I later found out that this, or something similar, was a fairly regular occurrence. Normally if he touched the computer Robert would be there somewhere but on this occasion he was away from the office. Simon decided that he would book the seats on the plane for the four golfers with his credit card. Now I wasn't paying too much attention to what he was doing until I heard him offer an expletive and wondered why. Apparently he had pressed a button on the computer so many times that he had virtually booked all the seats for that flight. Luckily for him Robert arrived back and managed to undo all his bookings and that weekend only the four of them went golfing.

I was recruited to find a new way of delivering the weather forecast to sell to customers and I was well known after being on the television for the last 25 years. When, on that fateful afternoon, I was offered a Directorship of the Company together with a salary of £1,000 a month for working one day a week I took it and we all adjourned to the pub across the road again to celebrate. In fact if I remember correctly that was where we held most of our Board Meetings in the early days.

My task was to simplify the weather forecast so that the recipients could understand it quickly and without too much difficulty. Most outdoor activities are affected by the weather, but before you make a decision to take part in them you have to weigh up all the different elements of the weather that affects it. For instance, just going for a walk with the dog, you have to consider the temperature, the chance of rain or snow and to a lesser extent the wind. What I planned to do was to incorporate all these elements into a single index from 0 to 100 where the nearer the index was to 100 the better the weather for that activity. This was a completely new and novel way of describing the weather and in due course the company acknowledged this and changed its name to The Weather Index.

We decided on a few activities that we wished to target with our new approach and they included sailing, golf, gardening and hill walking with astronomy and flying small aircraft coming later.

I had meetings with dingy sailors as well as members of The Royal National Lifeboat Institution on the elements that were important to sailors of small boats. I had a pretty good idea beforehand, since I was brought up in a village on the banks of the River Dart at Dittisham where we were messing about in boats from a very early age. Once I had decided what weather factors were important to these sailors I had to work out an empirical equation to take them into account as well as weighting their importance. The problem, especially for those with little or no experience, taking part in any new activity, was that they had to weigh up all of the weather elements before deciding whether to take part on any particular day. By me being able to give them the answer in one number, it did all the calculations for them. For instance in sailing the wind strength was all important as well as the direction since that enabled me to calculate the waves and swell. I had to take the temperature into consideration but to a much lesser degree than the wind. After considering all the relevant elements I would end up with an equation which when the forecast weather was inserted would give an answer from 0 to 100. The higher the answer the better it would be for the sailors so, for example, if on a Thursday they weren't sure whether to go sailing on Saturday or Sunday all they needed to do was to put in the forecast figures and it would give them the answer as to the best of the two days. I even refined the index so that just considering novice sailors, if the answer was less than 50, they should not go out but on the other hand a very experienced sailor was fine with an index of only 30.

Wind Speed (Kt)	Index	Visibility (m)	Index	State of Sea	Index
Calm	00	0-200	00	Smooth	100
1-5	30	201-500	05	Slight	75
6-7	50	501-700	10	Moderate	50
8-10	70	1001-1200	15	Rough	25
11-13	90	1201-1500	20	Very Rough	00
14-17	100	1501-1700	30		

18-20	75	1701-200	35
21-24	55	1701-2000	40
25-30	30	2001-3000	50
31-35	20	3001-5000	60
>35	00	5001-10,000	80
		>10,001	100

My proposal for the sailing index, once they have launched and got into the open water is 4x wind speed index + 4x visibility index + 2x state of sea index all divided by 10. The individual indices are as above.

If the forecast is for rain, the index is multiplied by 0.9. If the temperature is between 10°C and 15°C the index is multiplied by 0.9, between 5°C and 10°C by 0.8 and if below 5°C by 0.75. For example if the wind forecast was 10Kt, visibility 4,000m and state of sea moderate the sailing index would be 4 x 70 + 4 x 60 + 2 X 50/10 then the sailing index would be 62.

If the forecast was for rain the index would drop to 62 x 0.9 = 56 and if raining with a temperature of 9°C the index would be 47. So a reasonably pleasant index of 62 would drop to 56 in the rain and 47 in early Spring.

BILL: *Over the following months we became more and more ambitious with the weather indices and added Golf Clubs and Flying Clubs. Golf proved a very complicated area to sort out since it was just not an index for people playing the game but for the green keepers needing the weather forecasts for cutting greens and fertilising them. That depended on whether they were using dry fertiliser or wet, when the ideal weather conditions were so different. The only problem was that Simon didn't fully understand the limitations of weather forecasting and would offer services that I could not possibly execute. I do remember him offering to be able to tell one Oxfordshire Golf Club that we could give them an hourly forecast some two weeks ahead, which was totally out of the question.*

I got in touch with Heather Couper CBE, former President of the British Astronomical Society, an eminent astronomer who has the ability to make quite a complicated subject very understandable. She lived just down the road from me so I arranged to meet her in her local the 'Pink and Lily' public house, which I already knew quite well.

The forecasts that we give on BBC Television have a short duration so it was impossible to cater for some specialist activities and I am thinking of Surfers, Glider pilots and Stargazers. I thought that we might be able to adapt an index for those that wished to watch the stars at night. I obviously knew that the cloud amounts overnight were important but needed to find out from Heather all the other astronomical elements that were to be considered as well.

As in all things, Heather was very interested and threw her full weight behind the project and after copious amounts of delicious red wind we came up with a formula that would give all future star gazers a much better idea of which nights it would be worth looking up to the heavens.

Once we had started to compile all these new indices we had to 'sell' them to the relevant customers and one of the ways was to put them on our website. Robert, our computer expert, was far too busy with other things so I wracked my brains as to who we could get to fill that post when it suddenly dawned upon me who it should be. I knew someone at the BBC Weather Centre who had plenty of spare time at the weekends and who was fully up to date with websites and the way they operated - his name was John Teather. I spoke with John about joining the company for one weekend day a week but he wasn't at all convinced that the indices worked and he said he couldn't afford the time until I pointed out to him that for that one day a week he would be paid £250, and with two children at university he readily agreed. We continued working on the indices over the following year and John continued with us after he retired from the BBC. We were both still only working as Directors of WPIndex for one day a week but now both on the same day.

Simon, by this time was floating in and out visiting clubs that he thought might want to take our services but it was a very difficult environment. He did make the mistake, against my advice and unbeknown to me or John, of visiting the Met Office at Bracknell and discussing our future plans with them hoping for a joint venture. This turned out to be the fatal blow in that they then knew exactly our plans and could counter them in the weather market and this was shown up by a slow decline in our sales.

Nonetheless, even though times were getting difficult we still had some long and expensive lunches at restaurants that were purported to be top class but to a village lad like me who enjoys simple food they were worryingly sophisticated. I remember one restaurant, which we all went to on a regular basis and on looking down through the menu found nothing I wanted.

All I was after was a beer and cheese sandwich but all I could find were things like Spinach and Spleen, and Roast Squirrel. I would look across at John who had the same look of disbelief on his face as I did. I glanced at the person opposite who was tucking in with relish on squid cooked in its own ink. One of the other restaurants Simon used to take us for long lunches reminded me of school dinners where we all sat on long tables but here I must admit the food was very much to my liking.

It was obvious to the people and companies that had invested in us that things were going downhill and one of them, a delightful man called John Redman, called me and another investor to a secret meeting to decide what to do. Sigma Capitol Group also investors had decided that we needed someone new at the helm so we sat down to contemplate who, but even at this stage it looked almost impossible to be able to turn the company around.

At my suggestion John was made Managing Director but even for him, after great success at the BBC Weather Centre, it was an impossible task and so on the 6th May 2004 we went into voluntary liquidation. That was the end of WPIndex but I still believe there is a lot of mileage yet in the concept.

During this period John suggested to Bill that they form their own company to jointly represent their interests. So the Weather People Ltd was formed in November 2002, with a view to provide a vehicle through which they could make programmes, sell data and procure training contracts. We had mixed fortunes, working hard to sell a weather programme to ITV West Country, which, unfortunately never got off the ground.

BILL: *Previous to this, I had been approached by David Atkins, a freelance television producer, who did a lot of work for ITV West Country Television. David had the idea of making a series of programmes that used the general overall reasons for, and consequences of, climate change. We could then put the details on for each ITV region of the country. We did two full half hour programmes for the far southwest of England and one centred on Bristol which were very well received but we never managed to get any others commissioned. While making these programmes the evenings were spent in hotels and bars and the conversation eventually got around to the weather and climate change itself.*

I enjoyed making these programmes so much that I discussed with John the possibility of the Weather People Ltd (of which we were the Directors) making some weather programmes ourselves. We already had vast experience making many "Weather Shows' for the BBC and I had done some adverts as well so we sat down to think about it. We came up with the idea of a series of half hour programmes for the ITV network, which minus the adverts, would only amount to some twenty three or twenty four minutes.

It was to be personality based using the well-known weather presenters who would each talk about their passions and hobbies. Mine, for instance would be cooking and gardening. Incidentally many years later I was invited to be a contestant on "Ready Steady Cook" against, would you believe, Michael Fish and I beat him and still have the winner's plate hanging in my kitchen to prove it!

We had planned to invite John Kettley, Sian Lloyd from ITV, Jim Bacon who now worked for his own weather company in East Anglia, Suzanne Charlton and Michael Fish who would all decide on their topics. After costing it all out and working out when we could do the filming we discussed it down in Plymouth with the commissioning editor but, as we were told, because of staff changes they were making, it was not a runner. We abandoned it unfortunately, but even to this day I believe it would be a very interesting series of programmes even though we've all got a lot older!

We were then contracted to run a training session at WMO in Geneva. Their idea was that the training could be filmed and we would then produce a comprehensive training DVD. The problem though is that you can't learn to drive a car watching a video. It is an interactive process and weather presenter training is no different. The training week was held in February 2006, with a mixed bunch of candidates. We had developed a training package called 'Ten Steps to Good Broadcast Meteorology'. We had originally called it the Ten Commandments, but realised that may not be too attractive to some religions and countries.

In Geneva, at the World Meteorological Organisation, we discovered they had a fully fledged radio and television studio and after much hard work in convincing the hierarchy of the need to use it, Haleh Kootval, Chief of the Public Services, persuaded them to agree to hold a television and radio broadcast course there. English speaking forecasters from developing countries were invited to join (many other courses were conducted in Spanish by the well known Barcelona weatherman Tomas Molina).

We arrived in Geneva a couple of days before the course started to make sure everything was in order and in place. We went down to the studio full of optimism only to find that the studio was not fully equipped and that there was only a camera and a graphics system supplied by Gerald Fleming of RTE. It was an old graphic system called WeatherOne from the Norwegian company Metaphor, but would suit our purposes. But, as John quickly found out there was no vision mixer, which is used to interface between the camera and the graphics device. We had no idea what to do as the course started in a couple of days, until someone suggested we try to hire one from a company in Geneva.

Bill managed to persuade a local TV equipment hire company to lend us a mixer for the duration of the course on the understanding that WMO might purchase it, or something similar, at a later date. Well at least that got us over the immediate problem.

The course students duly arrived very excited to be coming from their homelands to Geneva and as guests of the WMO. There was a mixture in so much as most of them were raw recruits never having broadcast before, at least on television and a few who had been broadcasting quite a long time. We always stressed that experienced broadcasters should appear on courses, since many had developed bad habits and needed to be shown the error of their ways.

BILL: *The course started as usual with the one-minute test, when they all had to speak for exactly one minute on any subject they wanted but it had to have a beginning, middle and an end making sure that they talked to the camera and not to the ceiling or floor. This always proved shattering to them and to me because John, who would be behind the camera, quite often said, "Bill will show you how to do it". If only I had been bright enough to have my story well rehearsed it would have been less nerve wracking!*

205

The first one who made a pretty good attempt as did many of the ones that followed until one somewhat older forecaster from Ghana, who had been broadcasting for 10 years, stepped up to the camera - his name Steve Quoi. He was very confident as he started his one-minute test. I gave him the hand signals showing he had half a minute to go, then fifteen seconds, and finally counted him out on my fingers for the last ten seconds. He took no notice whatsoever but ploughed on for nearly three minutes.

Although there was admiration from some of his fellow students that he had not hesitated, it was not what we had planned. On questioning Steve he revealed that he was a great friend with the President of Ghana and no one would dare cut him off air before he had finished and to crown it all he was a Church Minister and was used to giving long and involved sermons. Since then we have got to know Steve very well and he has taken a very active part in the International Association of Broadcast Meteorology in Africa.

Steve proved to be a very pleasant well educated man and at the end of the course presented John and me with a native costume. We tried these on and mine fitted perfectly. When John had not met me in the bar for our pre-dinner drink I went up to see why, thinking he might not be feeling too well. What I saw was amazing, John at 6' 6" was standing beside his bed with the Ghanaian costume half off and half on. It came down to the middle of his chest and was obviously stuck. He couldn't get it on or off. I just laughed and left. A little while later he came down carried the said garment and mentioned it to Steve who duly took it off him and promised to get a much larger one made and send it on. It duly arrived.

The World Meteorological Organisation is well known for its hospitality, which it uses to great effect for networking and we were always invited to the events. Looking out from the glass building over Lake Geneva was a particular joy and meeting with the good and great in world meteorology was a bonus. At these events the resident photographer would be flitting around taking pictures of everyone and everything. On one particular occasion John, who trained at college for three years as a professional photographer, said to Bill "Look at the photographer, he's taking all these photographs and hasn't taken the lens cap off".

That same evening the United States Ambassador strode up to us and said that he had heard from colleagues in the US about the way that we had run the BBC Weather Centre as a prime example of good practise between the broadcasting company and the State Met office. We had met him previously when some of us were invited to an evening at the US Embassy. It was a large chateau with gardens cascading down to the shores of Lake Geneva and we had a magnificent evening with beautiful food and wine to match whilst huge uniformed marines wandered back and forth. This was in stark contrast to our visit to the Russian Embassy where equally large men patrolled wearing loose fitting dark suits obviously to hide the guns they were carrying. It frightened the life out of us.

The Ambassador said he would be honoured if we would come and stay at his official residence the following night to continue the conversation. We had to say no as our flights were booked and Bill had to be on duty the following day. Some you win and some you lose.

The IABM had been working hard to stage a World Conference on Broadcast Meteorology and finally did in 2004 held in Barcelona as part of the Universal Forum of Cultures. Tomas Molina, a Catalan weather presenter and a star in his own country was one of the founding members of IABM.

He persuaded those running the Universal Forum to both host and fund a conference. They realised that with so many broadcasters coming from around the world, it would be excellent publicity. This was a staggeringly large event running for 141 days and consisted of building multiple facilities including many exhibition and conference halls, a complete tram system into the centre of Barcelona and an ambitious urban development scheme with building a university. The total cost was $2.3 billion.

Our part was a weeklong event starting with a broadcast training session that Bill and John organised and ran, then followed by a three-day conference. This was all held in a brand new conference centre with every conceivable facility. Because we still had many good contacts and friends throughout the world we were able to amass a brilliant range of speakers. John Zillman, who was a previous Chairman of WMO, old friend Julian Hunt who gave a stunning presentation, Geoff Jenkins a leading world expert on climate change from The Met Office's Hadley Centre, and John Kermond an expert on El Niño.

We had known John for many years. He had many grand titles such as a University Corporation for Atmospheric Research (UCAR), and visiting Scientist at the Climate Program Office of the National Oceanic and Atmospheric Administration (NOAA). Prior to that he was with the NOAA Office of Global Programs, and for many years represented the Marine Division of the National Association of State Universities and Land Grant Colleges (NASULGC) in Washington D.C. (pause for breath). An Australian by birth, he had adapted well to the American way of life, and when we got to know him, he was actively involved in research into the El Niño/La Niña effect. There was little or no observational data available, so NOAA funded a project to place a row of automatic buoys across the Pacific Ocean. However, the Americans call then "boo-ies" which just made us laugh. John Kermond had a very witty and acerbic way of describing things that stripped away all of the padding and got straight to the point.

He was also fascinated by the Bill and John double act and our 'English sense of humour'. Having known one another for so many years we easily slipped into our little double act. Every time we met him, he would say, "you guys ought to go on American TV, they just love that English humour". We would smile politely and think nothing more of it. However, he was insistent that there was potential, and after we retired we thought it might be worth a go.

We did some filming in London at Buckingham Palace and the Tower of London that went quite well. All silly humour really, about Tony Blair trying to become President of Europe and living in Buck House and Phil the Greek mowing the lawns each morning. John K liked the material and suggested that if we could get to Washington, he could film us doing some more.

We had a few pennies left in the Weather People account following the WMO Training contract, so we thought we would speculate on that. However, the hotel was a real bucket-shop job.

It was was so bad that the air-con packed up and we slept in rooms at a temperature of over 100°F. But we had some fun filming, in particular with the commissionaire of a block of flats called Blair Towers when we were asking him for an appointment with Cherie Blair. However, just after this time John K retired and moved to Florida. Our hopes of stardom went with him.

But inevitably Bill and John's involvement in weather took a back seat as other opportunities came along. Coincidentally with John leaving the BBC he had moved down to the south of England and his wife started working at a local Prep School. After a while John also started at the school and the opportunities for Bill and John to do any weather projects became limited to school holidays.

But our interest in the IABM has not waned and both are still committee members. Bill writes articles for the in-house magazine UP FRONT, which John produces and edits.

A meeting of the Executive Committee of WMO held in the Council Chamber in their headquarters in Geneva

A reception in the top floor restaurant in the WMO Headquarters

Filming in front of Buckingham Palace

At the Tower of London we got moved on for not having a filming permit

A Climate of Change

CHAPTER 20

WE DIDN'T START OUT FROM THE SAME PLACE

Both Bill and John came from very different backgrounds and experience. If more by luck than judgement, the skills they picked up on the way was exactly what was needed to form this strange partnership. When, later on circumstances brought them together they found a real meeting of minds and a collection of experiences and talents that allowed for the lasting partnership to thrive.

BILL: *Having lived in a beautiful remote part of Devon for all of my formative years I was always interested in the weather but the subject really started to become an obsession while I was away at Queen Elizabeth's School, Crediton.*

It was at my boarding school in my 5th year that I decided on it as a career. I was amazed that I had stayed there that long because I nearly ran away after the first day. It was a cold September day when I arrived, a shy retiring scholarship boy to find a rigid routine in place at St Martin's House run by the Assistant Headmaster and chief Latin master Mr. Sharp and his wife. I found out that we had to bath three times a week and in twos, under the guidance of the matron and that my first taste of this was on my first evening there. I duly arrived at the appointed time only to find the other chap already in the bath. I got undressed and sat in the tap end and though since I was sharing a bath with him the least I could do would be to introduce myself. Of course we only used surnames so I said "I'm Giles" to which his reply was "I'm Piddler." I've never jumped out of a bath so quickly in all of my life only to find out later after I had calmed down, that in fact he was called Piddler, Brian Piddler, which was a well respected name from mid-Devon.

Five years later two of us in my form, myself and a tall lad called Routley, decided that the Met Office would be good for us. He had his interview one week before I did and since he came from north Devon went to the Main Met Office in Gloucester for it. He was successful and briefed me as to what it consisted. The Chief Met Officer there was a sports fanatic and since Routley and I were in the same rugby fifteen and cricket eleven at school I thought it would be a doddle.

Coming from south Devon I had to go to Plymouth for my interview by a man called Wilf Saunders who, I found out later, was a stickler for protocol and scientific knowledge since he spent most of his career writing research articles on many different aspects of weather. The first question he asked me was not about rugby or cricket but the answer to $\cos^2 x + \sin^2 x$. Luckily I was keen on maths so didn't take long to give him the answer of 1.

He looked at me and said twice "are you sure?" I stuck to my answer since if that was wrong I had no other and at last he said "Well done boy." He tried all the tricks of the trade to catch me out even by standing up half way through to see if I would do the same but eventually I left successful.

On the 31st December 1956 I travelled from my home to some digs in Clyst Honiton, a small village just below Exeter Airport and on the very next day January 1st (which was not a bank holiday at that time) I started work as a Scientific Assistant.

Over the next year or so I studied hard at Exeter under a senior scientific assistant called Johnny Meadows. He was an excellent teacher but a hard man who wouldn't suffer fools gladly. I gained confidence under him to such an extent that when I saw people were needed to go to Christmas Island to act as observers during the H-bomb tests, I readily volunteered. After a further course at Hemsby in Norfolk to learn about measuring temperature, pressure, humidity and the wind velocity by tracking huge hydrogen filled balloons and a further short course at Dunstable tracking thunderstorms, I was on a plane to the south Pacific calling in at New York, Tulsa, San Francisco, Hawaii and finally Christmas Island itself.

The work there, Operation Grapple, was done on three islands, Christmas, Fanning and the one that I later went to, Malden, which was my first journey south of the equator and there we travelled on a shaky old Dakota aircraft. Once there we set to our task of sending very large hydrogen balloons up into the atmosphere to at least 60,000 feet with instruments tied underneath recording the height of the package, temperature, humidity and the all important wind velocity. These balloons were sent up from all three islands simultaneously so we could calculate when it was safe to explode the bombs. We also used the triangulation to observe and collate data on thunderstorms in the area.

There were only 31 of us in total on the Island consisting of Met Office personnel, some from Decca Navigation and the rest RAF. The Officer in charge of the island was a Flight Lieutenant - the only officer- but we had two messes one for Officers and Senior NCOs (which we came under) and other ranks. In the informality of a tiny tropical island and a small number of people, we still dressed for dinner and were served by RAF stewards with a napkin over their arm.

On the island we certainly enjoyed our leisure time; my favourite pastime was crayfishing. We would gather ourselves in teams of three. One would be wearing a thick glove similar to that used by a wicket keeper in cricket, the second would have a torch and the third a sack. Then as the sun went down we would stretch out in a line and walk along the reef. When a crayfish was spotted the person with the light would shine it directly onto it, the second man would swoop down with his gloved hand and pop it into the sack carried by his colleague.

After a while all the teams would retire to the shore where a large drum of water was boiling to cook our catch. During the fishing the line of people would break as a sea snake rushed through and it was only later that I discovered that the snakes were amongst the most venomous in the world.

Back in the UK some four months later I was again posted to Exeter Airport under Johnny Meadows. I had only been there a very short time when he announced that it was time for me to learn to drive so I duly signed up for some lessons. What I hadn't realised was that he wanted to sell his old Austin 7 and decided it was me who was going to buy it.

A Climate of Change

When I said that there was no way I could afford such a machine he got me detached for a few weeks to another office where I was entitled to large amounts of subsistence which he duly claimed as the price of buying his car.

The next three years I spent in Germany, firstly at RAF Gutersloh then to RAF Wildenrath with a short stay at RAF Bruggen whilst the runway at Wildenrath was being repaired. I had three very happy years in Germany (although I have to confess that in all that time the only words of German I learned were beer and sausage!)

Postings back from overseas were always fraught with danger. You tried to get somewhere close to your relatives or in an area in which you wanted to settle, so it was good news for me when I was posted to the small Met Office at Filton on the outskirts of Bristol.

Two things stand out in my memory from that time at Filton, first was the boss, a Mr. Jones who travelled in every day from the wilds of South Wales. He was a very mild man who didn't over work but suddenly realised than he was retiring in about eighteen months and because he only worked Monday to Friday would have the absolute basic pension. To boost this he decided to come onto shift working, including nights and weekend work but it nearly killed him. Although I must say that many years later I used a similar tactic – modified of course.

The second memory was of a young assistant, a distant relative of 'Mad' Major Draper whose claim to fame was that he flew his Tiger Moth airplane over the Thames and under Tower Bridge. The young lad had a fixation with time and could only try to start his car after leaving his shift at precisely ten to or twenty past the hour. Not too much trouble you would have thought, but he had a very old car which took some starting on cold mornings and it was not unusual to see him still there waiting to go three or four hours after his shift had finished.

This was the same guy whom I met a few years later at the Met Office headquarters and was given compulsory retirement on medical grounds and I used to sit and think who was the brightest him or me because there was I, having to work another twenty five years and he had retired on full pension!

Whilst at Filton I studied Advanced Mathematics and Physics at Bristol College of Science before being promoted to Assistant Experimental Officer and went on the first of my forecasting courses at Honeypot Lane, Stanmore in Middlesex. Incidentally this is where John Teather was born and brought up, although he was still in short trousers when I was there.

On promotion I was sent on the Initial Forecasting Course. This, in the Met Office, was a huge step and in military terms was going from a Sergeant to an Officer which in those days didn't happen very often so I worked like a demon on the course, even refusing the end of course party in favour of more revision for the final exam. I came top of the class and was posted to Main Met Office Gloucester under the Chief Experimental Officer (the next thing to God) Gwyn Evans.

I had been there just a few weeks and was told that my posting was to be made permanent so I could sell my house near Bristol and buy in Gloucester. I duly started looking but was called back into the boss' office to be told that I was returning to the training school as an instructor.

Two and a half years spent there, travelling up and down to Bristol every weekend, were followed by the Advanced Forecasting Course, promotion to the newly created grade of Higher Scientific Officer, and a posting to RAF Strike Command at High Wycombe.

Strike Command was an interesting place to work - always underground and often far underground. One of my tasks was to brief the air staff in the morning and to do this you had to go well down in the lift. I was shown the ropes the first time then left on my own after that. I remember going down in the lift clutching my charts and standing in front of a mirrored door but before I knocked on it to be let into the briefing room.

I stood there combing my hair and making ridiculous faces in the mirror to get myself psyched up only to find, on entering, that it was a two way mirror. The young lady airwoman who let me in couldn't contain her laughter so I entered the holy of holies very red faced.

The briefing consisted of a close circuit television system with a duty airman pushing the maps into view on cue from me. There was one airman who always got it wrong and you could almost guarantee that when you wanted to be telling the viewers about the weather in the Middle East he would put up a chart of Gibraltar. To this day I am sure he was trying to work his passage out of the RAF, if not, then he was very stupid.

During the advanced course we all sat a voice test. This consisted of writing a radio script that was read out to three people from the Met Office (most of whom had never broadcast in their life) and we were then judged whether we would be any good as a radio broadcaster.

There were three categories. Firstly no good at all, in which case you had the rest of the day off, suitable for local radio and finally OK for national radio. I was deemed suitable for the latter but nothing was then done about it and I was duly posted to RAF Strike Command near High Wycombe as the United Kingdom Forecaster. The notion of being posted is an interesting one and it came about because we were part of the Ministry of Defence. In that regard we all had equivalent RAF ranks and worked on the military principle of you go where you are told to go without question.

I used to hate the system in the early days because there was little you could do about refusing, but as time went by and I climbed the managerial ladder, I found I was in a position to post someone from one place to another and then I thought it was a wonderful system. I suppose it wouldn't work now because it would be against their human rights!

Any rate, there I was at Strike Command as a junior weather forecaster. Actually being a forecaster in those days was great when the main job of the Met Office was to try and forecast the weather, unlike today when it appears to be selling products especially hardware and software.

Bill just before he left for the Christmas Islands

The only problem with being a forecaster then was that you had to agree to work a 24-hour shift pattern, 365 days a year, anywhere they decided to send you. But in agreeing to that, you got an extra 20% on top of your salary and extra money for working at weekends.

After being at Strike Command for about six months, settling into the job and learning a lot from some of the Chief Forecasters, I received a letter from on high that there was a vacancy for a forecaster at London Weather Centre to do national radio and that since I was recommended on my advanced forecasting course, I should attend this audition with the BBC. I didn't want to go to work in London for the simple reason that I enjoyed my position where I was dealing with the RAF and the fact that I only lived a short distance away from the office. So I wrote a letter saying thank you, but no thank you.

Before I could send it on its way, my boss called me into his office and told me he wanted me to stay there as his Admin Manager. My first reaction was wonderful since in that post I would have an office of my own above ground (because all the forecasting was done in offices several floors underground). I would also have my own car parking space and could have my lunch in the Officer's mess instead of bringing in my sandwiches. It seemed too good to be true - and it was. However, it meant working only Monday to Friday and I would lose 20% of my salary for not working shifts, no Saturday or Sunday money so I tore up the letter I had written and wrote another reply to the audition invitation saying "Thank you for the offer, I would be delighted to attend".

Of course, as there was so much at stake, no one else at that audition stood a chance of beating me!!! I got the job and was duly posted to London Weather Centre in High Holborn as a trainee radio broadcaster. That's how most people ended up at London Weather Centre kicking and screaming except Michael Fish - he loved it there.

One of the most successful things we ever did at the London Weather Centre was that we had four telephone lines that the general public, could ring and speak to a forecaster. So we cut that to one and no one answered it! It saved a lot of awkward questions. Seriously, though, it was a great shame because we used to get some very interesting questions from some lovely people. I well remember a young lady ringing up one Wednesday lunchtime and she asked me a very simple question."

I'm getting married at the weekend what's it going to be like?" I was lost for words at first but then replied "If you don't know by now you're in for one hell of a shock". She laughed as she put the phone down. But I am still asked that very question from time to time and always give the same answer "Warm and close with a little sun later!" It generally goes down well.

We had many great characters at London Weather Centre, which has sadly been closed now and none more so, than Vic Walters. When I first arrived there as a trainee radio forecaster, Vic took me under his wing (probably because we both came from Devon) and I listened and learnt from him. He was very laid back and I remember one instance in the radio studio where he was giving a two way broadcast with an announcer from Radio 2, when he dropped all his notes and weather maps off the table and they crashed onto the floor.

The BBC Announcer asked what the noise was and Vic replied that it was his assistant (not me!) bringing the latest weather information to him. Quick as a flash came the reply from broadcasting house "I see and it sounded as though he'd thrown it at you from the doorway."

Graham Johnson was another very good radio broadcaster that never graduated to television. One Sunday morning he went into the studio with a written three minute script for Radio4 but half way through the broadcast realised that it was only a two minute broadcast and with only one minute remaining and he still had two minutes of script left to read. Instead of throwing his script away and adlibbing for the last minute he chose to read it all, so he got through a two-minute script in just one minute.

After the broadcast he came back into the office and asked if I would care to go in and listen to what he had done, since we taped all the broadcasts in case there was a query. I listened and the last minute of his broadcast sounded just like a take off of the Chipmunks but strangely enough nothing was ever said about it.

Jack Cohen was one of my favourite senior forecasters. He was a lovely Jewish gentleman who, as senior forecaster on duty, should have been helping and advising us juniors about the forecast but Jack plodded on with his own work, mainly forecasting for oilrigs in the North Sea, without saying a word to anyone.

This happened throughout the whole of his eight-hour shift on virtually every shift, until one memorable night. One of the young assistants had started going out with an Israeli girl and we were teasing him saying that he would have to have the operation. Jack suddenly sat up straight and said "Well if that is the case I hope what happened to me doesn't happen to you." I couldn't let his remark go since this was one of the first times Jack had said anything on duty, so I said to Jack "What did you mean? What did happen to you when you had it done?" He replied without the hint of a smile "When I had the operation I swear they threw the wrong bit away"

In those early days, when we were opening Weather Centres in many cities across the country, one of the elements that we had to include was a shop facility where people could come in and look at the weather forecast or just buy some of the many items on sale. I remember getting into very hot water on this aspect of the shops when, many years later, I was in charge of buying merchandise for them.

I had decided to liven things up a bit and that we needed more novel and interesting things to sell instead of the usual thermometers, barometers and satellite pictures. I arranged for some different thermometers to be sent to my office in Bracknell. I was away on leave when they arrived and the boxes were duly opened by my staff, who reported them immediately to my boss. On my return I was confronted by a hostile department who didn't see the advantage of selling my new thermometers because they were in the shape of Mickey Mouse. I didn't agree, but was well and truly overruled and so instructed my assistant, David Lee, to pack them up and send them back. I was way ahead of my time!

It was important to make sure that the shop managers were in tune with the general public after all they were the face of the Met Office, but a big mistake was made on this occasion at the London Weather Centre. The first mistake was that the person appointed hated the general public.

He would try very hard to stop people actually coming into the shop but if they did he would stride around with a face like thunder. He would stalk them as they browsed the information or goods on sale giving monosyllabic answers to any who were brave enough to ask a question until they felt intimidated and left. On the other hand he had his favourites who would come in for detailed scientific discussion when he would give them all the time in the world. Suffice to say the shop's revenue went down to such an extent that there was a lot of discussion about the value of the Weather Centre shop before the reason was discovered. The manager ended up in the library at headquarters.

The monthly roster was pinned upon the wall to give us some six-week's notice of our duties and on one spring day in 1975 I was standing looking at it when I noticed a letter 't' against my name on one of the days. I asked my boss, Dick Ogden, who had just put the sheet up what it meant." You are going for an audition at the BBC Television Centre" he said "because there is a vacancy for a television weatherman".

My reply was that I was more than happy as a radio forecaster based at London Weather Centre. He said that I had better go because it was on the roster. My reply was, it was there because he had just put it there. "In that case" he said, "You had better go." And that is how I "volunteered" to go for a television audition. The rest is history!

Once there, being an experienced forecaster, the weather side of it was no more difficult than anywhere else in the Met Office, but you had to learn, and learn quickly, the art of presenting it to over 10 million viewers. I was put with Keith Best for a week to learn my trade and then you were on your own. I well remember my first live unscripted broadcast. It was at teatime and we had the arrangements of a minimum time or fill to cover the gap left by the news. The minimum time they gave you at the broadcast was 30 seconds and as a joke, I asked how often we were cut to that bare minimum. "Oh about once every six months" was the reply from the gallery. Well obviously the six months was up and I went on air frowning like mad but completed the forecast on the three maps in that very short time. Afterwards, being very pleased with myself for not overrunning I asked Keith what he thought. Now Keith has a very dry sense of humour and his reply was "Well I know what to do next time I am cut to thirty seconds. Miss out half the country". Apparently in the whole of the forecast I had never mentioned either England or Wales. But that was the start of 25 years on National television and over 10,000 separate broadcasts.

Obviously John's journey into weather was a very different one from Bill's as his was a broadcasting career and not in meteorology. His arrival at weather broadcasting was much more by luck than judgement and one of those happy flukes of life.

JOHN: I suppose we never really know what early influences shape our lives and make us what we are. But there were certainly three profound moments that pointed me in the right direction.

For my 5th birthday my parents gave me a Pelham string puppet, and as I added more puppets in later years, that led me to putting on shows for the local kids, writing the script, organising my friends, making the sets and doing the lighting and sound. Then at primary school we had a new teacher, John Springall, who was mad keen on drama, and introduced me to a lifelong obsession with putting on shows. He was also in to multimedia and later on I was introduced to film making. Finally there was my Uncle Derry who was a keen amateur photographer, and he taught me not only how to take photos, but also to process them in my own darkroom.

So, when I finished school, I was not destined for an academic career and university was not for vocational subjects. But the local Technical College was offering a three-year full time photographic course, and after applying for a grant I was accepted. In some ways, 'I had been there and done that' as I had already been taking and processing film for some years and, although I can't say I was bored, there was something missing. The second year of the course introduced us to film, and I found that much more stimulating. By the third year I embarked with student friend Chris Young on a project to make a mini-feature film on a spy theme with the title of 'Albatross' and starring Hans Linder our tutor.

Complete with an especially composed music score and ending with the army storming the college (spy headquarters) it won the silver medal at the prestigious Cannes Amateur Film Festival.

After the euphoria, it was down to earth and time to look for a job. The obvious place for me was the BBC, although everyone said it was very difficult to get into. I applied for one job and was turned down, but then I was called for an interview for my second application. At the tender age of 20 I arrived one cold November morning for my interview. It wasn't really the job I wanted as it involved working in Cardiff. But everyone had told me that I should just get in the BBC and then I could move around.

The interview was in a faceless set of offices that looked at the side of Broadcasting House in Portland Place London and sat to the side of the Langham (now a hotel, but then BBC offices). The job was a Regional Film Technician based in Wales. The idea was that you would be trained up so that you could become a cameraman, sound recordist or film editor. At the appointed time I was ushered into a large room with high ceilings and windows that went down to the floor. Against all good practice I was shown to a seat facing the windows and a long table with five people sitting behind. I could hardly see their faces from the glare of the light from the windows, and I swear my chair was lower than theirs!

As with all interviews – they never ask the questions you think they will, and I found my powers of 'bullshit' being put to the test. At this time, recruitment of staff was made by a central department that technically employed all staff. Although the area of the BBC who needed the staff had a say, it was the Personnel Department that really made the decision.

The BBC was a career based organisation and Personnel was looking much further forward that just the job in hand.

They were looking to the future and wanted to ensure that new entrants to the BBC were the stuff that would make future managers and senior staff.

Well, they obviously thought I might make the grade and I started in January 1966 in Cardiff. My first time away from home in a strange land of foreign peoples and living in digs run by Edna and her sister. I had to share a bedroom with another BBC chap – to say I lived in fear would be an understatement!

But in the end I got used to it and if nothing else the house was spotlessly clean. Edna was obsessed with cleanliness, so much so, every Friday she would take the back off the television set to hoover the dust off the valves! Both sisters were spinsters, Edna ran the home and her sister went out to work at the local tax office. Their attire was straight out of Coronation Street and Edna had a straight-face delivery that scared all of us inmates until you got to know the measure of her. I felt at times that I was living a part in a Wednesday Play!

So the process of discovering my true calling began at the BBC Wales Film Unit. It didn't take me long to realise that I was not suited to be out on the 'road'. Filming sheep and male voice choirs – always in the rain and with the oddest people you were ever likely to meet.

The vast majority of the crew were either English or from South Wales. The production staff were all from North Wales who, although they spoke English, would always speak in Welsh. It gave them the endless opportunity to insult the crew without them knowing! To a man or a woman, I swear they didn't have any sense of humour. Unlike those from South Wales who were always good fun - those from the north thought fun was a sin!

These were the early days of radio mics, and in the evening the crew would entertain themselves in the local pub playing a game with the locals where sound recordist Ted Doule would go out of the room, the locals would agree a secret word and Ted would come back in and guess it having listened to it via a radio mic hidden in the bar. He did a very good job of groaning and peering into the future, but the locals were simple folk and never realised that technology was behind it! The crew never needed to buy a round. However after one of these sessions, a cameraman full of free beer, woke up in his hotel bedroom and needing the toilet, decided, as usual, to pee out of the window, but in the dark got confused and relieved himself in the wardrobe all over his own clothes! He was a sorry sight at breakfast.

So, the warmth and dry of a film cutting room was calling me and soon I was editing films. However, Sunday afternoon rugby did provide a challenge for me. The afternoon match was filmed and after it had been developed I had to edit the black and white negative film with a magnetic sound stripe that carried the commentary. On transmission it would be phased reversed back to the proper tones. But making any sense of the pictures was really hard. Keeping it free from dust and scratches and making the correct edit was enough of a challenge, but the producer was the famous Welsh player, Cliff Morgan, who later became a very successful Head of BBC Sport.

Not only was I rather an innocent young man but also I lacked any knowledge of rugby, and I struggled with this. But I did develop my vocabulary very quickly "don't f*****g cut there you silly c**t" was Cliff's favourite phrase!

A Climate of Change

All this against the clock, as the finished programme had to be down the road to Telecine in another building (the machine that turned film into TV) ready for transmission at 6.00pm.

The good thing about regional television was that you worked on all types of programmes from schools to documentaries. I had a favourite Producer Nan Davies, and I think I was a favourite of hers. She always asked me to edit her documentaries. I loved cutting film to music, and she loved using music in her films, so it was a good working relationship. She would arrive with some wonderful tracks such as Vaughan-Williams Fantasia on a Theme by Thomas Tallis. "Use it on that bit there dear" and then would promptly fall asleep whilst I cut the film. I had never seen anyone 'power-nap' before, but she would come round after 20 minutes to see how I was getting on.

The strange thing about working on a programme in the Welsh language and not speaking a word of it is that you develop a sense of the rhythm. So it is pretty easy to hear sentences and stops and starts. None of the film editors at the BBC Wales Film Unit spoke Welsh, but that didn't stop them producing some first class work. But we did have to become multilingual in gibberish! Many of the programmes were made for schools and often there would be long sections of film without sound. So we would go into the dubbing studio and invent the sound of people speaking in their own tongue.

One film was about desert dwellers and a sequence showed Arabs building a house. By the time we had finished you would never have guessed that they were not speaking to one another in Arabic – unless of course, you were an Arab!

But as much as I enjoyed working on programmes like this - I was homesick and desperate to get back to London. In the end it took four years, when after many attempts I was finally successful, although once back, for the next couple of years I was at the mercy of the Film Allocations Clerk and worked at Ealing Film Studios, Lime Grove Studios, East Tower Television Centre and Kensington House. Working on a variety of programmes from 'Some Mothers do 'Ave 'Em!' to documentaries such as 'One Pair of Eyes'.

Then the fickle finger of fate struck. Going on leave, I said to the Allocations Clerk, Ian Brindle, whatever you do, I do not want to go to the Promotions Cutting Room on my return. Guess where I was placed when I came back!

Promotions was the posh name for programme trailers and were the responsibility of the huge Presentation Department which also transmitted all the BBC's programmes, and also made programmes such as 'Late Night Line-up' and the 'Old Grey Whistle Test'. It was also responsible for the Weather. Far from hating it – I loved it. There was so much variety working on both 16mm and 35mm film with a great number of production staff. It was always busy and no time to be bored. Doing a trailer for 'Casablanca' in the morning and Hi-de-hi' in the afternoon.

The production staff became great colleagues with people such as Albert Barber, Martin Everard, and Pam Masters (later Head of Department) and the never to be forgotten, Head of Promotions, Pat Hubbard. Happy days.

Then Pat suggested that I might like to apply for an attachment as an Assistant Producer in the department. I was successful and stayed in that department until 2001 when Weather was taken over by News Division. As an A.P. you were trained to be a Network Director (directing the transmission of programmes) and on a Promotions Team making trailers. This was wonderful. At the end of the 6 month attachment, I was offered a substantive post (a fulltime job).

Although, from the appointment board, to actually being told I had the job, took over six weeks. I subsequently learnt that it was probably because I was being positively vetted by the security services. Never thought of it at the time when I was asked to sign the Official Secrets Act, but as Presentation had a central role in times of war, then it's reasonable to hope that your staff are batting on the same wicket!

Network directing was a high pressure area, and excellent at teaching bowel control. This was so different from what I had ever done before, but I suppose years of doing lighting and sound in amateur theatre had at least taught me how to push button on cue.

At that time it was considered a sin not to get to the News on time. It was always preceded by a clock. You will notice that since TV has gone digital that the clock has gone, and that is simply that all the processing required, means that the signal received in Scotland would be two and half seconds late.

The early evening News junction (the bit between programmes) was always a challenge in the days of Blue Peter, the famous children's show. The great matriarch Biddy Baxter who ran the programme didn't believe in autocue and she expected the presenters to learn the script she had written. She also thought the whole planet centred on her programme and the rest of the schedule really didn't matter. The sequence of events was out of Blue Peter, into a trailer, then a 10 second clock ident with the continuity announcer saying "it is 5.40 and now the early evening news with ....

The network director would agree an out time with the studio gallery, and if all went well we would hear the countdown on talkback from the production assistant and when she got to 11 seconds push the button to run the video tape machine for the trailer that would start 10 seconds later. But the first time I directed this junction, John Noakes stumbled over his words and started adding some because he couldn't remember the script. I could hear the countdown start.

Then at 5 seconds to go she restarted her count. By then I had run the trailer. The result was a mess and I was late to the News. I had my hand well and truly slapped for that! When I spoke to gallery I was put on to Biddy who gushed that it was a live show and "these things happen!" I pointed out that she needed to find a way to provide some flexibility at the end of her show so that she could finish on time. More gushing and more excuses.

The next week I was on the same shift doing the same junction. They overran again, but this time, by luck, at the time I was due to go to the trailer, there was only one credit left to go. So I quickly said the vision mixer "fade down and fade up trail". It all looked very smooth. Once into the News, I waited for the red light of the Blue Peter studio phone to flash.

It did and I answered. "John why did you fade my credit screeched Biddy"? Sorry Biddy but you overran again. We had the same meaningful conversation. The next week the same happened but this time I faded the entire end credits. So I held the world record for having faded Blue Peter three times. But Biddy learnt the lesson and she added a buffer to the end of the programme and after that they always ran to time!

The department also did lots of other things, and Hugh Sheppard as Senior Assistant Special Projects, was in charge of all this. The Weather came under his remit. At that time the weather team was Jack Scott, Keith Best, Michael Fish and Barbara Edwards, Bert Foord and Graham Parker. The weather broadcasts were directed by the promotions team (there were three teams that worked a rotating schedule). The duty team operated out of one of the two presentation studios A&B. 'A' was for promotions and 'B' for programmes. So directing the weather was one of the duties and the most frightening thing I have ever done in my life!

All weather broadcasts were live at peak times following the news. They were followed by a trailer that was on video tape that had to be cued 10 seconds before it went on air. Pres 'A' was a self operate studio where the director also did the vision mixing.

Usually News would 'hand-over' to the Weather and at this point the Network Director would cut from the News studio to Pres 'A' which would then be live 'on air'. The weather presenter would start as soon as they saw themselves 'on-air'. The director in the studio would then calculate an 'out-time' which was normally 1 minute and 30 seconds from the start. This was done by watching the large studio clock as we went 'on air' and doing a calculation as to when the weather would finish. The strange thing about this was that some directors discovered that they were 'clock blind' in particular in the back half of the minute, ie the bit from the 30 seconds up to the top of the clock. Many seemed unable to quickly do the calculations in this segment. However, once the director had worked it out, they would relay this to the floor assistant over headphones, as they would be giving the visual clue to the weather presenter when they had to stop talking. This they did by putting their finger over the segment of a smaller clock on a stand in the studio.

So, if I said over talkback "weather out at the next 50" then the floor assistant would place their finger at the 50 second mark and the weather presenter would talk until the second hand lined up with the finger.

Very crude – but effective. In the gallery the video tape for the trailer would have been run at the 40 second mark and always supposing the weather presenter stopped on time, then to the viewer the weather would fade down and the trailer would appear. If the presenter over-ran then invariably they would be faded to meet the trailer as it was by then too late to reset it. Mike Fish of all the team got faded more often than anyone else.

Calls would come through to the Duty Office (also part of Presentation) from viewers complaining that we had faded the weatherman. The truth was that he had not stopped on time.

Early in my training, I directed a 'live' lunchtime weather with Graham Parker.

The floor clock had been positioned a bit too far down the studio, and he wore quite thick spectacles. I calculated the time and told the floor manager the out point, but when he got to it – he didn't stop.

He hadn't seen the finger on the clock and just carried on talking. Waving didn't work and shouting was not possible. Eventually he finished after 3 and half minutes on a broadcast that should have been 2 minutes!

The next pressure was to do the vision mixing – not in itself difficult – but with a shaking hand? There were two cameras in the studio, one fixed on the big Atlantic Chart and one manned that could pan from the Tonight Chart to the Tomorrow Chart. Before the broadcast a cue word would be agreed with the presenter at which point the director would cut from the Atlantic Chart to the Tonight Chart. The key word was invariably 'tonight'. For one broadcast, I had agreed with Bert Foord (famous for his very dour presentation) that indeed we would use the normal key word. We went on air and Bert said "tonight" when standing talking about the Atlantic, so I cut to the Tonight Chart and waited for him to walk into shot. When he didn't, I cut back to the Atlantic Chart. In the meantime he had realised what had happened and walked to the Tonight Chart. It was only a short broadcast and after the initial opening he was never seen again that night!

I eventually found myself attached as an Assistant Producer to Hugh Sheppard. This suited me fine as it was as a day worker and other jobs in the department were shift working. I had become more heavily involved in the local arts scene where we lived in Harrow (on the outskirts of London). On shift it would have been impossible for me to either direct or act in an amateur production of a play. Basically Hugh looked after everything that the rotating three teams could not. One particular aspect was Eurovision. As the largest broadcasters in Europe, the BBC covered many events that other broadcasters would show on their own stations. They would send to the UK a commentator and Hugh and his team would provide the facilities for them to broadcast live back to their own countries. So, over many years, I would get to attend the great sporting and social events of the time, from Royal Weddings to Wimbledon, From Jeux sans Frontières to The Grand National.

Often the event required that the visiting commentators needed a briefing, so for example, for a Royal Wedding they would be driven along the route and then a walk through Westminster Abbey. I was very lucky to be part of this, as over the years I had privileged access to some of the greatest events of our time.

With Weather as part of Hugh's remit I got more involved with this, including the launch of the new weather symbols in August 1975. This whole area of weather graphics is a story by itself and is dealt with in a chapter of its own.

In May of that year, at one of the regular audition sessions that I directed, there was a chap who I had heard on the radio who seemed to have potential – it was Bill Giles. I would l love to say that his future stardom was evident at that time – but in reality his audition lacked sparkle.

However, off screen he seemed to be very focussed and determined and out of the others we saw that day – by far the best.

A Climate of Change

We decided to take him, and unbeknown to both of us, at that time, it started a working relationship that has survived to this day, based on a shared passion for excelling in the art of broadcast meteorology. Indeed a perfect working relationship where television and meteorology melded together to provide something truly greater than each organisation could manage themselves.

But weather was still very much a part time job for me. With only three live broadcasts each day and one recording for closedown, our job was very much supporting the forecaster in the background. It was really providing the means and then letting the duty forecaster get on with it. So, I started directing the end of the year shows, and helped with the design of new steel maps for the new weather symbols. But I had other duties and Eurovision kept me occupied, together with an increasing involvement in planning the daytime schedule into a format ready for transmission. It was the job of the channel controllers to place the programmes, but then Presentation made it work in detail, placing trailers, pointers to next programmes, menus showing what was coming up next, and getting the timings right so that went to the News on time.

Eventually I took over planning all daytime schedules from the start of programmes until the early evening News when the operational team took over the task. I had the grand title of Co-ordinator Daytime Operations and sat in large open plan office together with researcher Shirley Edwards, who also over the years acted as Production Assistant on many of the end of year Weather Reviews.

In the middle of this I was asked to take over as Head of Visitor Liaison for three months. This was the most unusual job I ever did in my time at the BBC. As the world's biggest broadcasting organisation at that time, there was a constant stream of people from around the world wanting to come to Television Centre and see the sights and meet senior staff. Our job was to arrange this. So we would meet and greet, tour, lunch and take them to high level meetings. Incidentally, the unit also arranged the hospitality for all the Eurovision events, so I already knew the staff well.

There was no hand-over and so I arrived on a Monday morning to my palatial new office, to be greeted by Roz Raites, a larger than life lady of Caribbean decent, who wanted to take my order for the week! She told me I was low on Gin in the hospitality cabinet and asked what brand of cigarettes I required! Oh dear, I thought, I am glad it is only for three months or I would be an alcoholic by the end!

One day I was asked to host a lady who was a senior diplomat in the Philippines Embassy in the days when Ferdinand and Imelda Marcos were running the country. She had provided facilities for a Panorama film team to go to the country. However, the resulting film when shown was very critical of the regime and its human rights record. There was a witch-hunt and she was very frightened over her involvement.

Over coffee I tried to give this charming lady some reassurance – but her replies were always whispered, and would look round the room before replying. I then realised how frightened she was, as she explained that she was scared that I might be recording our conversation. I managed to reassure her that she was in a free country and an independent BBC.

After that we had a very useful meeting. But it has concerned me ever since, how lucky we are to live in a free and open democracy, as many in this world do not.

Weather was still there in my life. In 1985 I led the team that introduced electronic graphics, the first self-operated weather studio in 1986, and the first commercial weather forecast for SuperChannel in 1989. However, I didn't go full time on weather until the BBC Weather Centre opened in 1991, but that's all in another chapter!

CHAPTER 21

CONCLUSIONS

JOHN: *It may appear that I have been rather hard on the BBC, but I am still one of its greatest supporters. The concept of public service broadcasting, where programme making is not driven by commercial imperatives has served the British public extremely well. However, in the 1990s a new breed of leadership took over at the BBC.*

One morning one of my Producers arrived in the office, white-faced, to say that he had just been chucked out of one of the lifts in Television Centre by a group of 'minders'. They wanted the lift exclusively for their boss. It was John Birt the new Director General. The fact that he was not prepared to be in the same lift as ordinary people really seemed to sum up his whole attitude to BBC staff and how he would go on to irrevocably change the BBC's culture. His immediate predecessors, Mike Checkland and Alasdair Milne would enjoy being in the same lift as staff and would have chatted with them.

As an example of one of Birt's changes, was how staff would be paid. Until his arrival all monthly paid staff were on incremental pay grades. With this system you started at the bottom of the grade and each year, if your work was judged as satisfactory, you were awarded an increment until you reached the top of the grade. This meant that everyone knew how much everyone else earned. It was open and transparent. But that all changed with personal salaries being negotiated and bonuses awarded. It was a system of patronage, where, if you got on with your boss, then you were rewarded. This change led directly to the excessive pay rates that have shocked us all, in particular Director General Mark Thompson being paid £834,000 in 2010. A ridiculous amount for what is basically a public servant. Of course the usual excuses are trotted out that the BBC is in a competitive market when recruiting staff.

But this undermines the real qualities of all those dedicated people who worked for the BBC and built it up over the many years. None of us worked for the BBC for the money. We worked for it, because we had a shared vision of public service broadcasting and how we could make the best programmes in the world. This new concept of 'noses in the trough' was as alien to us as much as the idea of the BBC taking advertising!

Greg Dyke, who shared Birt's pedigree, with a background in commercial television, followed him as DG. I remember showing him around the BBC Weather Centre only after a few weeks of him being in post. He was completely disinterested, and kept questioning "what is all this about – what are you showing me?" He obviously couldn't get a grasp of what public service broadcasting was all about and why we needed to do weather forecasts at all.

Oh dear – it really was that the culture of commercial television was an unbridgeable chasm.

There is a danger of 'it was better in my day' syndrome colouring some of the comments I have made about the BBC Weather Centre since I left in 2001. A great deal of what we see these days is very, very good. The move to the new News Studios at Broadcasting House in central London has enabled the completion of the work to go fully High Definition. The results on-screen are stunning. The content still suffers with unnecessary fly throughs and editorially still doesn't lead with the 'weather story'. The lack of forecasts looking further forward than 2 days is a serious problem that needs attention.

But all that said, my congratulations to all, both past and present, in having crafted a true public service. Until now!

BILL: *Like John, I may have appeared to be a little harsh in my criticism of the Met Office but it is the Met Office that gave me a terrific career for which I am very grateful.*

In the last fifty years I have seen some enormous changes within the Office, some of which I agree with and some I don't. The biggest change started when the title of Director General was replaced by Chief Executive when it felt to one and all that we had started to move away from our core business of making weather forecasts available free of charge to all persons in the UK, to selling our products to the highest bidder, and this has continued a pace since then.

I was very privileged to run a team of broadcast meteorologists that were as good an any in the world despite the fact that in the early days, the Met Office had little or no interest in who appeared on screen to deliver the weather message. That is still a huge problem in many parts of the world where the national weather service does not "talk" to the national broadcasting company and many meteorological services still cannot understand why they get bad publicity for incorrect forecasts.

John and I realised this problem very early on and developed a great understanding between the Met Office and the BBC, which through the World Meteorological Organisation and the International Association of Broadcast Meteorology has been the model used all around the world.

Using this co-operation, and understanding the model used in the United States of America where the weather information is free and freely available to all their citizens, we made the BBC Weather Centre the envy of the world both in delivery of the forecast and especially in training of potential weather broadcasters around the world particularly in the developing countries.

If John and Bill leave a legacy at all, it will be that they changed the face of weather broadcasts worldwide and showed that to do this, meteorologists have to talk to the broadcasters.

Having spent so many evenings working together, we even developed the knack of knowing what each other would order for dinner!

Retirement does have some benefits!

ACKNOWLEDGEMENTS

Bill and John would like to thank those who helped make this book possible.

To our wives Suzanne and Maureen, who supported us whilst we put pen to paper.

To Roger Hunt, Liz Varrall, Tom Hartwell, Gerald Fleming and others who filled in the facts that we had long forgotten.

To MJ Teather for the cover photography and designs.

To the many dear friends and colleagues that we met along the way.